Freud's
Moses:

Judaism Terminable

and Interminable

9.8.1934 Der Mann Moses.
Ein historischer Roman.

First page of Freud's 1934 manuscript draft of *Moses and Monotheism*.

Freud's
Moses:
Judaism Terminable
and Interminable

Yosef Hayim Yerushalmi

Yale University Press
New Haven and London

Published with assistance from the foundation established in memory of William McKean Brown.

Grateful acknowledgment is made to the following for permission to reprint: excerpts from the 1934 manuscript draft of *Moses and Monotheism* and from unpublished correspondence of Freud and facsimile of first page of 1934 manuscript draft of *Moses and Monotheism,* by permission of A. W. Freud et al.; excerpt from "East Coker" in *Four Quartets,* copyright 1943 by T. S. Eliot and renewed 1971 by Esme Valerie Eliot, by permission of Harcourt Brace Jovanovich, Inc., and Faber and Faber Ltd.; excerpt from "The Death of Moses Sequence," *The Penguin Book of Hebrew Verse,* trans. T. Carmi (Allen Lane, 1981), copyright © T. Carmi, 1981, by permission of Penguin Books Ltd.; excerpt from *Philosophical Investigations* by Ludwig Wittgenstein, copyright 1953 by Macmillan Publishing Company, copyright © renewed 1981, by permission of Macmillan Publishing Company and Basil Blackwell Ltd.

Library of Congress Cataloging-in-Publication Data
Yerushalmi, Yosef Hayim, 1932–
    Freud's Moses: Judaism terminable and interminable / Yosef Hayim Yerushalmi.
      p. cm.
    Includes bibliographical references and index.
    ISBN 0–300–04921–8 (cloth)
        0–300–05756–3 (pbk.)
    1. Freud, Sigmund, 1856–1939. Der Mann Moses und die monotheistische Religion. 2. Moses (Biblical leader) 3. Egyptian literature—Relation to the Old Testament. 4. Monotheism. 5. Psychology, Religious. 6. Judaism—History. 7. Psychoanalysis—History. 8. Freud, Sigmund, 1856–1939.
I. Freud, Sigmund, 1856–1939. Der Mann Moses und die monotheistische Religion. II. Title.
BS580.M6   1991
222'.1092—dc20   90–23859

A catalogue record for this book is available from the British Library.

The paper in this book meets the guidelines for permanence and durability of the Committee on Production Guidelines for Book Longevity of the Council on Library Resources.

To the indelible memory of

Arthur A. Cohen

Theologian, Novelist, Bookman,
who asked the difficult questions
with grace, wit and passion

and

For Mortimer J. Ostow, M.D.

whose uncompromising commitment
to psychoanalysis and to Judaism
is as moving as it is exemplary

But when I make a statement about Moses—am I always ready to substitute some *one* of these descriptions for "Moses"? I shall perhaps say: By "Moses" I understand the man who did what the Bible relates of Moses, or at any rate a good deal of it. But how much? Have I decided how much must be proved false for me to give up my proposition as false? Has the name "Moses" got a fixed and unequivocal use for me in all possible cases?—Is it not the case that I have, so to speak, a whole series of props in readiness, and am ready to lean on one if another should be taken from under me and vice versa?

—Ludwig Wittgenstein,
Philosophical Investigations

The Death of Moses [excerpts]

2.
[*He pleads with God for his life*]
"While I was yet in my mother's
    womb
You marked my perfection and chose
me as your spokesman—
why then should I die?"

"Lest it be said: the man of God went
up to God,
and he has become like God."

"When Israel labored with clay and
with mortar, I was put into a wicker
basket. And I fulfilled Your word—
why then should I die?"

"Lest it be said: He spoke to God
face to face and then the skin of his
face shone,
and he has become like God."

"You led the tyrant's daughter to the
Nile, brought her in haste, so that my
life might be prolonged—
why then should I die?"

"Lest it be said: He exulted when he
was sent to the treasured people and
brought them out of Egypt joyfully,
and he has become like God."

6.
[*He takes leave of his people*]
"This day is my last; thus has He
ordained, who is both First and Last;
I shall be gathered to my kin as
    was my
brother Aaron. My people, be at
    peace."

"Such is the fated course; both high
and low must take it; who shall live
    and not
see death? Our shepherd, go in
    peace."

*He was buried in a valley in Moab
opposite Beth-peor, but to this day
no one knows his burial place.*

—Anonymous,
from the Death of Moses cycle in
the Roman Jewish Liturgy

Contents

Illustrations

Frontispiece: First page of Freud's 1934 manuscript draft of *Moses and Monotheism*. Courtesy of Sigmund Freud Copyrights, Freud Archives, and the Library of Congress.

following p. 80

1. Jakob Freud's bilingual inscription in Hebrew and German in the family Bible. Courtesy of the Freud Museum, London.

2. Jakob Freud's Hebrew dedication in the family Bible. Courtesy of the Freud Museum, London.

3. "Moses coming from Mount Sinai throws the tablets of the Ten Commandments to the ground," engraving after a painting by Rembrandt. Courtesy of the Freud Museum, London.

4. Rembrandt van Rijn, *The Jews in the Synagogue*. Courtesy of the Freud Museum, London.

5. Antiquities and two kiddush cups in Freud's consulting room at Berggasse 19. Photo © Edmund Engelman.

6. Detail of the kiddush cups. Photo © Edmund Engelman.

7. Bronze Hanukkah menorah, from Freud's private collection. Courtesy of the Freud Museum, London.

8. Picture postcard sent by Freud from Rome to Karl Abraham. Courtesy of Sigmund Freud Copyrights, Freud Archives, and the Library of Congress.

9. Reverse of postcard to Karl Abraham.

Acknowledgments

My thanks first to the members of the Research Group on the Psychoanalytic Study of Anti-Semitism, who welcomed a lone historian into their midst and whose friendship and discourse have meant so much to me: Drs. Jacob Arlow, Martin Bergmann, Kenneth Calder, Joseph Coltrera, Sidney Furst, Alexander Grinstein, John Hartman, Milton Jucovy, Eugene Mahon, Peter Neubauer, Mortimer Ostow (chair), Winfred Overholser, Bernard Pacella, Annemarie Weil, George Wiedeman.

I am grateful to Professors David Ruderman and Albert Solnit of Yale University for inviting me to give the Franz Rosenzweig Lectures under the appropriately joint sponsorship of the Program in Judaic Studies and the Gardiner Program in Psychoanalysis and the Humanities and to Professors Paula Hyman, Geoffrey Hartman, William Hallo, and John Hollander for making my trips to Yale so pleasant and memorable. Similar thanks are due to Professor Harold Garrett-Goodyear of Mount Holyoke College and Professor Howard Adelman of Smith College for enabling me to repeat the lectures at their institutions, and to Professor Lois Dubin of Smith and her husband, Professor Benjamin Braude of Boston College, for their exceptional hospitality. I take this occasion also to express my indebtedness to Professor François Furet, who first brought me to teach what has become an annual seminar at the École des Hautes Études en Sciences Sociales in Paris, to its current president, Professor Marc Augé, and to Dr. Nancy Green of the École, who has smoothed my path at every turn.

Information, leads, and scholarly help of various kinds were generously provided by Peter Swales, Professor Paul Schwaber of Wesleyan University, Ernst Pawel, Professor Dr. Laetitia Boehm of Munich, Professor Dr. Anna Maria Accerboni Pavanello of Trieste, Professor Lucien Dobroszycki and Mme. Dina Abramovich of the YIVO Institute, Professor Josephine Woll of Howard University, Dr. Lynn Gamwell, Director of the Art Museum at the State University of New York at Binghamton, and my colleagues Professors Andreas Huyssen and David Weiss-Halivni of Columbia. For their invaluable help in the transcription of Freud's Gothic handwriting I have to thank two of my doctoral students, Ms. Evelyn Erlich, now Librarian of the Leo Baeck Institute, and Mr. Michael Brenner. My good friend Catherine Goetschel acceded readily to my last-minute request for a final review of the German appendixes. Ms. Malka Gold, my administrative assistant at Columbia for the past decade, put the manuscript of this book into its final computer shape with her customary patience, skill, and devotion. Three other doctoral students of mine, Jonathan Karp, Nancy Sinkoff, and Miriam Wielgus, shared with me the arduous task of proofreading.

For permission to consult and reproduce manuscript material in their possession I thank the Freud Archives and the Library of Congress in Washington, D.C., the YIVO Institute for Jewish Research in New York, as well as the Central Zionist Archives in Jerusalem.

I am most grateful to Mr. Mark Paterson, Director, Sigmund Freud Copyrights, Wivenhoe, Colchester, England, for granting permission to reproduce material from the unpublished correspondence of Freud and from the 1934 manuscript draft of *Moses and Monotheism* as well as the facsimile of the first page of that draft. I thank the Freud Museum, London, for permission to reproduce photographs of objects in their collection that belonged to Freud.

I am especially pleased to have my book appear under the imprint of Yale University Press and thus join its distinguished list of publications in the field of psychoanalysis and its history. Charles Grench, my editor, has shown the most sympathetic understanding and encouragement at every turn. My manuscript editor, Lawrence Kenney, has been an ideal arbiter of questions of style and grammar, while his extraordinary eye for detail has saved me from many a pitfall.

Finally, I want to thank Mr. Russell Knapp of New York for his quiet support at a difficult juncture. A sabbatical from Columbia University and a Fellowship from the John Simon Guggenheim Memorial Foundation in 1989–90, for which I am particularly grateful, enabled me to complete this book.

Prelude for the Listener

"Prelude" rather than "introduction," for in all essential respects the work must introduce itself along the way; "listener" rather than "reader," for the text that follows remains exactly as it was delivered orally. Except that my lectures have become chapters I have altered nothing, in the hope that some echo of the spoken word will somehow survive the transition onto the printed page. Tempted though I was to dispense with any further apparatus, my scholarly superego (as well as my own frequent frustration in trying to trace the sources of others) has induced me to add a full garland of notes, most of them intended to allow those who are so inclined to check my sources, others to amplify or further qualify a point. The appendixes consist of a number of hitherto unpublished texts, most by Freud, one by his father, all of them discussed in the body of the work, which I thought should now be made publicly available in the original German (with one in Hebrew). The bibliography is linked directly to the notes and makes no attempt at completeness. Most of my listeners may be content with the main body of the text and forego the rest.

Even these, however, may be surprised to find a book on Freud's *Moses and Monotheism* by a historian who has generally been known as a student of Sephardic Jewry and may therefore have some interest in how this book came to be. Undoubtedly there is a tangle of unconscious motives of which I myself have only the slightest intimation but which may be related to the existential fact that I have been the son of a father and am myself the father of a son. My last book, published two years before my father's death, was dedicated to both my father and my son and spoke in terms of a transmission of past into future in which all three of us were implicated.

It is, of course, easier for me to delineate in retrospect some of the conscious factors of which I am aware. Like any educated person of my generation I had read Freud sporadically and thought of myself (prematurely I now realize) as knowledgeable in at least the rudiments of psychoanalytic theory. Whatever vague fascination I had always felt for Freud received a sharp new focus in 1981, when Dr. Mortimer Ostow invited me to join the Research Group on the Psychoanalytic Study of Anti-Semitism. The group, composed of some fifteen eminent analysts, had been meeting for about a year and had decided they needed a historian of the Jews in order to pursue their work effectively. Thus began for me an association which, through monthly meetings over the past nine years (the group has just now disbanded), has been a new and vital source of intellectual stimulation which was bound to affect my own thinking and the direction of my work. Shortly after joining the group I began to read and reread Freud systematically, both in English and in German. Initially I did this out of a desire to increase my psychoanalytic literacy the better to follow the discussions in the group, but soon my reading of Freud developed its own momentum. At a very early stage it became evident to me that although, bereft of professional training and experience, I would not have anything significant to say about the clinical aspects of psychoanalytic theory, I might have some contribution to make in various areas of applied psychoanalysis and the history of the psychoanalytic movement. Indeed, when I reread *Moses and Monotheism* for the first time in some thirty years, it occurred to me that it was precisely my training and knowledge as a Jewish historian that might enable me to understand this book in ways not accessible to psychoanalysts or literary critics. My prior preoccupation with the nature of Jewish collective memory also made me see Freud's book in an entirely new light. In this sense my work on *Moses and Monotheism* may be regarded as a natural extension of themes that had already surfaced in my *Zakhor.*

Meanwhile another seemingly fortuitous event occurred which was to influence the trend of my thought. In 1982 I was invited by the Leo Baeck Institute, which is devoted to research on the history of the Jews in the German-speaking lands, to give the 26th Leo Baeck Memorial Lecture. The topic I chose—"Assimilation and Racial Anti-Semitism: The Iberian and the German Models"—was an exercise in comparative historical phenomenology. Looking back, I now think it also marked, symbolically, the transition of my interests from medieval Hispano-Portuguese to modern Central European Jewish history. Even more unexpected and influential was my subsequent election to the presidency of the New York Leo Baeck Institute, with its incomparable library and archival resources on German and Austrian Jewry, a milieu particularly congenial and sustaining for anyone working on Freud. The walls of my office at the Institute are adorned with paintings and sketches of Felix Mendelssohn-Bartholdy, Arnold Schoenberg, the Rosé Quartet, and—a virtually unknown oil portrait of the young Bertha Pappenheim (Freud's Anna O) in which she is sufficiently beautiful to explain why Breuer abruptly broke off her treatment in order to save his marriage.

Various strands, then, came together when I was invited at Columbia, my own university, to deliver one of the annual Lionel Trilling Seminars for 1986. After much initial hesitation I decided to overcome my qualms and to present my work-in-progress publicly in a lecture which I entitled merely "About Freud's *Moses and Monotheism.*" Given the late Lionel Trilling's well-known engrossment with Freud and the problematics of his own Jewish identity, I thought such a topic appropriate to the occasion. At the same time I wanted to test the waters and see how my work would be received. To my genuine relief I found the audience interested and receptive. It was also my good fortune to have as my commentators two distinguished scholars, Robert Alter of

Berkeley and William McGrath of Rochester, whose sympathetic criticisms were entirely constructive and of considerable use to me. The Trilling Lecture, never published, already contained the nucleus of all that I would subsequently elaborate. My own feeling was that it had been too long for a lecture and too short to present the materials I had already gathered. It was clear to me that I would have to write a book.

It was just around the time I came to this decision that the most attractive of alternatives presented itself. I received yet another invitation, now from Yale University, to deliver the Franz Rosenzweig Lectures. The luxury of a series of five lectures on Freud's *Moses* in such a setting seemed to me an ideal and irresistible solution. Even so, it was three years before I could finish the manuscript. In the meantime I did manage to publish an article, "Freud on the 'Historical Novel,'" in the *International Journal of Psycho-Analysis* (September 1989) that, I should stress, contains material on the genesis of *Moses and Monotheism* and on Freud's attitudes toward psychoanalysis as art or as science that I have not included here.

The Rosenzweig Lectures were delivered at Yale over a three-week period in October-November 1989. They were repeated in a three-day marathon at Mount Holyoke and Smith Colleges in March 1990 and, somewhat paraphrastically, in French at my annual seminar at the École des Hautes Études en Sciences Sociales in Paris two months later. The lectures are the book. The warm response of my three audiences has encouraged me to publish it.

I am, of course, under no illusion that the warmth was unanimous or that my work will find the same favor in other quarters. The book that has emerged through the process I have sketched is as vulnerable as any in what has become the perilously mined field of Freud studies. Nor am I so naive as to think I can sway my potential critics by anticipating them here. I would merely hope that I shall be criticized for what I have said and done, not for what I never intended to say or do. Indeed, old-fashioned as it may sound, the question of an author's conscious intentionality and the belief that such intentions are to a large extent recoverable by the reader are among the pivots of this book. This does not mean I hold that the effort at linkage between reader and author exhausts the possibilities of the act of reading. For the record, then, I would indicate those of my intentions that are most liable to be misunderstood, and I shall do so in the most succinct manner possible, by stating them negatively. Thus:

1. This book is not an attempt to prove that psychoanalysis is "Jewish," though eventually it is concerned to inquire whether Freud thought it to be so, which is a very different matter.

2. The book is not intended as an exploration of Freud's life or Jewish identity except insofar as these become vital to explore the meaning of *Moses and Monotheism*.

3. Except for the depth and intensity of Freud's Jewish identity and commitment, and a rejection of any interpretation that would regard *Moses and Monotheism* as a repudiation of that identity or even ambivalence toward it, this book does not attempt to reach closure on any of the themes of which it treats. On the contrary, one of its central purposes is to reopen questions concerning Freud which have been generally regarded as foreclosed in the scholarly literature.

4. I have not attempted an exhaustive analysis of Freud's book. Many aspects, worthy of independent treatment, have not been included.

5. This book is not a polemic, though I have had to take issue explicitly with a number of important scholars on some major points of disagreement. Nonpolemical by nature, I have done so with considerable restraint and without going into every detail to which I object. Not to have mentioned some of the students of Freud whose views differ from mine would have been a disservice to the reader and a worse insult to them.

6. It has not been my aim to deny or disparage the validity of a psychoanalytic exegesis of Freud's writings or, for that matter, of any other texts. I insist only that without taking conscious intentionality into consideration and without the elementary controls provided by traditional historical and philological critical methods, the results will all too often be merely capricious.

7. The fact that, within a Jewish historical context, I have arrived at a positive evaluation of Freud's intentions in *Moses and Monotheism* does not mean that I necessarily share any of his views on Jews or Judaism.

It remains for me only to make a technical observation. The problem of quoting the existing English translations of Freudian texts and correspondence has often proved difficult. Writing in English, I have had no choice but to use James Strachey's translations of the canonical works precisely because they are, for the English-speaking world and even beyond, the "Standard Edition." Strachey's devotion and achievement are not to be minimized. I am, however, certainly not the first to go back to Freud's original German and to discover how misleading Strachey's translations can sometimes be. Moreover, in the case of *Moses and Monotheism* there is another complete English translation available, that of Katherine Jones, published simultaneously with the first German edition in 1939 and still in print. A comparison of the Jones and Strachey translations has convinced me that while the latter is generally closer to the literal German text, the former is often more felicitous in capturing its tone and spirit. Considering the various alternatives, I have generally resisted the temptation to provide my own translations from *Moses and Monotheism*, which would then add an unauthorized third to the two translations already available and thus confuse the reader even more. To merge Jones and Strachey would produce a hybrid. In the end I decided to use the Standard Edition throughout, so long as the issue of translation involved relatively minor points.

I have made an exception on only a few occasions where I have either introduced a modification into the Strachey translation or simply quoted that of
Katherine Jones. Wherever I have exercised this option I have so indicated in
the notes. I should add that throughout I have clung stubbornly to Freud's
(and James Breasted's) "Ikhnaton," rather than Strachey's "Akhenaten," as
the adopted name of the heretical pharaoh Amenhotep IV.

Yosef Hayim Yerushalmi

Columbia University
July 4, 1990 / 11 Tammuz 5750

Addendum (February, 1993):
    For this paperback edition several technical errors have been corrected. I
wish to note also that in the first edition I was unaware that part of the
German text of the Freud-Herzl letter (Appendix III, no. 1) had already been
quoted by Peter Loewenberg in his "Freud as a Jew: A Study in Ambivalence
and Courage," *Journal of the History of the Behavioral Sciences*, 7 (1971),
and that the complete German text was first published by Avner Falk in his
"Freud und Herzl: Die Geschichte einer Beziehung in der Phantasie,"
Zeitgeschichte, 9 (1982). While Dr. Falk thus has obvious priority, I differ
from his reading of the name Max "Neuda" which, following Ernst Pawel
[(1989), p. 456], I read as Max Nordau. Finally, the exhibition of Freud's
collection of antiquities with the addition of the newly discovered Jewish
objects mentioned in my "Provisional Postscript" (pp. 111–112) was held,
after this book appeared, at the Jewish Museum in New York (November 7,
1991–February 18, 1992). See now my essay "The Purloined Kiddush Cups:
Reopening the Case on Freud's Jewish Identity," in the supplementary exhibition catalogue entitled *Sigmund Freud's Jewish Heritage*, ed. Lynn Gamwell,
State University of New York and the Freud Museum, London, (1991).

Freud's
Moses:
Judaism Terminable
and Interminable

1

The Fourth
Humiliation

> Aber wir vergessen zu leicht, dass wir
> kein Recht haben, die Neurose dort in
> den Vordergrund zu stellen, wo es
> sich um eine bedeutende Leistung
> handelt.
>
> [But we forget too easily that we have
> no right to place neurosis in the fore-
> ground wherever a great accomplish-
> ment is involved.]
>
> —Freud, at a meeting of the Vienna
> Psychoanalytic Society, January 12,
> 1910

In a conversation that must have taken place around 1908 Freud told Theodor
Reik the following joke:

> The boy Itzig is asked in grammar school: "Who was Moses?" and
> answers, "Moses was the son of an Egyptian princess." "That's not
> true," says the teacher. "Moses was the son of a Hebrew mother. The
> Egyptian princess found the baby in a casket." But Itzig answers:
> "Says she!"[1]

The joke catches our attention on two counts; first, because the precocious
Itzig seems already to display a talent for what Paul Ricoeur, referring to
Freud's own method, has elegantly called a "hermeneutics of suspicion";[2] and
second, because it was Freud, after all, who taught us to take jokes seriously.
Just how serious this one can be will become evident if we move Itzig from
his Galician *ḥeder* (the Jewish elementary school) to the University of Berlin,
from which the following came forth solemnly in 1922: "Die letzte und wich-
tigste Frage aller israelitisch-jüdischen Religionsforschung wird immer blei-
ben: Wer war Mose?" (The final and most important question for all research
into Israelite-Jewish religion will always remain: Who was Moses?) It is the
opening line of a book by Ernst Sellin on which Freud was to rely heavily, of
which more later on.[3]

Let me stress at the outset that my concern with Freud does not stem from any need to claim him for an already crowded Jewish pantheon. Long ago I serenely relinquished Columbus to Italy and Santa Teresa of Avila, despite her Jewish grandfather, to Spain. I could yield Freud with equal equanimity, but the nature of his life and work will not allow it. By this I do not mean to plunge into the premature and hitherto sterile debate as to whether psychoanalysis as a system of thought is organically rooted in Judaism (the Jewish origins of the psychoanalytic movement are another matter). Whatever one's stance on such tortuous issues, *Moses and Monotheism*[4] remains, at its core, a deliberately Jewish book.

Reactions to *Moses and Monotheism,* Freud's last major work, have ranged from its total acceptance as literal history to its outraged condemnation as a malicious attack upon the very foundations of Jewish existence.[5] On a more sober plane it has been rejected almost unanimously by biblical scholars as an arbitrary manipulation of dubious historical data, and by anthropologists and historians of religion as resting on long outmoded ethnological assumptions. Both these strictures, I hasten to add, are quite correct, and the details, available in the literature, need not concern us here.[6] The most obvious remaining course has seemed to lie in treating the book as a psychological document of Freud's inner life, itself to be subjected to psychoanalytic exegesis.

Yet although such an approach has yielded an occasionally provocative insight, it has more often fallen into the snare of the genetic fallacy, has confused motive and meaning, and has avoided the central question of what it was that Freud, writing and publishing the work ex cathedra, wanted to convey to his readers. Surely he himself did not intend the book as psychoanalytic confession. To move at this point into a theoretical discussion of textuality and exegesis would, however, distract me from more urgent tasks. Besides, my own instinct for survival whispers that to enter the enchanted forest of current literary theory would be to double the perils I already face. I will only propose that to read *Moses and Monotheism* merely as psychological autobiography without first exploring its conscious intentionality is to be reductive in a fundamental sense and to engage in a species of "wild analysis." If the book can be read as a final chapter in Freud's lifelong case history (I shall play with this option in chapter 4) it is also a public statement about matters of considerably wider consequence—the nature of Jewish history, religion and peoplehood, Christianity and anti-Semitism—written at a tragic historical juncture.

My own preoccupation with *Moses and Monotheism* arises out of a profound interest in the various modalities of modern Jewish historicism, of that quest for the meaning of Judaism and Jewish identity through an unprecedented reexamination of the Jewish past which is itself the consequence of a radical break with that past,[7] a phenomenon of which Freud's book is at once an exemplary and idiosyncratic instance.

I come, then, as a Jewish historian seeking a broader historical context, or rather a series of such contexts. That these must also take account of vital elements in Freud's personal history should require no special explanation. One need hardly adopt an initial psychoanalytic or "psycho-historical" posture to appreciate the relevance of Freud's life to his work. Beyond that my tools remain the humble ones of my craft in general, and the knowledge I bring to bear that of my discipline in particular.

What follows, however, is a very different exploration from that I had originally anticipated. When I started out I took it for granted that all the routine historical homework had already been done. It was some time before I realized that this was simply not the case, and that I would have to review the genesis of the work in considerable detail. To give but one example: because there was no mention of a manuscript, at least in the literature known to me, I had assumed that none had survived or that, if it exists, it is identical with the published text and therefore of no value. A skeptical inquiry to the Freud Archives at the Library of Congress eventually brought me, to my surprise, a photocopy of the original draft of *Moses and Monotheism* dated August 9, 1934, and different in significant ways from the published version.[8] We shall soon have occasion to profit from it. For the rest—I shall not pretend to have touched upon, let alone penetrated, every important aspect of what may well be the most opaque of Freud's works. The dictum of Ortega y Gasset concerning the *Quixote* of Cervantes is equally appropriate to *Moses and Monotheism*: Some books cannot be taken by direct assault; they must be taken like Jericho.

I presume that the bare plot (though not the essential drama) of Freud's *Moses* is, by now, notorious. Monotheism is not of Jewish origin but an Egyptian discovery. The pharaoh Amenhotep IV established it as his state religion in the form of an exclusive worship of the sun-power, or Aton, thereafter calling himself Ikhnaton. The Aton religion, according to Freud, was characterized by the exclusive belief in one God, the rejection of anthropomorphism, magic, and sorcery, and the absolute denial of an afterlife. Upon Ikhnaton's death, however, his great heresy was rapidly undone, and the Egyptians reverted to their old gods. Moses was not a Hebrew but an Egyptian priest or noble, and a fervent monotheist. In order to save the Aton religion from extinction he placed himself at the head of an oppressed Semitic tribe then living in Egypt, brought them forth from bondage, and created a new nation. He gave them an even more spiritualized, imageless form of monotheistic religion and, in order to set them apart, introduced the Egyptian custom of circumcision. But the crude mass of former slaves could not bear the severe demands of the new faith. In a mob revolt Moses was killed and the memory of the murder repressed. The Israelites went on to forge an alliance of compromise with kindred Semitic tribes in Midian whose fierce volcanic deity, named Yahweh, now became their national god. As a result, the god of Moses was fused with Yahweh and the deeds of Moses ascribed to a Midianite priest also called Moses. However, over a period of centuries the submerged tradition of the true faith and its founder gathered sufficient force to reassert itself and emerge victorious. Yahweh was henceforth endowed with the universal and spiritual qualities of Moses' god, though the memory of Moses' murder remained repressed among the Jews, reemerging only in a very disguised form with the rise of Christianity.

All this is quite shocking, of course, though it will be less so to those with a prior psychoanalytic orientation or with a certain fund of historical information at their disposal. To begin a proper evaluation of *Moses and Monotheism* requires not only an initial suspension of psychoanalytic disbelief, but the ability to enter provisionally, yet with empathy, structures of thought and modes of discourse as alien as those encountered by an anthropologist studying the Bororo or Nambikwara tribes in the Brazilian unknown or, if you wish, to pass like Alice through the rabbithole, into a world where everything is "curiouser and curiouser." The reorientation must, in any event, be radical.

To take an initiatory example: in December 1905 the young Otto Rank wrote a brief essay, found and published only in 1981, on a theme that has been a favorite of modern Jewish thinkers and scholars since the nineteenth century: *Das Wesen des Judentums* (The essence of Judaism). His conclusion was succinct: "The essence of Judaism is its stress on primitive sexuality." Should we be appalled? Was this an instance of so-called Jewish self-hatred? The discoverer of the text observes, drily and correctly, that it was "the highest praise he [Rank] could confer on any people."[9] Similarly, Freud's conviction that Judaism had its origins in the slaying of its founder will neither come as a surprise nor be perceived as a particular insult for anyone familiar with his *Totem and Taboo,* where not only religion but the whole of human civilization is rooted in a prehistoric murder of which the slaying of Moses is, on an unconscious level, a repetition.

Our perspective also changes as soon as we realize that the denial of the creation of monotheism by the Jews, let alone their divine election, represents for Freud only the last in a series of painful humiliations which the narcissism of mankind has had to endure in order to exchange illusion for reality: the "cosmological" blow delivered by Copernicus to the idea of the centrality of our planet in the universe; Darwin's "biological" blow to Man's supposedly privileged place in the hierarchy of creation; and—most devastating of all— Freud's own "psychological" blow to Man's last imagined refuge ("the ego is not master in its own house").[10] All three humiliations were noted by Freud with grim satisfaction, for ultimately they were not really humiliating, not loss but gain. Why, then, should the centrality of the Jews in history as God's Chosen People be exempt?

Nor were Freud's speculations concerning Egyptian origins as novel as they might seem. Goethe had already speculated that Moses may have been murdered, although he had in mind a political assassination committed by an impatient Joshua.[11] That monotheism derived from Egypt was argued before Freud by James Breasted and other Egyptologists.[12] Contrary to the impression Freud leaves with the reader, the Egyptian descent of Moses is itself no novelty. Not only had such a hypothesis been suggested by so diverse a company as the sociologist Max Weber, the anti-Semitic apostle of Bayreuth Houston Stewart Chamberlain, and in fictional form by Freud's beloved Joseph Popper-Linkeus;[13] it had a far more venerable history.

Thus, although Josephus Flavius in the first century has Moses as a Hebrew, he too rejects the biblical etymology of his name in favor of an Egyptian one.[14] That Moses was, in fact, an Egyptian is stated explicitly by such ancient pagan writers as Strabo, Manetho, Apion, Celsus.[15] Leaping forward, we find that in the seventeenth and eighteenth centuries the debt of Hebrew religion to Egypt was an important theme in the nascent critique of biblical history by John Marsham, John Spencer, and John Toland. Indeed, Toland speculated pointedly as to whether Moses had been "an Egyptian priest and king" who had "left his country because of dissent about the public state of religion."[16] In 1789 Friedrich Schiller, one of Freud's favorite poets, proposed in an elaborate essay that Moses as the foster child of an Egyptian princess was initiated into a purely monotheistic Egyptian mystery religion which he subsequently taught to the Hebrews.[17] Had we world enough and time it might be interesting to pursue these ideas and to situate them within the wider search for a pre-Mosaic Egyptian revelation that begins in European thought with the Hermetic traditions of the Renaissance. But that would not really facilitate an understanding of *Moses and Monotheism,* whose originality lies not in the discrete elements of its plot but, as Freud correctly insisted, in the use he made of them and the conclusions he drew.[18]

The only ostensible precursors within the psychoanalytic movement itself were Otto Rank and Karl Abraham. Rank's *Myth of the Birth of the Hero,* first published in 1909, already pointed out striking mythological parallels to the biblical birth of Moses and viewed them as projections of the psychoanalytic "family romance." Freud mentions the book as having been written under his influence, but the passage on the family romance was actually written by him, and he later reprinted it independently.[19] By contrast, Abraham's paper "Amenhotep IV: A Psycho-Analytical Contribution Toward the Understanding of His Personality and of the Monotheistic Cult of Aton" (1912)[20] directly anticipated certain aspects of *Moses and Monotheism,* yet Freud never mentions Abraham in the book.

The text of *Moses and Monotheism* seems to reflect the difficulties Freud experienced while composing it. It is riddled with apologies, hesitations, repetitions. Its publishing history is peculiar. Part I, which posits Moses' Egyptian origin through the Egyptian etymology of his name and a reinterpretation of the biblical story of his birth and rescue in light of the family romance, and part II, an attempt at a historical reconstruction of the events in Egypt and the wilderness, were published in 1937 in Vienna in two separate issues of the psychoanalytic journal *Imago*. The third part was withheld by Freud until the entire work was published two years later, after he had fled to London and shortly before his death.[21]

Since then many have asked how Freud could have brought himself to publish such a book at a time when European Jewry had already entered its darkest hour and despite repeated entreaties not to go through with it.[22] The answer, of course, will largely depend on one's prior image of Freud and especially on how one interprets the book as a whole. Though he knew, as he wrote to his son Ernst, that "Jewry will be very offended," he felt it would make no practical difference, and in the book he states that he could not "set aside truth in favor of supposed national interests."[23] The adjective is significant, and to offend was, after all, nothing new for Freud. Indeed, one senses that the degree of offense (translate: resistance) had long become for him one of the criteria for truth itself.[24] For us the question of interpretation is more imperative.

It has become something of a commonplace by now to regard both the content of *Moses and Monotheism* and its convoluted gestation as symptoms of Freud's deep "ambivalence" (that tired and evasive cliché) about his own Jewishness. Others have gone farther. For Marthe Robert the book represents Freud's climactic resolution of a lifelong Oedipal conflict with his father, Jakob, through a final repudiation of the Jewish past and of his Jewish identity, so that "he could say that he was neither a Jew nor a German . . . for he wished to be the son not of any man or country, but like the murdered prophet only of his life work." Even Ricoeur has written that "this book stands like an exorcism. It marks the renouncement on the part of Sigmund Freud the Jew of the value that his narcissism could still rightfully claim, the value of belonging to the race that engendered Moses and imparted monotheism to the world."[25]

Now while such interpretations have all the seduction and excitement of reading Freud contra Freud, it seems to me that the conclusions remain precarious at best and that the available evidence can be read in very different ways. To be sure, Freud identified with Moses at various stages of his life, but at the very time he was writing *Moses and Monotheism* he also identified repeatedly with Rabbi Yochanan ben Zakkai, the architect of Judaism after the destruction of the Second Temple.[26] Moreover, in the very first sentence of the book he carefully and solemnly declares himself a Jew: "To deny a people the man whom it praises as the greatest of its sons is not a deed to be undertaken lightly—*especially when one belongs oneself to that people.*"[27] How deliberately Freud penned these words is revealed only now by the manuscript of 1934, in which, after a discussion of the Egyptian etymology of *Moses,* the original sentence reads merely, "One will not easily decide to deny a nation its greatest man *because of the meaning of a name.*"[28] Why, then, should we doubt him? In a letter to the novelist Arnold Zweig, written shortly before Freud embarked on his study (the letter is typically not included in the published correspondence but was available to Max Schur), it is Zweig's Jewish ambivalence that is at issue and Freud who is telling him to deal with it. Schur writes, "Zweig had periodically been in analysis, and Freud, who had repeatedly advised him to leave Germany, had pointed out [in a letter of August 18, 1933] that some of Zweig's conflicts found expression in his ambivalent attitude toward being Jewish. . . . [Freud] continued: 'One defends oneself in every way against the fear of castration. Here a piece of opposition to one's own Jewishness may still be hiding cunningly. Our great master Moses was, after all, a strong anti-Semite and made no secret of it. Perhaps he was really an Egyptian.'"[29]

Would an Egyptian Moses make Freud any less a Jew? Does the assertion, as Marthe Robert insists, "declare a whole people illegitimate?" The Jews have never claimed descent from Moses, and Abraham, from whom they do claim it, was originally a Chaldean. Whether God or Moses made the Jews, they have been Jews ever since. Significantly, part III of the book is entitled "Moses, His People, and Monotheistic Religion," as if to say that, once he chose them, the bond between Moses and Israel was indissoluble. They were henceforth "his people" (*sein Volk*). Again—is the denial that Moses was a Hebrew a projection of Freud's own yearning for a different lineage? While Freud's concept of the family romance enabled him to bring a fresh approach to the biblical narrative, there are alternative ways to understand his need for Moses to be an Egyptian within the framework of his book, where it has its own logic. Freud was neither the first nor the last to have difficulty in grasping how monotheism could have arisen full-blown among a conglomeration of recent slaves. If, as he believed, monotheism did not evolve gradually, then it had to come to the Israelites abruptly and from the outside or, in his own words, it had to be "given" to them by a "great stranger." In this, as I shall have occasion to emphasize, he is in curious accord with the Bible, only there the great stranger is God himself.

And how crucial, really, is the Egyptian provenance of Moses? In 1934 Freud told Zweig, "The fact that I wrote at length to you in an earlier letter about Moses being an Egyptian is not the essential point, though it is the starting point."[30] To which Marthe Robert responds characteristically, "But for one who had so brilliantly demonstrated the significance of negation in the grammar of neuroses he seems to deny it too emphatically. The more he denies that his 'Egyptian Moses' was the main cause of his difficulties, the more one inclines to think it was."[31] Curiously, so far as I am aware, this denial occurs only once and quite casually, in the 1934 letter to Zweig. Though I shall myself have ample occasion to express my own skepticism about certain aspects of the persona that Freud displayed to the world, Robert's remark only sharpens the larger issue: Whether to approach Freud's explicit statements with but ordinary historical caution or with radical, admittedly Freudian, suspicion. I would suggest, provisionally, that if we first allow Freud to speak for himself we can trace a fully coherent development leading to *Moses and Monotheism* and arrive at a very different assessment of the book itself. Unless, of course, we greet every statement of Freud in the spirit of Itzig and murmur, "Says he!"

The difficulty in interpreting *Moses and Monotheism* is directly related to the difficulty in grasping the nature of Freud's Jewish identity. The problem reveals itself in exemplary fashion at a well-known point in his correspondence that will still bear reexamination.

In 1918 Freud wrote teasingly to his friend and follower the Swiss clergyman Oskar Pfister, who was also a psychoanalyst, "Quite by the way, how comes it that none of the godly ever devised psychoanalysis and that one had to wait for a completely godless Jew?" (*einen ganz gottlosen Juden*). Unruffled, Pfister replied, "Ah well, because piety is not yet tantamount to genius for discovery. . . . Besides, in the first place you are no Jew, something that in view of my unbounded admiration for Amos, Isaiah, Jeremiah, and the author of Job and Ecclesiastes, causes me great regret, and secondly, you are not godless, for he who lives for truth lives in God." Indeed, he went on to say, "A better Christian there never was."[32]

The gentle Pfister, of course, missed the point on both counts. Freud *was* godless and he *was* a Jew, a combination that Pfister, like many others then and now, could not fathom.

The exchange has other resonances. Pfister's good-natured "a better Christian there never was" (*ein besserer Christ war nie*) is an eighteenth-century echo from the heyday of the German Enlightenment. It is a direct quotation from Lessing's play of 1779, *Nathan der Weise* (Nathan the wise), that glowing testimony to his friendship with Moses Mendelssohn and a singular document of a moment when the future seemed full of promise for German-Jewish brotherhood in a mutual religion of tolerant reason.[33]

Three years later, Lessing's younger contemporary Herder published his *Vom Geist der ebräischen Poesie* (On the spirit of Hebrew poetry), in which, among other matters, he expressed his fervent admiration for the epic quality of the Moses narrative in the Bible and his astonishment that no one had as yet seen fit to make Moses a subject for German epic poetry. In a striking passage he asked that this neglect be redressed but insisted that he would like to arouse, not a German but a German Jew (he uses the delicate term "German Hebrew") to undertake the task ("*doch möchte ich . . . keinen Deutschen, sondern einen deutschen Ebräer geweckt haben!*").[34] Only a Jew would have the innate empathy and unmediated acquaintance with the biblical source to accomplish what was required.

Herder's call went not without a response. Between 1789 and 1802 an epic on Moses and the Exodus was published in five volumes in Berlin. It was the work of Hartwig Wessely (Naftali Zvi Weisel), himself a disciple of Mendelssohn and a leader of the movement for secular Jewish enlightenment in Germany known as Haskalah. Significantly, the poetry of this German Hebrew was actually in Hebrew, and his epic was entitled *Shirey Tif'eret* (Songs of glory). Within a very short time this would be less possible, for the language of the Haskalah in Germany shifted rapidly from Hebrew to German. These are not exotic details. That the figure of Moses should confront us at both the bright beginning and the dark end of the Jewish romance with German civilization is emblematic of our theme.

The story of Central European Jewry in the century and a half between Wessely's *Shirey Tif'eret* and Freud's *Moses and Monotheism* has often been told although, among historians of psychoanalysis, frequently misunderstood in some of its crucial aspects. For the moment it will suffice to recall that the Haskalah and the initial struggle for Emancipation led the vanguard of German Jewry to ruptures of varying degrees with Jewish tradition and a secularization of life and outlook often more radical than anything that the earlier apostles of Jewish *Aufklärung* had anticipated. From Königsberg and Berlin the Haskalah spread rapidly to Austria and eastward within the Habsburg Empire to Bohemia and Moravia, as well as to Galicia, where Hebrew was and remained its primary vehicle of expression (we shall travel back to Galicia in chapter 4). In the often turbulent process of social and cultural change that accompanied or succeeded the Haskalah, there emerged that modern species of "gottloser Jude" whom we know as the secular Jew.

One would think that by now the secular Jew would be so familiar as to require no special comment. Yet a blurb for a book on "Humanistic Judaism" in the *New York Times* still finds it necessary to proclaim, "You don't have to be religious to be Jewish"—an obvious parody of the immortal "You don't have to be Jewish to eat Levy's Rye," but without its inexorable logic. For to be a Jew without God is, after all, historically problematic and not self-evident, and the blandly generic term *secular Jew* gives no indication of the richly nuanced variety within the species. Throughout the nineteenth century, Jews who had lost faith in the God of their fathers sought and found a spectrum of novel secular Jewish surrogates. Some expressed their Jewish identity through a passionate devotion to the new critical historical scholarship (*Wissenschaft des Judentums*), others through varieties of Jewish nationalism, socialism, philanthropy, fraternal organizations, Hebrew or Yiddish culture. There were, and still are, ideological Jews, cultural Jews, even culinary Jews ("I love your cooking more than your religion," Heinrich Heine observed at one point). These are some of the broad categories; there are exquisite shadings and permutations in between. But then there have also been those many who have evinced no special need to define themselves as Jews or to embrace any particular form of visible Jewish commitment, but who have felt themselves to be somehow irreducibly Jewish nonetheless. They are perhaps best described if we temporarily appropriate and expand Philip Rieff's suggestive term and call them Psychological Jews. They are not, however, a Jewish counterpart to Rieff's Psychological Man, who is by definition a post-Freudian creature.[35]

The Psychological Jew was born before Freud. If, for all secular Jews, Judaism has become "Jewishness" of one kind or another, the Jewishness of the Psychological Jew seems, at least to the outsider, devoid of all but the most vestigial content; it has become almost pure subjectivity. Content is replaced by character. Alienated from classical Jewish texts, Psychological Jews tend to insist on inalienable Jewish traits. Intellectuality and independence of mind, the highest ethical and moral standards, concern for social justice, tenacity in the face of persecution—these are among the qualities they will claim, if called upon, as quintessentially Jewish. It is therefore no accident that the first great culture-hero of modern secular Jews was Spinoza (to be joined later by Marx and eventually by Freud himself). Without attempting a complete typology, I should at least mention one other feature. Psychological Jews tend to be sensitive to anti-Semitic prejudice in a particular way. Floating in their undefined yet somehow real Jewishness, they will doubly resent and fiercely resist any attempt on the part of the surrounding society to define them against their own wishes. The worst moments are those in which, as a result of anti-Semitism, they are forced to realize that vital aspects of their lives are still determined by ancestral choices they may no longer understand and which, in any case, they feel they have transcended or repudiated.

Though Freud may seem at first glance an exemplary specimen of the genus *Judaeus Psychologicus*, being Freud he also displays some strikingly mutant traits. Thus, in choosing a wife Freud does not turn outside the faith or, for all his fierce ambition, to some lavishly dowered daughter of the Viennese Jewish upper bourgeoisie. In effect, he reaches upward, but to what may be properly considered the aristocracy of German-Jewish orthodoxy. Certainly he fell in love with Martha Bernays, but he was also fully aware of her family background, so different from his own.

Martha was the granddaughter of the renowned Haham (Chief Rabbi) Isaac Bernays of Hamburg. Her father, Berman, was a businessman. Both he and his wife scrupulously maintained the orthodox tradition, and Martha grew up in a deeply pious home. By 1879, when Berman died, the family finances were virtually ruined, and one wonders if, had it not been for this fall of fortune, Freud would even have been considered as a suitor, especially when the engagement faced other obstacles as well.[36]

In the course of the long engagement Freud virtually bludgeons Martha into abandoning the Jewish rituals of her upbringing if she is to be his wife. Their correspondence is romantic and passionate, but he rails against her because, to spare her mother's feelings on the Sabbath, she writes her letters in the garden, using a pencil. She must, he insists, consent to eating ham and break with her mother's observances, for he is going to make "a heathen" out of her. In the end he wants a civil marriage in Germany, but this would not be recognized in Austria. Furious, he tells his friend and collaborator Joseph Breuer that rather than face a Jewish religious ceremony he would formally change his confession, a momentary overreaction from which Breuer was able to dissuade him by pointing out gently that this was "too complicated."[37]

Yet all this was only one side of the coin. In a letter of 1882 the same Freud assures Martha that "even if the form wherein the old Jews were happy no longer affords us any shelter, something of the core, of the essence of this meaningful and life-affirming Judaism will not be absent from our home."[38] What that core or essence might be he did not specify, then or later. But the same syndrome—an insistence on a Jewishness that resisted definition—surfaces repeatedly. It is vividly present, for example, in his early correspondence with Karl Abraham.[39]

We could readily concede that in the course of his life Freud may occasionally have experienced conflicts and ambiguities about his Jewish origins (few modern Jews of his type have been immune to them),[40] and that these may have been linked to unresolved Oedipal conflicts (though Jakob Freud seems a poor candidate for a Jewish Laius; one almost wishes that Freud's father had been Hermann Kafka). But let me postpone these speculations as well. The essential fact remains that unlike so many of his Viennese Jewish contemporaries Freud never acted out whatever negative impulses he may have harbored in the one way that really counted—to disavow his Jewish identity.

Quite the opposite. By 1925 Freud had arrived at a public formulation of his Jewish identity that he would repeat, with minor variations, to any subsequent inquiries. Thus, to the *Jüdische Presszentrale* in Zurich: "I can say that I stand as far from the Jewish religion as from all other religions. . . . On

the other hand, I have always had a strong feeling of belonging together with
my people and have always nurtured it in my children as well. We have always
remained in the Jewish denomination" (*wir sind alle in der jüdischen Konfession verblieben*).[41] To Enrico Morselli, an Italian neurologist, in 1926: "Although I have been alienated from the religion of my forebears for a long time,
I have never lost the feeling of solidarity with my people and realize with
satisfaction that you call yourself a pupil of a man of my race—the great
Lombroso."[42] To the Vienna lodge of B'nai Brith: "What bound me to Judaism was . . . not the faith, not even the national pride. . . . Whenever I have
inclined toward feelings of national exaltation I have tried to suppress them
as harmful and unfair, frightened by the warning example of those peoples
among whom we Jews live. But there remained enough over to make the attraction of Judaism and the Jews irresistible, many dark emotional powers all
the more powerful the less they could be expressed in words, as well as the
clear consciousness of an inner identity, the familiarity of the same psychological structure."[43]

Let us note that, by his own admission, national pride was at least sufficiently strong in Freud to require suppression. In fact, however, it was never
completely suppressed. On January 4, 1898, he wrote to his intimate friend
Wilhelm Fliess, "On Wednesday we shall go with your entire family . . . to a
Jewish play at the Carltheater—a first night, which has already played a role
in my dreams."[44] The play was Theodor Herzl's *Das neue Ghetto,* and apparently Freud had read it before the Viennese premiere. Its impact was sufficiently powerful to provoke the "My Son the Myops" dream, which would
soon find its way into *The Interpretation of Dreams.* Even the manifest content
of the dream reveals Freud's deep anxiety over the possibility of anti-Jewish
persecutions and the necessity "to remove the children to safety" because they
do not have "a country of their own."[45] Beyond that Peter Loewenberg has
provided an astute argument for seeing here "a hidden Zionist theme." For
Das neue Ghetto, written four years earlier, was not a play about persecution,
but about reconciliation between Jews and non-Jews. To produce the dream
content Freud must also have read or at least been thoroughly aware of Herzl's
Der Judenstaat (The Jewish state), published in 1896.[46] And indeed, Freud's
attitude toward Herzl the Zionist is confirmed in a letter of September 28,
1902, in which Freud wrote that he had asked his publisher to send Herzl a
copy of *The Interpretation of Dreams* for review in the *Neue Freie Presse.*
However, Freud added, even if the book is not reviewed, he begs Herzl to keep
the copy for himself "as a token of the high esteem in which for years now I
like so many others have held the writer and fighter for the human rights of
our people."[47]

Freud never formally declared himself a Zionist, though he willingly lent
his name to the board of governors of the Hebrew University and on occasion

expressed his sympathy for the Zionist cause. Martin Freud declares that when he first joined Kadimah, the student Zionist organization at the University of Vienna, he hesitated to tell his father because "Jewish citizens in distinguished positions had a strong prejudice against Zionism and, so far as I knew, he might easily regard my joining this club with disapproval. . . . As it turned out he was plainly delighted . . . and I may say now that many years later he himself became an honorary member."[48]

Obviously Freud's suppression of his occasional feelings of "national exaltation" varied with the time and circumstances. In 1930, following the Arab riots in Palestine, he received an appeal by the Jewish Agency to prominent European Jews for public criticism of British policy on Jewish access to the Western Wall in Jerusalem and on Jewish immigration to Palestine. Ever wary of nationalism, doubly so when it involved some religious elements, in a letter to Dr. Chaim Koffler Freud responded,

> I cannot do what you wish. I am unable to overcome my aversion to burdening the public with my name and even the present critical time does not seem to me to warrant it. Whoever wants to influence the masses must give them something rousing and inflammatory and my sober judgment of Zionism does not permit this. I certainly sympathize with its goals, am proud of our University in Jerusalem and am delighted with our settlement's prosperity. But on the other hand, I do not think that Palestine could ever become a Jewish state, nor that the Christian and Islamic worlds would ever be prepared to have their holy places under Jewish care. It would have seemed more sensible to me to establish a Jewish homeland on a less historically burdened land. But I know that such a rational viewpoint would never have gained the enthusiasm of the masses and the financial support of the wealthy. I concede with sorrow that the baseless fanaticism of our people is in part to be blamed for the awakening of Arab distrust. I can raise no sympathy at all for the misdirected piety which transforms a piece of an Herodian wall into a national relic, thus offending the feelings of the natives. Now judge for yourself whether I, with such a critical point of view, am the right person to come forward as the solace of a people deluded by unjustified hope.[49]

On the other hand, with Nazism rampant in 1935, Freud wrote to L. Jaffe of the Keren Ha-Yesod, the financial arm of the World Zionist Organization, "I well know how great and blessed an instrument this foundation has become in its endeavor to establish a new home in the ancient land of our fathers. It is a sign of our invincible will to survive which has, until now, successfully defied two thousand years of severe oppression! Our youth will continue the struggle."[50]

The fact to ponder is that even when not actually suppressed, such feelings were always expressed privately, in letters or in conversation. Freud's public posture remained essentially the one he had adopted in his response to the *Jüdische Presszentrale* and, ironically, it found its most powerful formulation in the preface he wrote in 1930 to the Hebrew translation of *Totem and Taboo*:

> No reader [of the Hebrew version] of this book will find it easy to put himself in the emotional position of an author who is ignorant of the language of Holy Writ, who is completely estranged from the religion of his fathers—as well as from every other religion—and who cannot take a share in nationalist ideals, but who has yet never repudiated his people, who feels that he is in his essential nature a Jew and who has no desire to alter that nature.

And he continues:

> If the question were put to him: "Since you have abandoned all these common characteristics of your compatriots, what is left to you that is Jewish?" he would reply: "A very great deal, and probably its very essence." He could not now express that essence in words; but some day, no doubt, it will become accessible to the scientific mind.[51]

Six years later, in the midst of revising *Moses and Monotheism,* Freud wrote in a letter of condolence to the British psychoanalyst Barbara Low on the recent death of her brother-in-law David Eder, himself an analyst, "We were both Jews and knew of each other that we carried that miraculous thing in common, which—inaccessible to any analysis thus far—makes the Jew."[52]

Common to all these pronouncements is Freud's stubborn insistence on defining himself *via negationis,* by a series of reductions. He is not a Jew by religion, or in national terms, or through language (though there is evidence, yet to be considered, that he was by no means as linguistically ignorant as he claimed), and yet in some profound sense he remains a Jew. Similarly we have seen him emphasize proudly that he and his family had not converted to Christianity, a declaration that would be greeted today with a shrug but which had considerable significance in Freud's Vienna. When Max Graf, father of the Little Hans whom Freud immortalized in his classic case history, asked him whether, given the prevalence of anti-Semitism, it would not be preferable to raise the child as a Christian, Freud replied, with obvious reference to his own experience, "If you do not let your son grow up as a Jew, you will deprive him of those sources of energy which cannot be replaced by anything else. He will have to struggle as a Jew, and you ought to develop in him all the energy that he will need for that struggle."[53] The same thought is emphasized in the

B'nai Brith letter and in the so-called *Autobiographical Study*: "As a Jew I was prepared to join the Opposition and to do without agreement with the 'compact majority' "[54] (the phrase is lifted from Ibsen's *An Enemy of the People*). This was the farthest he was prepared to go. Beyond that it was all "dark emotional powers," "essence," "inner identity," "psychological structure," none of which this most articulate of men could express in words.

There the matter might well have remained had it not been for the advent of Hitler and the Nazis. For Freud, as for so many others, the shock of the anti-Jewish barbarism brought the question of what it means to be a Jew to a new pitch of existential urgency, and there can be no doubt that it was this that provided the immediate impulse to the actual writing of *Moses and Monotheism*. The transition is reflected with the utmost clarity in Freud's correspondence with Arnold Zweig. In 1927, after receiving Zweig's *Caliban,* a study of anti-Semitism that Zweig dedicated to him, Freud wrote, "With regard to anti-Semitism I don't really want to search for explanations; I feel a very strong inclination to surrender to my affects in this matter and find myself confirmed in my wholly non-scientific belief that mankind on the average are a wretched lot."[55] In 1929 he asked Zweig if he owns a copy of *The Future of an Illusion,* and added, "I shall probably not publish anything further unless I am definitely pressed to do so."[56] Nor is there as yet any indication of a plan for a new book in the extraordinary letter Freud sent after Zweig returned from a visit to Palestine in 1932, in which he writes in a tone of fascinated exasperation:

> How strange this tragically mad land . . . must have seemed to you.
> Just think, this strip of our mother earth is connected with no other
> progress, no discovery or invention. . . . Palestine has never produced
> anything but religions, sacred frenzies, presumptuous attempts to
> overcome the outward world of appearance by means of the inner
> world of wishful thinking. And we hail from there (though one of us
> [Zweig] considers himself a German as well, the other [Freud] does
> not); our forebears lived there for perhaps half perhaps a whole mil-
> lennium . . . and it is impossible to say what heritage from this land
> we have taken over into our blood and nerves. . . . Oh, life could be
> very interesting if we knew more about it.[57]

Within a year both men witnessed the precipitous crumbling of the world they had known. Zweig fled Germany and made his way to Palestine, a wistful exile ill at ease in the land of his ancestors. Shortly after his departure he dashed off his *Bilanz der deutschen Judenheit 1933* (Balance-sheet of German Jewry, 1933), an impassioned, if futile, attempt to awaken the world to the reality of what was happening. The attack against the Jews also brought a frontal assault against psychoanalysis as a "Jewish science," a microcosm of the larger tragedy. Most of the Jewish members of the Berlin Psychoanalytic Society, Vienna's most vigorous offspring, rapidly joined the exodus. The Berlin Psychoanalytic Institute dragged on a shadowy existence before disappearing completely three years later, to be replaced by the Deutsches Institut für Psychologische Forschung und Psychotherapie, headed by Matthias Heinrich Göring, a cousin of Reichsmarschall Hermann Göring.[58] As recently as 1930 Freud had been awarded the Goethe Prize by the city of Frankfurt am Main. By the end of May 1933, his works were being burned at German universities, and on the last day of the year Max Eitingon, founder and director of the Berlin Institute, abruptly left for Palestine.

After the *Anschluss* of 1938 the inevitable liquidation of psychoanalysis in Vienna was rapid and complete. Forced to seek refuge in England, Freud would compare the loss of the Viennese matrix to the destruction of Jerusalem. Decades earlier he had repeatedly expressed his anxiety lest the psychoanalytic movement be regarded merely as a "Jewish national affair." Suddenly, and in a way he could not have foreseen, in 1933 the fate of psychoanalysis had intertwined directly with the actual fate of the Jewish people. For a man of Freud's intellectual intensity the earlier vague phrases about Jewish identity could no longer suffice. He had finally to confront what he would soon call "the fateful content of the religious history of the Jews."

On September 30, 1934, Freud informed Zweig that he had embarked on a new venture:

> The starting point of my work is familiar to you—it was the same as that of your *Bilanz*. Faced with the new persecutions, one asks oneself again how the Jews have come to be what they are and why they have attracted this undying hatred. I soon discovered the formula: Moses created the Jews. So I gave my work the title: *The Man Moses, An Historical Novel* [Der Mann Moses, ein historischer Roman].[59]

Freud's declaration of motive is unequivocal, the projected themes are clear. The only ambiguity lies in the provisional subtitle, which seems almost an invitation to exegetical somersaults. If it is a "novel," then indeed why not interpret the work as a personal fiction, especially when *historischer Roman* seems to link so nicely in German with "family romance" (*Familienroman*)? The authentic history in Freud's historical novel would thus turn out to be autobiographical, the manifest historical content a fictional code. But what did Freud really mean by the term? Perhaps we can find some enlightenment in the manuscript draft of 1934. Here, in a rather literal translation, is the original introduction that Freud never published:[60]

As the sexual union of horse and donkey produces two different hybrids, the mule [*Maulthier*] and the hinny [*Maulesel*], so the mixture of historical writing and fiction gives rise to different products which, under the common designation of "historical novel," sometimes want to be appreciated as history, sometimes as novel. For some of them deal with people and events that are historically familiar and whose characteristics they aim to reproduce faithfully. They derive their interest, in fact, from history, but their intent is that of the novel; they want to affect the emotions. Others among these literary creations function in quite the opposite way. They do not hesitate to invent persons and even events in order to describe the special character of a period, but first and foremost they aspire to historical truth despite the admitted fiction. Others even manage to a large extent in reconciling the demands of artistic creation with those of historical fidelity. How much fiction, contrary to the intentions of the historian, still creeps into his presentation, requires little further comment.

When I, however, who am neither a historian nor an artist, introduce one of my works as a "historical novel," then this term must allow for yet another definition. I have been trained to the careful scrutiny of a certain domain of phenomena. To me fiction and invention are easily associated with the blemish of error.

My immediate purpose was to gain knowledge of the person of Moses, my more distant goal to contribute thereby to the solution of a problem, still current today, which can only be specified later on.

A character study requires reliable material as its basis, but nothing available concerning Moses can be called trustworthy. It is a tradition coming from one source, not confirmed by any other, fixed in writing only in a later period, in itself contradictory, revised several times and distorted under the influence of new tendencies, while closely interwoven with the religious and national myths of a people.

One would be entitled to curtail the attempt as hopeless, were it not that the grandeur of the figure outweighs its elusiveness and challenges us to renewed effort. Thus, one undertakes to treat each possibility in the text as a clue, and to fill the gap between one fragment and another according to the law, so to speak, of least resistance, that is—to give preference to the assumption that has the greatest probability. That which one can obtain by means of this technique can also be called a kind of "historical novel," since it has no proven reality, or only an unconfirmable one, for even the greatest probability does not necessarily correspond to the truth. Truth is often very improbable, and factual evidence can only in small measure be replaced by deductions and speculations.

I would submit that, coming at this stage, such a statement is as lucid as it is modest. Freud is saying that he has called his work a historical novel, not because it really has anything in common with that genre as ordinarily conceived, not because he has any imaginative agenda beyond the quest for a historical truth, but only in the sense that, given the extreme paucity of reliable historical facts concerning Moses, his reconstruction must be based to such an unusual extent on psychoanalytic probability. Quite incidentally we are also given a clue to a possible earlier stage in his thinking. The term *character study* (*Charakterstudie*) suggests that Freud had toyed with the notion of writing a psychoanalytic study of Moses himself, something akin to his *Leonardo*, and there is evidence at one point in the manuscript that he had even thought to deduce the character of the Jews from that of Moses.[61] By now, however, he had discovered more profound channels through which Moses had "created the Jews." The character study of Moses receded to the background. The novelistic subtitle *ein historischer Roman* was eventually dropped, and so this introduction, having become irrelevant, was scrapped as well. Three months after composing his draft Freud wrote to Max Eitingon in Jerusalem, "I am no good at historical novels; let us leave them to Thomas Mann."[62] And in 1938, after the first two parts had been published in *Imago,* he declared in a letter to his son Ernst, "It is my first appearance as a historian; late enough!"[63]

2

Sigmund Freud,
Jewish Historian

That which hath been is that which
shall be. And that which hath been
done is that which shall be done.

—*Ecclesiastes* 1:9

In my beginning is my end.

—T. S. Eliot, *East Coker*

That Freud should have turned to history to solve his Jewish riddles comes as
no surprise. Historicism of one kind or another has been a dominant characteristic of modern Jewish thought since the early nineteenth century, while
the "historical" bent of psychoanalysis itself is, theoretically and therapeuti-
cally, part of its very essence.

But if *Moses and Monotheism* presents itself ultimately as history, what
kind of history could Freud possibly be expected to write? In 1934 he was
seventy-eight years old. His major discoveries lay behind him and had been
integrated into a coherent whole. Predictably, the only Jewish history that
could be of moment to him was the history of the Jewish psyche, and it was
not through the scrutiny of an endless series of texts and documents that it
could be fathomed. Here, as always, the crucial task was to lay bare its roots.
In 1937 he wrote, "Several years ago I started asking myself how the Jews
acquired this special character and, following my usual custom, I went back
to the earliest beginnings." Origin, then, is the primary goal, the origin of the
Jewish religion that has made the Jews what they are and given them their
"special character." In order to recover it, Freud the historian employed a
blatantly ahistorical, even anti-historical method, at least as we ordinarily con-
ceive the rules of the game.[1]

Freud's psychology of the individual had been anchored in direct experience
with his patients and in his own self-analysis. Of necessity, however, his application of psychoanalysis to religion and culture had always proceeded by
deduction and analogy from individual to group phenomena. The earliest hint

of what was to come is present in a letter to Wilhelm Fliess on October 15, 1897, in which Freud writes,

A single idea dawned on me. I have found in my own case too [the phenomenon of] being in love with my mother and jealous of my father, and I now consider it a universal aspect of early childhood even if not so early as in children who have been made hysterical. (Similar to the invention of parentage [*Abkunftsroman*—almost a synonym for *Familienroman*] in paranoia—heroes, founders of religion [*Religionsstifter*].)[2]

In the *Psychopathology of Everyday Life* (1901) he affirmed his belief that "a large part of the mythological view of the world, which extends a long way into the most modern religions, *is nothing but psychology projected into the external world.* The obscure recognition . . . of psychical factors and relations in the unconscious is mirrored—it is difficult to express it in other terms, and here the analogy with paranoia must come to our aid—in the construction of a *supernatural reality,* which is destined to be changed back once more by science into the *psychology of the unconscious.* One could venture to explain in this way the myths of paradise and the fall of man, of God, of good and evil, of immortality, and so on, and to transform *metaphysics* into *metapsychology.*"[3]

The *Minutes of the Vienna Psychoanalytic Society* for March 20, 1907, summarized and recorded by Otto Rank, yield this deliciously Olympian exchange:

Brecher: raises only the question how metapsychology is related to the psychology harbored by the philosophers. He asks, for instance, whether the need for causality issues *exclusively* from unconscious factors.

Häutler: repeats that the scientific law of causalities was taken over from religious life, which links guilt and punishment.

Freud: religion would then correspond to an obsessional neurosis, and the philosophical system to a delirium.[4]

In his essay of the same year entitled "Obsessive Actions and Religious Practices" Freud underscored the affinities between the rituals of the neurotic and the ceremonies of the religious, postulating that obsessional neurosis could be regarded as an "individual religiosity" and religion as a "universal obsessional neurosis."[5] Though he was aware of the significant difference between the shared, communal ritual of religion and the private, isolated ritual of the neurotic, he was never to retreat from this fundamental position although, as we shall yet see, he eventually added to it. In *Totem and Taboo* the analogy was carried a large step farther. If individual neurosis is the result of repressed childhood trauma, the same must also be true of religion. Religion originates in the Oedipal murder and devouring of the primeval father by the horde of his rival sons; their repression of the memory of the deed; their unconscious remorse and consequent worship of the father in the guise of the totem animal; and the guilty though veiled recollection of the murder itself through its periodic reenactment in the totem feast. Viewed in strictly immanent terms *Moses and Monotheism* would seem merely to represent the final telescoping of a series of analogies. If the origin of religion in general lies in the slaying of the primeval father, then the origin of Judaism requires a comparable patricide—the murder of Moses by the Jews.

And yet, although inconceivable without the earlier work, *Moses and Monotheism* is far more than applied *Totem and Taboo.* We have already found that it might never have been written had it not been for the events of the Hitler years. Moreover, it is significant that Freud should have styled himself a "historian" only in relation to *Moses and Monotheism* and not to *Totem and Taboo,* for this seemingly casual remark points to a fundamental difference between the two books.

In *Totem and Taboo* Freud did not have to be a historian, for the pivotal event it presupposes does not really take place in historical time. It would be as absurd to ask Freud to date the primal patricide as it would be to inquire in what year Cain murdered Abel, the primal fratricide. Insofar as these are "events" they occur in the dreamtime of mankind. Not so with *Moses and Monotheism.* The man and the religion he established are situated within history and are therefore legitimately subject to the historian's insistent demand for specific historical proofs. Freud was aware of this problem from the start, and it put him under an unprecedented tension. On the one hand he was convinced that through a profound analytic intuition he had hit upon a genuine historical truth concerning the origins of monotheism. But he also realized that, unlike *Totem and Taboo,* this new reconstruction of the past had to be grounded in some concrete historical evidence, however oblique. The unusual hesitations that accompanied every stage in the composition of *Moses and Monotheism* are commonly attributed to Freud's alleged ambivalence over his own Jewish identity. Be that as it may, the expressions Freud employs in his correspondence and in the book itself point consistently to the more intrinsic dilemma. For the first time he must attempt to corroborate a psychoanalytically derived truth with historical facts quite beyond the purview of psychoanalysis.

Thus, to Arnold Zweig on November 6, 1934: "I need more certainty, and I should not like to endanger the final formula of the whole book by founding it on a base of clay."[6] A month or so later: "Nor is it any uncertainty on my part, for that is as good as settled, but the fact that I was obliged to construct so imposing a statue upon feet of clay, so that any fool could topple it.''[7] And wistfully, on May 2, 1935: "In an account of Tel-el-Amarna, which has not been fully excavated, I noticed a comment on a certain Prince Thotmes, of whom nothing further is known. If I were a millionaire I would finance the continuation of these excavations. This Thotmes could be my Moses, and I would be able to boast that I had guessed right."[8] The central metaphor returns in the book. "Like a bronze statue with feet of clay," he calls it, in an obvious effort to preempt the potential critic.[9]

It is the recurring metaphor that catches our attention. The weak base (or feet) of clay is clearly a reference to parts I and II of the book, which, as the manuscript draft of 1934 reveals for the first time, originally constituted the "historical novel" proper.[10] The "imposing statue" refers to part III, the aim and raison d'être of the entire work, which, as a result, is rendered vulnerable to "any fool." But the choice of image, which might otherwise seem natural enough, is especially significant in light of Freud's prior work on Moses. It cannot but conjure up for us the essay he wrote in 1914 entitled "The Moses of Michelangelo," an association whose subjective, psychological ramifications will be considered in their proper place. Here I will focus on only one aspect. If, as Freud seemed to believe, his interpretation of Michelangelo's statue of Moses was correct, then he and the great sculptor have one thing in common: both are, in effect, biblical exegetes who radically violate the plain sense of the text—Michelangelo by presenting a Moses who contains his anger and does not shatter the Tablets, Freud by making him an Egyptian and having him killed by the Jews. In the Michelangelo essay Freud had written,

> But here it will be objected that, after all, this [Michelangelo's Moses] is not the Moses of the Bible. For that Moses did actually fall into a fit of rage and did throw away the Tablets and break them. This Moses must be quite a different man, a new Moses of the artist's conception; so that Michelangelo must have had the presumption to emend the sacred text and to falsify the character of this holy man. Can we think him capable of a boldness which might almost be said to approach an act of blasphemy?[11]

Indeed. And was this not precisely what Freud was doing now? But with the vital difference that, after all, Michelangelo's statue did not purport to be other than an act of the individual imagination while Freud's *Moses,* even at the stage of calling itself a historical novel, let alone after that phrase was expunged, claimed to have recovered a historical reality.

At this juncture we would do well to remind ourselves that modern biblical criticism did not begin with Freud, but with Spinoza, and that the nineteenth

and early twentieth centuries had left a turbulent legacy of conflicting interpretations at least as radical as Freud's, and sometimes more so.[12] Attempts,
generally reductive, to explain biblical ideas and institutions as borrowings
from other Near Eastern cults and cultures were a commonplace. Indeed,
following the discovery by archaeologists in 1901 of the Code of Hammurabi,
Babylonia, not Egypt, had dominated such discussions, and "Babel und Bibel"
(the title of an influential book published by Friedrich Delitzsch in 1902) became, for some, an obsession. Freud himself delivered a lecture on Hammurabi to the B'nai Brith in 1904 and, according to one eyewitness, it was entirely
in Delitzsch's spirit.[13] Thus the notion of foreign influence on the Bible was
hardly new. The novelty in *Moses and Monotheism* was Freud's psychoanalytic
approach, but he knew from the outset that it alone would not suffice to make
his case.

In *The Interpretation of Dreams* Freud remarked that he had treated
dreams "like a sacred text" (*wie einen heiligen Text*).[14] What would be more
natural for him than to treat the sacred text like a dream? But the dream itself,
in Freudian perspective, also contains "day-residues," elements from our experiences while awake. If the hermeneutic Freud applied to the biblical narratives was essentially that of his dream-interpretation, could he at least find
some historical day-residues behind the narrative distortions?

Freud's desperate attempts to find support for his truth in the historical
and archaeological literature were inevitably frustrated. Throughout the nineteenth century the dominant trend in German biblical scholarship had been
to deny that Moses was a historical person or, at best, to grant him a grudging
and minimal historicity. No extrabiblical source mentions him, and what is
reported of him in the Pentateuch was considered anachronistic. If Moses was
a historical figure, he was not a lawgiver; at most he created a covenant between Israel and a deity named Yahweh. The early religion of Israel was not
monotheist. The evolutionary bias of the Higher Criticism demanded a gradual development from polytheism to henotheism to monotheism. Pure monotheism was the late creation of the prophets.

Early in this century there were several attempts to rescue Moses from the
scholarly bullrushes and to concede some historical concreteness to his person. In *Die Israeliten und ihre Nachbarstämme*, Eduard Meyer concluded that
Moses must have been a Levite priest at the oasis of Kadesh. Georg Beer proposed in *Mose und sein Werk* that the historical Moses was essentially a ma-
gician. In *Mose und seine Zeit*, Hugo Gressmann argued that Moses was also
a leader and founder of a religion. However, Gressmann still based himself
entirely on an analysis of the Moses narratives in the Pentateuch, which, according to the regnant Graf-Wellhausen chronology, were themselves late and
reflected the spiritual development of later ages.[15]

In the 1934 draft of *Moses and Monotheism*, after summarizing the plot of his "novel" and before proceeding to the material that would become part III, Freud added a "Critical Appendix" (*Kritischer Anhang*) which was eliminated from the final version. "I did not know," Freud began, "that it would be so difficult to compose a historical novel. Now that it is completed, my conscience demands that the standard of more sober historical writing be applied to it."[16]

This *Anhang* is largely devoted to a critique of Gressmann's book as representative of the best in modern critical biblical scholarship, thus also affording Freud an opportunity to compare it with his own venture. The key points in Gressmann's reconstruction with which Freud took issue were his acceptance of the Hebrew origin of Moses and especially his interpretation of the biblical miracle of the splitting of the Red Sea.

According to Gressmann and others, the Hebrews were forced to cross, not the Red Sea proper, but the Gulf of Akaba. Mount Sinai, or Horeb, which, judging from the biblical description, was surely a volcano, could not have been in the Sinai Peninsula, which contains no volcanic mountains, but must have been situated on the other side of the gulf, near the northwest coast of the Arabian Peninsula. This was the territory of the Midianites who worshiped Yahweh, the god of the volcanic region, as their chief deity. Just as the Hebrews were crossing the gulf they found the Egyptians in hot pursuit. But in the very midst of their terror something unheard of occurred. Suddenly volcanic eruptions sent the waters in turmoil, casting the Egyptians back and enabling the Hebrews to reach land safely. The impression upon them of this "miracle" was overwhelming and indelible.

From the Midianites of the region they now learned that the name of the god who had intervened to save them was Yahweh. It was then that the intuition flashed in Moses' mind that this god had chosen Israel to be his people, and that therefore the people must choose this god as its own. When Moses communicated this to them their spirits were fired as well. As soon as the Hebrews came to Kadesh in the Sinai Peninsula, where they united with kindred tribes who had lived there for ages since leaving Canaan, Yahweh was officially declared to be their only God. A Midianite priest, Jethro, was invited to Kadesh to teach Moses the details of Yahweh's service. With the transportation of Yahweh's holy ark from Midian to the Israelite camp, the implantation of the new religion was complete.

Freud pointed out that Gressmann's explanation of the miracle

is also only a historical novel, no more certain than the one constructed by us. One cannot easily subscribe to the notion that the adoption of a new religion is to be traced back to a fortuitous coincidence such as the appearance of a volcanic phenomenon . . . so long as other explanations are possible. A sudden volcanic tidal wave which only washed away the Egyptians and which left the nearby Israelites unmolested remains a process that is hard to imagine and extremely unlikely, actually not much different than a miracle.[17]

If biblical scholarship did not offer what Freud sought there was, nevertheless, one striking exception.

In Ernst Sellin's *Mose und seine Bedeutung für die israelitisch-jüdische Religionsgeschichte* (Moses and his significance for the history of Israelite-Jewish religion), published in Berlin in 1922, Freud found the thesis that Moses had been slain by the Jews advanced by a scholar with no psychoanalytic orientation whatever, but with an international reputation as a biblical historian and archaeologist. Freud's own remarks in *Moses and Monotheism* leave no doubt as to how important Sellin was to him: "To my critical sense this book . . . appears like a dancer balancing on the tip of one toe. If I could not find support in an analytic interpretation of the exposure myth and could not pass from there to Sellin's suspicion about the end of Moses, the whole treatise would have to remain unwritten."[18] Most of the commentators on Freud's *Moses* dutifully mention Sellin's book in passing but show no sign of having read it. Had they taken the trouble to do so, they would have found it is not merely about the murder of Moses, and that Freud's debt was greater than is commonly supposed.

Sellin's originality lay in his rejection of the evolutionary assumption and his attempt to prove that Moses was already a monotheist. He believed he had found traces of an ancient and authentic Mosaic tradition in the prophets themselves, notably in the prophet Hosea, who lived some five centuries after Moses. Specifically, Sellin detected in the text of Hosea vestigial recollections of a man who had led Israel out of Egypt and through the wilderness, a prophet who left a divine set of laws hewn in stone. That man, Sellin concluded, could only have been Moses, the laws must have been the Decalogue. This Moses was indeed the founder of Israelite monotheism. Unfortunately, nowhere in the admittedly difficult Hebrew text of Hosea do any of these elements actually appear. The reconstruction depends entirely on Sellin's exegetical method, which combined form criticism with his own often drastic and arbitrary emendation of words and phrases.

But Sellin was not content with salvaging the essential Moses from the skepticism of his predecessors. Applying the same method, he claimed to have discovered yet another covert memory preserved by Hosea—that Moses had been killed by his own people, who could not assimilate his message then or later. As soon as they reached Shittim they lapsed into the local idolatry of the Baal of Peor. Opposing them, Moses was murdered. The true religion of Moses, the belief in one invisible God and in the supremacy of morality over cult and ritual, remained alive as an esoteric tradition only among a small circle of followers whose successors in later ages were the prophets. "His ideas," Sellin wrote, "did not die out completely, but here and there, in complete silence, they worked upon belief and practice until, sooner or later, under the impact of exceptional experiences or through personalities who were especially gripped by [Moses'] spirit, they broke forth ever more powerfully."[19]

Having discovered evidence of these traditions in Hosea, Sellin found it comparatively easy to trace them in the prophets who preceded and followed him. A culmination is reached, according to Sellin, in Deutero-Isaiah. The enigmatic "Suffering Servant" in Isaiah 53 is none other than Moses, whose martyrdom was now endowed with messianic implications. Whereas Hosea knew only of his suffering and death, Isaiah foresees his eschatological return, when he will not only lead his people back to their land as long ago, but will bring his message and the Kingdom of God to the entire world. According to Sellin, this new hope for a *Moses redivibus* eventually provided the ground out of which emerged the faith of Jesus and his disciples.

Thus the essential history of Israel reveals one great leitmotiv—the suffering and martyrdom of the prophets. Moses brought a teaching to his people of which they were unworthy, then and later. Led by its priests the people only strayed ever farther from the essential message, which remained an esoteric tradition that surfaced only sporadically. Finally, a second Moses arose who, like the first, was slain, but whose message went forth to the nations.

If all this, despite the scholarship and ingenuity, has a distinctly Christian ring to it, that is hardly fortuitous. Sellin's entire book has a Christian theological subtext which becomes manifest at the very end:

> Yes, this man at the end of the thirteenth century was too great, not only for his own time, but above all for his people. . . . He truly belongs, as Deutero-Isaiah interpreted him, to mankind. . . . That which he and his disciples the prophets announced . . . experienced a new revival in the Gospel. It became the foundation upon which Jesus could proclaim a new commandment to the world, intended to bring salvation to the peoples of the earth.[20]

But that is not what interested Freud. The salient elements in Sellin's reconstruction must have captivated him. Indeed, the correlations to *Moses and Monotheism* are so striking that we must wonder if Sellin's work merely confirmed Freud's prior intuitions or whether it was the reading of the book that triggered his own thinking. Beyond the slaying of Moses, Freud found in Sellin the historicity of Moses and the purity of his monotheism; a hidden link between Moses and the rise of Christianity through the expectation of his messianic return; the parallel between the murder of Moses and that of Jesus; above all, the survival of Moses' teaching and the memory of his murder as subterranean traditions ("in complete silence"—*in aller Stille*) that reemerged only after a lapse of centuries. Against these fundamental affinities we can also appreciate Freud's departures from Sellin: the Egyptian origin of monotheism and of Moses himself; a very different evaluation of the fate of monotheism among the Jewish people and in post-Pauline Christianity; above all, the attempt at a psychodynamic interpretation of the hidden Moses tradition and of both murders.

⸺

While Sellin's book helped significantly to allay some of Freud's concerns over the weakness of his historical foundations, it did not dispel them completely. Freud knew very well that Sellin's reconstruction was itself highly speculative and had not been generally accepted.[21] But there was yet another major source of anxiety. In the first preface to part III, written in Vienna before the *Anschluss* of March 1938, Freud explains that he is withholding this part out of fear that it will jeopardize psychoanalysis in Austria by arousing the hostility of the Catholic church, which at that time he regarded as the only bulwark against a Nazi takeover (he would soon call it a "broken reed").[22] It was, in fact, a worry that had plagued him from the inception of the book. As early as 1934 he had written to Zweig that he might not publish the work at all, especially not the volatile third part, but here he spelled out the details: "For we live in an atmosphere of Catholic orthodoxy. They say that the politics of our country are determined by one Pater Schmidt. . . . He is a confidant of the Pope, and unfortunately he himself is an ethnologist and a student of comparative religion, whose books make no secret of his abhorrence of analysis and especially of my totem theory."[23]

Freud went on to blame Schmidt for the banning in Italy of Edoardo Weiss's *Rivista Italiana di Psicoanalisi*. To publish *Moses* would be to risk the ire of "this inimical priest" and a ban on psychoanalysis in Vienna that would deprive his Viennese colleagues of their livelihood. In addition "there is the fact that this work does not seem to me sufficiently substantiated, nor does it altogether please me. It is therefore not the occasion for a martyrdom."

Freud's reference to Pater Schmidt has been noted perfunctorily in the literature on *Moses and Monotheism* but has not been explored further.[24] That is a pity, for the matter is worthy of our fullest attention.

Wilhelm Schmidt was a leader of the Vienna school of historical ethnology, a university professor, an ordained priest, and a member of the missionary Society of the Divine Word (Verbum Dei). An ethnologist of world renown, from 1927 to 1939 he was director of the Papal Ethnological Museum at the Lateran in Rome. His lifework was the gargantuan *Ursprung der Gottesidee* (Origin of the idea of God), twelve massive volumes of some thousand pages each, in which he tried to prove with ethnological data from around the globe that religion was originally a belief in one Supreme Being, an *Ur-Monotheis-*

mus that only later degenerated into polytheism. It is not without interest and irony that both Freud and Schmidt were obsessed with religious origins and that the first volume of *Ursprung* appeared in 1912, the same year as Freud's *Totem and Taboo*.[25]

Freud is not mentioned in any volume of Schmidt's *Ursprung*, and I confess that at first I thought that his worries might have been exaggerated, perhaps even a bit paranoid. In 1930 Schmidt published a one-volume manual of comparative religion. To be sure, this did contain a concise and sharp rejection of *Totem and Taboo*, essentially recapitulating the criticisms of the American anthropologist A. L. Kroeber. Yet there was nothing personal here, nor anything that exceeded the normal bounds of scientific invective.[26]

Not so, however, in a now-forgotten lecture that Schmidt gave in Vienna in November 1928, which he published the following year in a Berlin periodical called *Nationalwirtschaft* as "Der Ödipus-Komplex der Freudschen Psychoanalyse und die Ehegestaltung des Bolshewismus" (The Oedipus complex of Freudian psychoanalysis and the condition of marriage in Bolshevism). If the title is disquieting, the contents are appalling.

Much of the article, only one of several by Schmidt attacking psychoanalysis,[27] is an ethnological critique of Freud along Kroeber's lines. The tone is relatively restrained—until Schmidt comes to Freud's notion in *Totem and Taboo* of the Christian communion as a reenactment of the primal slaying and incorporation of the Father. Schmidt calls this "the limit of atrocity," a crossing of what is intellectually and emotionally unbearable.[28]

The crucial section is the one that links Freud and Bolshevism. Here Schmidt states explicitly that he will now allow his affects to take over in view of the revolting origin that Freud ascribes to religion, morality, and society. He does not say that Soviet communism is directly indebted to psychoanalysis for its social theories. Nevertheless, Freud and the Bolsheviks have the same end in mind: the destruction of the family. The Oedipus complex can be abolished only in two ways—by removing the prohibition of incest or by removing the newborn infant from its parents. According to Schmidt both processes are well under way in the Soviet Union. Nor are Freud's other theories merely theoretical. *The Future of an Illusion* calls for the elimination of religion; the Freudian notion of religion as illusion is but a variant of the Marxist dogma of religion as opium. Between Freudianism and Bolshevism there is "an entente cordiale."[29]

In Italy, Schmidt must have alerted the Vatican to pressure the Fascist government to put an end to the Italian psychoanalytic movement. It would seem that the Vatican chose as its emissary Father Agostino Gemelli, professor of psychology and rector of the Università Cattolica of Milan, because of his long-standing friendship with Mussolini. In fact, Gemelli had been active together with Mussolini in the Socialist movement before they took their separate paths, the one becoming a Franciscan and a psychiatrist, the other the leader of Italian fascism.[30]

Though I have not been able as yet to further reconstruct the details of Schmidt's activity against psychoanalysis in Italy, surely there was already enough in his published articles to indicate that Freud had ample cause for genuine alarm. Coupled with his continuing nervousness about his historical proofs, Freud's hesitations and conflicts over the writing and publication of *Moses and Monotheism* become quite comprehensible. Under the same circumstances who would not be "ambivalent"? But let us return to the book.

Its title notwithstanding, the book is not about the origins of monotheism per se. Freud himself admitted that in ascribing monotheism to Ikhnaton that problem was only pushed back one step and not resolved.[31] *Moses and Monotheism* is concerned specifically with the origins of Judaism, and since, like most good nineteenth-century German-Jewish rationalists, Freud was convinced that monotheism was the very essence of Judaism, that meant the origin of monotheism among the Jews.[32] Parenthetically, the same rationalist bias will explain why Freud presents such an antiseptic view of monotheism and such a sanitized Moses, as well as the bizarre duality of his plot. That biblical monotheism could contain anthropomorphic elements and its One God be capable of passions, or that the lofty Moses might also perform magic with a serpent of brass, was inconceivable to him. All that he found repugnant was shunted onto the Midianite Moses and his volcanic demon-god.[33]

But Freud did not stop there. What readers of *Moses and Monotheism* have generally failed to recognize—perhaps because they have been too preoccupied with its more sensational aspects of Moses the Egyptian and his murder by the Jews—is that the true axis of the book, especially of the all-important part III, is the problem of tradition, not merely its origins, but above all its dynamics. "Only thus," Freud observes at the end of part II, "would an interest in our purely historical study find its true justification. What the real nature of a tradition resides in, and what its special power rests on."[34] We may easily translate—once it came into being—what gave Judaism its extraordinary hold over the Jews, with all its "fateful consequences?" Jewish tradition itself, to which the power of its truths was self-evident, emphasized their unbroken transmission: "Moses received Torah from Sinai and delivered it to Joshua, and Joshua to the Elders, and the Elders to the Prophets, and the Prophets delivered it to the Men of the Great Synagogue." Thus the opening of the Mishnaic tractate *Avot* which would flower in the Middle Ages as the "Chain of Tradition" (*shalshelet ha-qabbalah*).[35]

Always the psychologist, Freud could not accept such answers to his problem. In *Totem and Taboo* he had asked, "What are the ways and means employed by one generation in order to hand on its mental states to the next one? I shall not pretend that . . . direct communication or tradition are enough to account for the process."[36] Now he wrote, "A tradition that was based only on [direct] communication could not lead to the compulsive character that attaches to religious phenomena. It would be listened to, judged, and perhaps dismissed, like any other piece of information from outside." Ever the Freudian, Freud concluded, "It must first have undergone the fate of being repressed, the condition of lingering in the unconscious, before it is able to display such powerful effects on its return and force the masses under its spell."[37]

And so he took his most audacious step. "I hold," he wrote, "that the concordance between the individual and the mass is in this point almost complete. The masses, too, retain an impression of the past in unconscious memory traces." In short, between the psychic life of the individual and that of the group there is not merely an analogy but a virtual *identity*.[38] Collectively the group too represses the memory of profound events experienced early in its history and transmits them phylogenetically through the unconscious, "independent of direct communication," until what was repressed occasionally breaks forth much later in distorted form but with utterly compelling force.

What may therefore properly be termed Freud's psycho-Lamarckism was neither casual nor circumstantial. It is the dominant theme of his "Overview of the Transference Neuroses," the long-lost twelfth metapsychological paper of 1915 discovered and edited by Ilse Grubrich-Simitis and published only a few years ago as *A Phylogenetic Fantasy* (the phrase, though not the title, is Freud's).[39] In this extraordinary document, written under the palpable influence of Sándor Ferenczi, Freud attempted nothing less than a historical view of the neuroses as phylogenetically inherited mechanisms originally developed by all of primeval humanity in order to meet the real, perilous exigencies of the Ice Age and its aftermath. True, Freud himself did not publish this paper. But Lamarckian assumptions are woven throughout his work, and, as *An Outline of Psychoanalysis* confirms, he clung to them fiercely to the very end.[40]

Nowhere is Freud's Lamarckism more striking and radical than in *Moses and Monotheism*. Even if we temporarily suspend our scientific disbelief, beguiled by Freud's own passing definition of scientific creativity as the "succession of daringly playful fantasy and relentlessly realistic criticism,"[41] the Lamarckism in *Moses and Monotheism* makes the most difficult demands on fantasy itself. For it is one thing even to imagine the formation of a phylogenetic heritage in the remotest prehistoric ages when, ostensibly, the structures of the human psyche were still in an early and fluid process of evolution, and certain overwhelming and universal experiences, repeated again and again over enormous periods of time, eventually left psychological imprints that could somehow be transmitted somatically to future generations.[42]

Here, however, trauma in the form of a unique cluster of historical events, their encoding within the genetic legacy of a particular group, collective repression, and the "return of the repressed" all take place in relatively recent historical time within the brief span of some five to eight centuries. Moreover, not only the traumatic slaying of Moses, but the content of his religious teaching is alleged to have undergone this fateful and intricate process. The archaic heritage of human beings, Freud insists in *Moses and Monotheism,* "comprises not only dispositions but subject matter—memory traces of the experience of earlier generations."[43] At which point even the most ardent and loyal admirer of Freud can only whisper to himself, "Certum, quia absurdum est."

Though the truly decisive revolutions in molecular biology and genetics were not to take place until after his death, Freud was always aware that Lamarckism was under sharp scientific attack. Nevertheless, and despite the urgent pleas of Ernest Jones that he expunge these embarrassing elements from the Moses book, he held fast. How to explain this particular stubbornness? While carefully avoiding any speculation as to unconscious motives, Grubrich-Simitis offers a number of plausible reasons for it, some of them advanced by Freud himself.[44]

Yet I find myself wondering whether, beyond the reasons that have been proposed, Freud's Jewishness may not also have played a role in his Lamarckian predilections. No, I am not implying that Lamarckism is "Jewish." I rather have in mind its subjective dimension, the feeling, harbored and expressed by committed and alienated modern Jews alike, of the enormous weight, the gravitational pull, of the Jewish past, whether it be felt as an anchor or a burden. Deconstructed into Jewish terms, what is Lamarckism if not the powerful feeling that, for better or worse, one cannot really cease being Jewish, and this not merely because of current anti-Semitism or discrimination, and certainly not because of the Chain of Tradition, but because one's fate in being Jewish was determined long ago by the Fathers, and that often what one feels most deeply and obscurely is a trilling wire in the blood. In this connection we may well recall Freud's own words to Zweig about the Land of Israel— *and we hail from there . . . our forebears lived there for perhaps a whole millennium . . . and it is impossible to say what heritage from this land we have taken over into our blood and nerves.*

Heinrich Heine, I think, harbored similar feelings. In a footnote to a passage in *Moses and Monotheism* on the alleged Egyptian origin of Jewish circumcision, Freud writes, "And, incidentally, who suggested to the Jewish poet Heine in the nineteenth century A.D. that he should complain of his religion as 'the plague dragged along from the Nile Valley, the unhealthy beliefs of Ancient Egypt'?"[45] The original lines are to be found in Heine's *Das neue Israelitische Hospital zu Hamburg* [The new Jewish hospital in Hamburg], which begins:

A hospital for sick and needy Jews,
For those poor mortals who are triply wretched,
With three great maladies afflicted:
With poverty and pain and Jewishness
[*Mit Armut, Körperschmerz und Judentume!*]

The worst of these three evils is the last one,
The thousand-year-old family affliction,
The plague dragged with them
From the valley of the Nile,
The old Egyptian unhealthy faith
[*Der altägyptisch ungesunde Glauben*].

But the next stanzas are even more interesting:

Incurable deep-seated hurt! No treatment
By vapor bath or douche can help to heal it,
No surgery, nor all the medications
This hospital can offer to its patients.

Will Time, eternal goddess, some day end it,
Root out this dark misfortune that the father
Hands down to the son? And someday will the grandson
Be healed and rational [*vernünftig*] and happy?

I do not know . . .[46]

Heine's point, of course, had nothing whatever to do with the Egyptian origins of Judaism. What suffuses these lines is the oppressive feeling of the longevity and irremediability of being Jewish. Paradoxically, the sense that Jewishness is both inherited and indelible could be shared equally by Jews who, like Heine at this moment, would discard their Jewish identity if they could, as well as by Jews who passionately affirmed that identity.

To appreciate this, let us momentarily leap back several centuries in time. The *Shevet Yehudah* (The scepter of Judah), a book unknown to both Heine and Freud, is a remarkable interrogation of the meaning of Jewish history written largely in the form of fictional dialogues by a Spanish-Jewish refugee who was baptized by force in Portugal in 1497. There we read: "And what will it profit our lord and king to pour holy water on the Jews, calling them by our names, Pedro or Pablo, while they keep their faith like Akiba or Tarfon? . . . Know, Sire, that Judaism is one of the incurable diseases."[47] And in another passage the author, Solomon Ibn Verga, precociously shifts the question of Jewish identity from theology to psychology and has a Spanish king declare,

I shall tell you Tomás, that I am far from the opinion of the kings
who preceded me, who sought to force the Jews to believe in Jesus
and in the end they did not succeed, because *in the innermost cham-
bers of their imagination they are Jews in every sense.* . . . My reason
is as follows: The Jews who, *when their religion was given to them,*
witnessed those awesome and holy assemblies and those marvels and
fires from heaven, *had the image of all that so strongly impressed
upon them that it remains with them naturally.* Therefore it would be
almost unnatural for them to remove that primal image from their
hearts and to replace it with a new one.[48]

Bear in mind that conversion was the only possible mode of assimilation
for medieval Jews[49] or, if you are a bit venturesome, replace the marvels and
fires with the murder of Moses, and do we not have here a fifteenth-century
analogue to the psycho-Lamarckism of *Moses and Monotheism*? But enough.
I have no intention of pressing this provisional juxtaposition into yet another
phylogenetic fantasy.

Whatever its motivations, the Lamarckian assumption lies at the very heart
of Freud's history of the Jews. That the transmission of acquired characteristics had been rejected by the biologists and that it seemed to bring Freud
perilously close to Jung's "collective unconscious" was brushed aside impa-
tiently. Only such an assumption, Freud insisted, makes possible the transition
from individual to group psychology.[50] As for Jung—the specific concept of
a collective unconscious is superfluous since "the content of the unconscious,
indeed, is in any case a collective, universal property of mankind."[51] And so,
at last, the secret of religious tradition is revealed. Its power lies precisely in
the return of the repressed, in the triggering of hitherto unconscious memories
of real events from the remote past. What I have called the essential drama of
Moses and Monotheism, as distinct from its external plot, lies here.

In the beginning the primeval father was slain by his sons. Ultimately, in
polytheism, he was completely forgotten, his memory repressed. In its very
essence, therefore, monotheism represented the return of that long latent
memory in the form of the one omnipotent God beside whom there is no other.
The tremendous impact of what Moses revealed to the Israelites lay, one might
say, in a shock of recognition, in their profound sense of reunion and reconciliation with the long lost Father for whom mankind had always unconsciously yearned. This, indeed, was the origin of their feeling of being the
Chosen People. But even then Moses' teachings could not become a "tradition." For this, in a repetition of the primal patricide, Moses had first to be
slain and his teachings forgotten. Only after another period of latency that
lasted some five to eight centuries did the Mosaic religion return to group
consciousness and grip the Jewish people for all ages to come.

Thus, as a historical essay *Moses and Monotheism* offers a singular vision of history as essentially a story of remembering and forgetting. To be sure, this is analogous to Freud's conception of the life history of the individual. What has been overlooked is how strangely analogous it is also to the biblical conception of history, where the continual oscillation of memory and forgetting is a major theme through all the narratives of historical events.[52] Periodically Israel forgets the God of the Covenant and lapses into idolatry; subsequently it remembers and is reunited with him. The primary biblical imperative is the command to remember, not to forget. It is more than coincidence that in the one place Freud actually chides the Jews for a failure, it is for a failure of memory that is almost a parody of the prophets: "Fate had brought the great deed and misdeed of primeval days, the killing of the father, closer to the Jewish people by causing them to repeat it on the figure of Moses, an outstanding father-figure. *It was a case of 'acting out' instead of remembering. . . . To the suggestion that they should remember, which was made to them by the doctrine of Moses, they reacted, however, by disavowing their action.*"[53]

The structural parallels do not end here. For both Freud and the biblical historians the true pulse of history beats far beneath its manifest surfaces, and the decisive tale is that of revolt against the Father. Even Freud's Lamarckism is, in a sense, implicit in the biblical narrative: "Not with you alone do I make this covenant and this oath, but with him who stands here with us this day before the Lord our God, and also with him that is not here with us this day" [Deuteronomy 29:13–14], on the basis of which the talmudic sages later asserted that the souls of all unborn generations of Jews were already present at Sinai. It may be of some interest that Hanns Sachs not only knew this legend but applied it to Freud in his affectionate memoir, *Freud, Master and Friend*: "It is as though Freud walked intuitively and unconsciously in the footsteps of his ancestors and followed one of the most ancient Jewish traditions: the belief that all Jews, born or yet to be born, were present at Mount Sinai, and that there they took upon themselves the 'yoke of the Law.'"[54]

What truly astonishes, however, is the extent to which Freud's reconstruction insists, like the Bible, that the Jews were chosen, that they were chosen from outside, that it was not the Jews who created their religion but their religion that created the Jews. In all these respects Freud turned his back on that modern secular-Jewish liberalism which, embarrassed by chosenness, spoke vaguely, yet with infinitely more arrogance than had Jewish tradition, of monotheism as a product of the "Jewish genius" or the "creative spirit of the Jewish people."

And more. In an important essay Martin Bergmann has grasped the larger significance of Freud's attribution of the return of the repressed to the Jews as, in effect, a unique event in world history. "Freud," he writes, "deprived the Hebrews of their discovery of monotheism but restored them psychologically to a central position: for among them alone the repressed returned with fateful results for the history of mankind."[55] If, for "central position" we substitute chosenness, we may say that for Freud the Jews are doubly chosen, first because Moses literally chose them and, more profoundly, because only among the Jews did the repressed actually return. If this is so, then the return of the repressed is the Freudian counterpart to biblical revelation, both equally momentous and unfathomable, each ultimately dependent, not on historical evidence, but on a certain kind of faith, in order to be credible. Once we recognize this we understand also that, vis-à-vis the Bible, *Moses and Monotheism* is not merely history, but a countertheology of history in which the Chain of Tradition is replaced by the chain of unconscious repetition. Indeed, that is perhaps why some will say that Freud has a better claim than Spinoza to be considered the archheretic of Judaism in modern times. For the *Theological-Political Treatise* is a mere demolition of the biblical view of history, from which it then detaches itself. Far more dangerous, as in all great heresies, *Moses and Monotheism* is a direct alternative, a new Torah in which Moses is, in effect, apotheosized and takes the place of God.[56] But to indict Freud for heresy is both premature and precipitous. Such rashness is alien to our more leisurely quest. In the next chapter I shall consider, among other matters, Freud's attitudes toward another "new Torah," proclaimed by a far more ancient Jewish heresy.

3

Father-Religion, Son-Religion, and the "Jewish National Affair"

As regards medicine the Jews of old boasted greatly, and they still do, and they are not ashamed of the falsehood. They claim that they are the oldest and first physicians. And indeed they are the foremost among all the other nations, the foremost rascals, that is. . . . God himself and his only Son they have rejected, and not recognized, and then they should know the works and powers of nature? God has snatched from them and taken away from their hands the art of medicine, condemning them and their children for all eternity and casting them away at the same time . . . and yet they vindicate for themselves all praise of medicine. Let us pay no attention to all that. . . .

For they are not born for medicine, nor are they educated in it. From the very beginning of the world it has been their task to wait for the divine Messiah . . . and whatever they have tried beyond this has been foreign to them and false. Medicine has been given to the gentiles.

—Paracelsus, *Labyrinthus Medicorum Errantium* [1553]

Freud's reading of Jewish history, centered around the return to group consciousness of the long repressed memory of the primeval Father, did not end with Moses or the Hebrew prophets. Yes, Moses created the Jews and Judaism by restoring the Father to them alone, through his own person and in the teaching of the one omnipotent God of the universe. Following his death this revelation was repressed in turn, only to reemerge from its state of unconscious latency in the teachings of the prophets, which would become the common patrimony of the entire Jewish people.

But, as we have seen, the twice-repeated return of the repressed among the Jews, however momentous, was incomplete. The father had returned, but not the recollection of his slaying. Even the slaying of Moses, although a repetition of the archaic murder, produced no such anamnesis. The repressed memory of the primeval murder and, by extension, that of the murder of Moses himself required yet a third repetition. This was achieved, albeit in a highly distorted way, only after the slaying of Jesus centuries later and above all through the interpretation of that event (if such it was; Freud is not sure) by the "Roman Jew" Saul of Tarsus, known as Paul. Significantly, except as victim, Jesus ("a political-religious agitator") plays no role here in the origins of Christianity. Not his teaching but his death is decisive, and this only because of the manner in which Paul interpreted it. The Crucifixion is at best a text of which Paul was the inspired exegete. And thereby "Paul, who carried Judaism on, also destroyed it."[1]

In Judaism the innate ambivalence toward the Father had been internalized into a powerful sense of guilt whose archaic source was not acknowledged. It was Paul who had the vague intuition that "the reason we are so unhappy is that we have killed God the father" and who proclaimed his truth in "the delusional disguise of the glad tidings: 'we are freed from all guilt since one of us has sacrificed his life to absolve us.' " "In this formula," Freud continues, "the killing of God [the primeval father] was, of course, not mentioned, but a crime that had to be atoned by the sacrifice of a victim could only have been a murder." The "shadowy [conception of] original sin" is itself none other than that "unnameable crime." In this sense—"that is, as regards the return of the repressed—and from that time on, the Jewish religion was to some extent a fossil." Judaism was fated to remain a "Father-Religion," Christianity a "Son-Religion," in which the Son was deified and, in effect, usurped and displaced the Father.[2]

If *Moses and Monotheism* thus went beyond *Totem and Taboo* by plunging into historical time, it also marked a partial retreat from *The Future of an Illusion,* or at least an important modification. Although religion contains no "material truth," Freud was now thrilled to acknowledge that it contained a "historical truth"—the memory, however distorted, of the primeval father and his murder.[3] Following the same lines, he ventured to state that there is even a "truth" in Christian anti-Semitism of which the anti-Semites are, of course, totally unaware. Beneath the Christian taunt to the Jews that "you killed our God," which refers on its manifest level to the Crucifixion (Freud dismissed that scornfully as "the supposed judicial murder of Christ"),[4] there is an unconscious reproach. Freud writes, "If it is brought into relation with the history of religions, it runs: 'You will not *admit* that you murdered God (the primal picture of God, the primal father and his reincarnations). . . . We did the same thing, to be sure, but we have *admitted* it and since then we have been absolved.'"[5] *right*

Now certainly there are phrases and formulations here which, heard in isolation, can easily grate on Jewish ears. Read closely and contextually, however, they may yet present a different aspect.

But I have already run far ahead of myself. Before continuing with the text it is vital that we not do so in a vacuum. We must first pause to examine Freud's relation and attitudes to precisely those aspects of the non-Jewish world with which he deals in *Moses and Monotheism*—Christianity, anti-Semitism, and gentiles in general. For Freud, all three aspects were linked and overlapped. Much has been written about the impact of anti-Semitism on Freud, without sufficient attention to these interrelationships, to the constants as well as the changes in his attitudes, to the frequent gaps between his private feelings and public postures.

━━━

We find in Freud a sense of otherness vis-à-vis non-Jews which cannot be explained merely as a reaction to anti-Semitism. Though anti-Semitism would periodically reinforce or modify it, this feeling seems to have been primal, inherited from his family and early milieu, and it remained with him throughout his life.

A striking illustration, though easily glossed over, can be found in a letter to Martha Bernays on September 4, 1883, in which he comments facetiously, "In the future, for the remainder of my apprenticeship in the hospital, I think I shall try to live more like the gentiles—modestly, learning and practicing the usual things and not striving after discoveries and delving too deep."

This equation is revealing even in the English translation, but the English reader cannot savor to what extent. The original German begins, "Ich denke, ich will in der nächsten Zeit dem Rest der im Spital, nach der Weise der *Gojim* leben. . . ."[6] Those who are content with the usual and do not delve too deep are not merely "gentiles." The word that comes naturally to Freud is *goyim*. The hand is the hand of Sigmund; the voice is the voice of Jakob. *voof*

With regard to Freud's personal encounters with anti-Semitism I shall not traverse all the familiar territory. I only want to emphasize that Freud's awareness of anti-Semitism antedates his experiences at the University of Vienna, or the end of the liberal Bürgerministerium and the rise of political anti-Semitism. This awareness is also an inheritance. It is tied, for example, to his first disillusion with his father:

> "When I was a young man," he [Jakob Freud] said, "I went for a walk one Saturday in the streets of your birthplace; I was well dressed, and had a new fur cap on my head. A Christian came up to me and with a single blow knocked off my cap into the mud and shouted: 'Jew! get off the pavement!' " "And what did you do?" I asked. "I went into the roadway and picked up my cap," was his quiet reply. This struck me as unheroic conduct on the part of the big, strong man who was holding the little boy by the hand.[7]

Jakob Freud told him the story when he was ten or twelve. How many other, unrecorded tales about anti-Semites must Viennese Jewish children, and Freud himself, have heard from their Galician fathers?

When Freud himself encountered anti-Semitic incidents in his manhood his reactions were aggressive and combative. There is the story, told to Martha, of how, in defiance of the anti-Semitic passengers in a train who wanted the windows closed, he insisted on keeping one open;[8] the scene at the spa when he waded into a hostile crowd brandishing his cane;[9] his joy when his friend and fellow-intern Carl Koller fought a duel with a surgeon who had called him a "Jewish swine" and Koller succeeded in wounding him. "Our friend is quite unharmed and his opponent got two deep gashes. We are all delighted, a proud day for us. We are going to give Koller a present as a lasting reminder of his victory."[10] How deeply thoughts about anti-Semitism were embedded in Freud's psyche can be gauged from the "My Son the Myops" dream, to which I have already referred.

As for Freud's own German identity, one should learn to distinguish the issues. That Freud's culture, though pan-European and cosmopolitan, was Germanic at its core is a fact so obvious as to be almost banal. But culture and identity are not necessarily synonymous. Certainly a vital part of him lived in a Germanic universe of thought, but this Germany of the mind and the imagination that he, like so many Central European Jews, cherished was that of the German Enlightenment, that of *Nathan der Weise* (Pfister as Lessing-Saladin, Freud as Mendelssohn-Nathan), of literature and philosophy, of nineteenth-century German science. Unlike so many of his contemporaries, Freud rarely confused this with the real Germany or Austria, even if part of him may have strongly wanted to do so. And this long before Nazism and Hitler. In 1886 he wrote to Martha from Paris describing a soirée at Charcot's: "Only toward the end I embarked on a political conversation with Giles de la Tourette, during which he of course predicted the most ferocious war with Germany. I promptly explained that I am a Jew [*Ich gab mich gleich als juif*], adhering neither to Germany nor to Austria. But such conversations are always embarrassing to me, for I feel stirring within me something German which I decided long ago to suppress."[11]

In 1926 he would say, retrospectively, "My language is German. My culture, my attainments are German. I considered myself German intellectually, until I noticed the growth of anti-Semitic prejudice in Germany and German Austria. Since that time, I prefer to call myself a Jew."[12] If, in the interim, at the outbreak of World War I he expressed some initial enthusiasm for the cause of the Central Powers, that was true of virtually all the intellectuals, from Thomas Mann to Martin Buber, who were swept up in the euphoria.[13] And Freud had two sons in the Austrian army.

The Wednesday evening group that met at Freud's home and evolved into the Vienna Psychoanalytic Society was, as is well known, originally composed entirely of Jews. It is beyond my present scope to probe the sociological and psychological reasons that brought these Jews to become adherents of psychoanalysis. The fact that these were Jews was certainly not accidental. I also think that in a profound though unacknowledged sense Freud wanted it that way. The only organized society in which Freud had felt at home prior to this was the B'nai Brith, and it is the merit of Dennis B. Klein to have meticulously examined his participation in the Vienna lodge and to have recognized the parallels and affinities.[14]

However, while Freud found it personally congenial to be among Jews, he also became increasingly convinced of the peril for the budding psychoanalytic movement if it continued to be regarded as composed exclusively of Jews and thus stigmatized as both Jewish and parochial. In order to be accepted as science, psychoanalysis must not only be universal; it must be perceived as such. To put it very crudely, Freud needed a goy, and not just any goy but one of genuine intellectual stature and influence. Miraculously, as it were, the apparently ideal goy did not have to be sought. It was Carl Jung who, in 1906, sought out Freud. Not long after, Ernest Jones turned up. But while Jones would prove endlessly useful then and later (we shall have occasion to see that he was also not unproblematic), for the time that Jung remained within the fold it was he who seemed to Freud to bring salvation to psychoanalysis from a seemingly Jewish insularity by opening doors to the Swiss and to the gentile world. In return, Freud was willing to bestow upon him the mantle of apostolic succession.

Of course, by 1913 it was all over between them. The rift was never healed, and its complex causes remain a matter of controversy. What is of moment for us is that apparently from the very beginning of their relationship, despite his genuine admiration and even love for him, Freud harbored suspicions about Jung apart from issues of psychoanalytic theory—worries about Jung's inherited Christian and even anti-Jewish biases, indeed his very ability as a non-Jew to fully understand and accept psychoanalysis itself. For the sake of the "cause" the same Freud who had been so militant about anti-Semitism and who had despised what he regarded as his father's weakness in the face of it, now deliberately squelched his misgivings and bent over backward to cultivate Jung and retain his allegiance, even if thereby he occasionally caused pain to some of his closest Jewish colleagues, Karl Abraham and Sándor Ferenczi among them.

How preoccupied Freud was in those years with the issue of "Jewish" and "Aryan" as it applied to psychoanalysis can be seen vividly in his mediating efforts in the frequent tensions between Jung and Abraham. In a letter to Jung written on August 27, 1907, we find Freud making his first inquiry about Karl Abraham, whom he had not yet met. "By the way," Freud asks, "is he a descendant of his eponym?" The delicately ironic circumlocution exudes an air of complicity, almost as though one gentile were writing to another. Jung confirmed that Abraham was, in fact, what his name implied.[15]

Once he came to know him, Freud was quick to recognize Abraham's gifts and loyalty. May 3, 1908:

> Please be tolerant and do not forget that it is really easier for you than it is for Jung to follow my ideas, for in the first place you are completely independent, and then you are closer to my intellectual constitution because of racial kinship [*Rassenverwandschaft*], while he as a Christian and a pastor's son finds his way to me only against great inner resistances. His association with us is the more valuable for that. I nearly said that it was only by his appearance on the scene that psycho-analysis escaped the danger of becoming a Jewish national affair [*eine jüdisch nationale Angelegenheit*].[16]

Freud's acute worry that psychoanalysis not appear to be a "Jewish national affair" remained, I am convinced, an abiding concern and source of inner conflict throughout his life. I believe it directly affected the images he presented to the world of himself, his background, and his teachings. It is certainly an important key to understanding the glaring disparity between the affect-laden expressions of his Jewishness in his private utterances and correspondence and the generally guarded, distanced tone to be found in his public pronouncements and published writings. How far Freud was capable of going in consciously restraining some of his most visceral Jewish feelings for the sake of the cause can be seen at this point in the letter he sent to Abraham on July 23, 1908:

> I surmise that the repressed anti-Semitism of the Swiss, from which I am to be spared, has been directed against you in increased force. But my opinion is that we must as Jews [*wir mussen als Juden*] if we want to cooperate with other people, develop a little masochism and be prepared to endure a little injustice. . . .
>
> Why cannot I harness Jung and you together, your keenness [*Ihre Schärfe*] and his *élan* [*seinen Schwung*]?[17]

Note that even here Freud attributes sharpness of intellect to Abraham, the Jew, and energy to Jung, the gentile. He must, he felt, keep them in tandem. On December 26 he writes to Abraham that the impending publication of the case of "Little Hans" will create an uproar: "German ideals threatened again! Our Aryan comrades are really completely indispensable to us, otherwise psychoanalysis would succumb to anti-Semitism."[18]

It was not to be. Both on intellectual and personal grounds the rift between Freud and Jung seems, in retrospect, to have been inevitable. At the height of the crisis, in 1912, Ferenczi sounded a general alarm: "It has seldom been so clear to me as now what a psychological advantage it signifies to be born a Jew and to have been spared in one's childhood all the atavistic nonsense. Putnam [James Jackson Putnam, the American psychiatrist] also may easily desert us; you must keep Jones constantly under your eye and cut off his line of retreat."[19]

But perhaps Freud's most important statement on Jew and Aryan came when he had done with Jung. On June 8, 1913, he wrote to Ferenczi telling him how to reply to a letter from the Swiss psychiatrist Alphonse Maeder which proposed that the scientific differences between the Viennese and the Swiss was the result of the former being Jews and the latter Aryans:

> Certainly there are great differences between the Jewish and the Aryan spirit. We can observe that every day. Hence there would be here and there differences in outlook on life and art. But there should not be such a thing as Aryan or Jewish science. Results in science must be identical, though the presentation of them may vary. If these differences mirror themselves in the apprehension of objective relationships in science there must be something wrong.[20]

These proved to be prescient words. Twenty years later, as we shall see, the "something wrong" erupted fully into the open.

New light on the impact on Freud of the break with Jung has come from the unexpected discovery and publication, in 1980, of the private papers of Sabina *archives*

Spielrein, including her diary, her correspondence with Freud, and her letters to Jung (his letters to her have been withheld by his heirs).[21] This discovery should also serve to remind us of how incomplete and tentative any conclusions must be in our reconstructions of the history of psychoanalysis, until the mounds of materials still unpublished or deliberately restricted are made available.

Sabina Spielrein was a brilliant young Jewish girl who came in 1904 from Russia to Zurich to study medicine. But soon her latent mental illness surfaced, and she was admitted as a patient to the renowned Burghölzli hospital, where Jung was then chief resident. Her treatment with Jung began when she was nineteen and he thirty. By 1906 she was well enough to leave the institution. She went on to pursue her medical studies, received her degree in psychiatry in 1911, and became a psychoanalyst. In 1923 she returned to Russia, where she continued her work but eventually disappeared, perhaps in the Soviet purges of the late 1930s, perhaps killed by the Germans after they invaded the Soviet Union.

The second time Jung ever wrote to Freud (October 23, 1906) he described Spielrein's case briefly without mentioning her name and, more important, without disclosing that he was involved in a love affair with her that must have begun while she was in the hospital and then continued after her release. The affair was at its height in 1908–09 and came to the attention of Spielrein's parents, almost certainly through Jung's wife, Emma. The mother wrote to Jung demanding that he end the affair. Whereupon Jung sent her the astonishing reply that in a normal doctor-patient relationship certain bounds apply, but since he is paid no fee, the relationship is not in the same category.

WHAT A DICK

Alarmed nonetheless, on March 7, 1909, Jung confessed to Freud in a letter that he was involved in an affair with a "woman patient" whom he had pulled out of a "sticky neurosis" and that she was now facing him with the prospect of a scandal. Still eager to retain him, Freud sided with Jung and, not much to his own credit, made light of the matter. When, in May, Spielrein wrote to Freud merely requesting a meeting, he put her off. On June 11 she wrote again, giving him the details of the affair. A week later Freud wrote another reassuring letter to Jung. The latter responded on June 21 with the fullest confession of which he was capable. By now, moreover, he realized that it was not Spielrein but his wife who had revealed the secret. "My action," he told Freud, "was a piece of knavery which I very reluctantly confess to you as my father."

The affair was now broken off, though Spielrein's love for Jung had not faded, and, despite his behavior, she continued to respect him and his work. At the same time, although she had been analyzed by Jung and supervised by him while writing her dissertation, in becoming an analyst she accepted Freud's teachings. Her great and lasting wish was to mediate between the two, convinced, in a touching if misguided way, that their differences could be reconciled. From October 1911 to March 1912 she lived in Vienna, attended Freud's Wednesday evenings, was accepted as a full member of the Vienna Psychoanalytic Society, and began to publish papers whose originality and significance are only now being recognized.[22]

What complicated the situation throughout was Sabina Spielrein's intense desire to have a child by Jung (she knew that marriage was out of the question). This desire was also deeply enmeshed in a symbolic fantasy. The child, to be named Siegfried, would represent the fusion of Jew and Aryan, hence also of Freud and Jung. Realizing finally that Siegfried was not to be, in 1912 Spielrein married a Jew, Dr. Paul Scheftel. *yeesh*

It is against this triangular background of tangled and unraveling relationships, the affair of Spielrein and Jung overlapping the deterioration and rupture of his relations with Freud, that we become privy to the larger implications of that rupture for Freud himself.

On August 20, 1912, Freud wrote to Spielrein,

> My wish is for you to be cured completely. I must confess, after the event, that your fantasy about the birth of the Saviour to a mixed union did not appeal to me at all. The Lord, in that anti-Jewish period, had him born from the superior Jewish race. But I know these are my prejudices.[23]

And a year later, having learned that she is pregnant:

> I am, as you know, cured of the last shred of my predilection for the Aryan cause, and would like to take it that if the child turned out to be a boy he will develop into a stalwart Zionist. He or she must be dark in any case, no more towheads. Let us banish all these will-o'-the wisps!
>
> I shall not present my compliments to Jung in Munich, as you know perfectly well. . . . We are and remain Jews. The others will only exploit us and will never understand and appreciate us.[24]

This rare glimpse into Freud's powerful emotions, triggered by the break with Jung, are sufficient to mark it as a kind of watershed in his perception of the non-Jewish world. The feelings that emerge here, though expressed ironically and often veiled later on, would remain unchanged.

We see it in 1923 when Erich Leyens, a young man who had been expelled along with all other Jews from the youth movement led by the anti-Semitic psychiatrist Hans Blüher, turned to Freud for advice. In the preceding year Blüher had called in his *Secessio Judaica* for the separation of all Jews from the German people.[25] Freud now replied to Leyens, *ugh*

I believe I understand you and your situation. That I have full sympathy for you requires no corroboration. But I would dissuade you from consuming yourself in the hopeless struggle against the present "spiritual" currents in Germany. Folk psychoses are immune to arguments. Precisely the Germans had the occasion to learn it in the recent World War. But they appear not to be capable of it. Let us leave them to themselves [*lassen wir sie*]. . . . Turn yourself toward the things that can lift the Jews over all these insanities and—don't take amiss the advice that is the upshot of a long life—don't impose yourself upon the Germans [*drängen sie sich die Deutschen nicht auf*]![26]

Meanwhile, despite the accelerating spread of the psychoanalytic movement, the convergence of anti-Semitism with the "Jewish national affair" did not abate. It was not a phantom of Freud's imagination but a reality. One out of numerous examples will suffice.

In 1921 Wilhelm Dolles, head of a progressive school who was interested in educational reform, published a book entitled *Das Jüdische und das Christliche als Geistesrichtung* [The Jewish and the Christian as spiritual direction]. Its basic premise was that the Jewish and the Christian are two radically different psychological types. Accepting Theodor Fritsch's thesis that Jesus was a Galilean Aryan, Dolles maintained that modern Christianity is a mixture of Galilean Christianity and Judaism. Racial theory has thus far not been successful in solving the Jewish problem because it is not a problem of *Religionsjuden* or *Rassejuden* (religious or racial Jews), but of *Gesinnungsjuden* (Jews by mentality).[27] In this sense he is also opposed to Christians whose psyches harbor Jewish elements.

I shall not attempt to follow Dolles's convoluted argument or his plethora of anti-Semitic canards. Only one section is relevant. According to Dolles, the striving of the Jews for unfulfillable aims has led to their extremely hysterical character. It is no accident, therefore, that psychoanalysis began with publications on hysteria and that most of its first practitioners were Jews. The patients in Freudian analysis are the typical Jews who are never content with themselves and who traffic with their souls.[28] Significantly, Dolles does not reject psychoanalysis per se. He sees in Jung and Marcinowski representatives of the Christian, and thereby the ethical, element in psychoanalysis. His ultimate aim is to purge the school system of the Jewish mentality that dominates it. For instance, he wants less emphasis on intellectuality and more on manual arts, for the book and the cult of the book are Jewish inventions. Still, though hatred of Jews is psychologically understandable, this does not justify actual persecution. Christians must help the Jews to overcome their Jewishness, not through the swastika but through the Cross. But whatever remains Jewish must be isolated from Christian society.

In 1932 German Jewry stood unwittingly at the brink of that isolation for which the Blühers, the Dolleses, and their cohorts had prepared the way. On May 29 Arnold Zweig wrote with a touch of nostalgia to Freud, "And we certainly have our Germanness in common—only it's a Germanness of the past it seems to me." Freud replied, "When you tell me about your thoughts, I can relieve you of the illusion that one has to be German. Should we not leave this God-forsaken nation to themselves?"[29]

More tantalizing is the following passage in a letter from Freud to Zweig on November 27, which, when its somewhat cryptic reference is pursued, yields yet another hint of Freud's inner feelings at the time: "I had a hand in the book which is going off to you at the same time as this. They are the letters of an uncle of my wife's who was a famous classical scholar and, it appears, an outstanding personality. His attitude toward the Jewish and Christian faiths is worthy of attention. . . . I beg you to read this little book."[30]

The uncle of Freud's wife was Jacob Bernays, one of the most formidable classical scholars of the nineteenth century. There has been, in fact, some speculation that Freud himself may have been influenced by reading Bernays's remarkable work on Aristotelian catharsis. A son of the Haham of Hamburg, Jacob Bernays remained a scrupulously observant Jew throughout his life. When his brother Michael accepted baptism to obtain a professorship, Jacob went through the traditional ritual of mourning for the dead.[31]

The book which Freud now sent Zweig and begged him to read was *Jacob Bernays: Ein Lebensbild in Briefen,* which had appeared in Breslau earlier in the year. Edited by Michael Fraenkel, it was dedicated to "Herrn Professor Dr. Sigmund Freud." The section to which Freud was drawing Zweig's particular attention because he obviously identified with it was undoubtedly the exchange of letters in 1852 between Bernays and his good friend Christian von Bunsen, then Prussian ambassador to London. The latter informed him that, after diligent efforts, there was absolutely no prospect for him, because he was Jewish, to obtain an academic position in Prussia. Bunsen, himself a devout Christian, now urged Bernays to convert, not for utilitarian reasons (that, he knew, would be beneath him) but as a fulfillment of his Judaism that would also put him in the mainstream of world history. In any case, whether as Jew or Christian, he was always welcome in his house.

Bernays's reply was firm. On the theological plane he cited Romans 11:25–26 as an indication that Paul held that the Jews have the right and even the duty to remain Jews, at least so long as not all the heathen have become Christians. On an inner level, Bernays told his friend, conversion was totally impossible for him. "He himself," Bernays wrote, "Jesus of Nazareth himself, were he now born a Jew, would not be able to do it, would be the least able to do it. I would not be able to respect him if I did not have to believe that he

Nersen

would rather allow himself to be crucified bodily by the whole row of church authorities, rather than going over to any of the denominations that call themselves after him."[32]

Nor did Freud keep his feelings entirely to himself. After Hitler's assumption of power he wrote on May 28, 1933, to Oscar Pfister, who, though an analyst, was after all also a Swiss Protestant minister: "Our horizon has become darkly clouded by the events in Germany. Three members of the family, with their families . . . are looking for a new country and still haven't found one. Switzerland is not among the hospitable countries. My judgment of human nature, especially the Christian-Aryan variety, has had little reason to change."[33]

The coup de grace came a month later with the beginning of Jung's ambiguous yet obvious flirtations with the Nazi regime. On June 26, 1933, in an interview on Radio Berlin, his criticism of Freudian psychology and stress on the youthfulness of the German as opposed to the West European soul could only have been gratifying to his Nazi listeners.[34] More serious was his collaboration with the newly reorganized German General Medical Society for Psychotherapy and his acceptance of the presidency of its international umbrella organization. Worst of all was the appearance in the 1934 volume of the society's journal, the *Zentralblatt für Psychotherapie und ihre Grenzgebiete*, of Jung's famous, indeed notorious, article "Zur gegenwärtigen Lage der Psychotherapie" (On the state of psychotherapy today).

Even earlier, in an editorial published in the December 1933 issue, Jung had alluded to "the differences which actually do exist between Germanic and Jewish psychology" and which are "no longer to be glossed over."[35] The effect of this statement was amplified all the more by the fact that in the same issue there had appeared a manifesto by Matthias Heinrich Göring calling upon German psychotherapists to adopt the ideological principles of Hitler (Jung later claimed he had not known that this would appear in the *Zentralblatt*).

But in 1934 Jung expanded on his theme with relish. "The State of Psychotherapy Today" was, in the first instance, a frontal attack against Freudian psychoanalysis in which Jung's pent-up resentment of Freud was expressed in the most extreme and sometimes crudest terms. Freud's approach to neurosis is characterized as a "soulless rationalism reinforced by a narrow materialist outlook," his emphasis on infantile sexuality is an "obscene caricature" which "merely demonstrates the adolescent smuttymindedness of the explainer." The vital portion of Jung's text deserves a more extensive quotation:

> Freud and Adler have beheld very clearly the shadow that accompanies us all. The Jews have this in common with women; being physically weaker, they have to aim at the chinks in the armour of their adversary, and thanks to the technique which has been forced on them

through the centuries, the Jews themselves are best protected where others are vulnerable. . . . As a member of a race with a three-thousand-year-old civilization, the Jew has a wider area of psychological consciousness than we. Consequently it is in general less dangerous for the Jew to put a negative value on the unconscious. The "Aryan" unconscious, on the other hand, contains explosive forces and seeds of a future yet to be born. . . . The still youthful Germanic peoples are fully capable of creating new cultural forms that still lie dormant in the darkness of the unconscious of every individual—seeds bursting with energy and capable of mighty expansion. The Jew, who is something of a nomad, has never yet created a cultural form of his own and as far as we can see never will, since all his instincts and talents require a more or less civilized nation to act as host to their development.

The Jewish race as a whole—at least this is my experience—possesses an unconscious which can be compared with the "Aryan" only with reserve. Creative individuals apart, the average Jew is far too conscious and differentiated to go about pregnant with the tensions of unborn futures. The "Aryan" unconscious has a higher potential than the Jewish; that is both the advantage and disadvantage of a youthfulness not yet fully weaned from barbarism. In my opinion it has been a grave error in medical psychology up till now to apply Jewish categories—which are not even binding on all Jews—indiscriminately to Germanic and Slavic Christendom. Because of this the most precious secret of the Germanic peoples—their creative and intuitive depth of soul—has been explained by a morass of banal infantilism, while my own warning voice has for decades been suspected of anti-Semitism. This suspicion emanated from Freud. He did not understand the Germanic psyche any more than did his Germanic followers. Has the formidable phenomenon of National Socialism, on which the whole world gazes with astonished eyes, taught them better?[36]

Now it is not my concern, and this is not the place, to judge Jung. His own explanations—many will say rationalizations—are on record and available.[37] The question here is not whether he was or was not an anti-Semite or a Nazi (certainly neither in any ordinary sense), or whether his retroactive explanations are satisfactory (no less a personage than Leo Baeck apparently accepted them after the war and thus enabled Gershom Scholem to overcome his previous qualms and to attend the Eranos conferences).[38] The question is how Jung's pronouncements sounded in 1934 and, above all, how they reverberated to Freud.

For while Freud never referred to Jung's article directly, and even if he did not read it, it is inconceivable that he should not have heard about it and about Jung's other activities. "The State of Psychotherapy Today" caused an international uproar. Even Jung's Swiss psychiatric colleague Gustav Bally and his disciple Gerhard Adler demanded an explanation (Jung replied with a public rejoinder to the one and a private letter to the other).[39] Assuming, therefore, that just as Freud was writing the first draft of *Moses and Monotheism,* or perhaps even before he began, all this came or was brought to his attention, it must have seemed like the closing of a circle, a confirmation of all the Christian anti-Semitism he had sensed in Jung from the earliest years and, given that Jung had once virtually represented the non-Jewish world for him, another proof of the generally negative judgment of that world which we have found running like a scarlet thread through most of his life. At this point we can return to the treatment of Judaism, Christianity, and anti-Semitism in *Moses and Monotheism* itself.

What is all too often missed by his readers is the dialectic that Freud establishes between Judaism and Christianity, and the difference in his view of Judaism as a religion and the Jews as a people.

For Freud Pauline Christianity was an advance, and Judaism thereafter a fossil, *only* with regard to the return of the repressed. After Paul, in all other respects, Christianity as compared to Judaism is a regression. "The Christian religion," he writes,

> did not maintain the height of spiritualization to which Judaism had soared. It was no longer strictly monotheist, it took over numerous symbolic rituals from surrounding peoples, it re-established the great mother-goddess and found room to introduce many of the divine figures of polytheism only lightly veiled, though in subordinate positions. Above all, it did not, like the Aton religion and the Mosaic one which followed it, exclude the entry of superstitions, magical and mystical elements which were to prove a severe inhibition upon the intellectual development of the next two thousand years. The triumph of Christianity was a renewed victory of the Ammon priests over Ikhnaton's god."[40]

And again: "It was as though Egypt had come to wreak her vengeance anew against the heirs of Ikhnaton."[41]

Nothing, as it were, came without a price. Christianity acknowledged the murder of the Father through the expiatory sacrifice of the Son but lost the Father by deifying the Son, and soon its Jewish monotheism degenerated into a virtually Egyptian paganism. Judaism stubbornly clung to the Father and thus retained a pure monotheism, but it paid for its continued repression of the Father's murder with an unending consciousness of guilt. And yet, precisely because it could not find release in the Christian myth of salvation (Freud calls it the "phantasy of atonement"), this very guilt was channeled into ever more rigorous ethical imperatives and so enabled the Jews to reach "ethical heights which had remained inaccessible to the other peoples of antiquity."[42]

The uncompromising monotheistic prohibition of images was, according to Freud, equally decisive in transforming Judaism into a religion of instinctual renunciation, "for it signified subordinating sense perception to an abstract idea; it was a triumph of *Geistigkeit* [the German word hovers between *intellectuality* and *spirituality*] over sensuality."[43] Even the belief in being chosen, despite the hostility this has naturally aroused, gave the Jews "a special trust in life, such as is bestowed by the possession of a secret gift; it is a kind of optimism. Religious people would call it trust in God."[44]

And so, if Christianity represented a certain psychological advance (*Fortschritt*), Judaism meant cultural, intellectual, spiritual progress. From what we know of Freud is there any doubt that "ethical heights," the sublimation of the sensual to the spiritual, the power of abstraction, were precisely the qualities he valued most, even as he deplored the price that had to be paid for them? These he attributed to the impact of Judaism, for all its tragic discontents, upon the character of the Jews.[45] Should we still have any reservations as to his priorities, one fact may help to dispel them. On August 1, 1938, the Fifteenth International Psychoanalytic Congress was held in Paris amid forebodings of the impending war and a general gloom over the uprooting of the psychoanalytic movement, not only from Germany, but now from Vienna as well. The complete and final version of *Moses and Monotheism* was at the printer's in Holland. Too old and ill to attend, Freud sent Anna from London to represent him by reading publicly only one section of part III. Of all he could have chosen, he selected the section entitled "The Progress in Spirituality" (Der Fortschritt in der Geistigkeit).[46] Thus, among other things, the delegates in Paris heard Anna Freud read the following in her father's name:

All such progress in spirituality results in increasing self-confidence, in making people proud so that they feel superior to those who have remained in the bondage of the senses. We know that Moses had given the Jews the exalted sense of being God's chosen people; by dematerializing God a new valuable contribution was made to the secret treasure of the people. The Jews preserved their inclination toward spiritual interests. The political misfortune of the nation taught them to appreciate the only possession they had retained, their literature, at its true value. Immediately after the destruction of the Temple in Jerusalem by Titus, Rabbi Yochanan ben Zakkai asked for permission to open at Yabneh the first school for the study of the Torah. From now on it was the Holy Book and the intellectual effort applied to it that kept the people together.[47]

If there was also a parable here for the new psychoanalytic diaspora, it rested squarely on what Freud regarded as a central Jewish experience, ultimately rooted in the qualities which the Jewish religion had impressed upon the Jews for all time. Needless to say, while granting these historically positive effects of Judaism Freud was not attempting to salvage the old religion for the present or the future. Despite its kernel of historical truth, religion was still illusion. Having forged the character of the Jews, Judaism as a religion had performed its vital task and could now be dispensed with. For, incredibly and outrageously, Freud was thoroughly convinced that once the Jewish character was created in ancient times it had remained constant, immutable, its quintessential qualities indelible. "According to trustworthy accounts, they behaved in Hellenistic times as they do today. The Jew was, therefore, already complete even then."[48] Though Freud does not put it into words, the conclusion is inescapable. The character traits embedded in the Jewish psyche are themselves transmitted phylogenetically and no longer require religion in order to be sustained. On such a final Lamarckian assumption even godless Jews like Freud inevitably inherit and share them.

If, by this token, Judaism as a religion is now a fossil in a double sense, the Jewish people retains its vitality. Having long ago internalized the ethical, spiritual, and intellectual qualities of Mosaic monotheism, the Jews continue to display them even now. To Jacob Meitlis of the London YIVO on November 30, 1938, four months after the Paris Congress: "We Jews have always known how to respect spiritual values. We preserved our unity through ideas, and because of them we survived to this day. Once again our people is faced with dark times requiring us to gather all our strength in order to preserve unharmed all culture and science during the present harsh storms."[49]

I trust I need not belabor the point that if the man who penned these lines wrote also of the "truth" in anti-Semitism, he was not offering a justification for anti-Semites but a partial psychoanalytic explanation of the price he felt the Jews have paid for remaining "chosen" rather than "saved." For a mind like Freud's there had to be an unconscious psychological truth within anti-Semitism in order to explain its extraordinary virulence, duration, and ubiquitousness. The specific truth he felt he had uncovered—the unconscious Christian charge "You won't admit that you murdered God. . . . It is true, we did the same thing, but we admitted it"—may be questioned. But in any case it implies that anti-Semitism is not incidental but endemic to Christianity, doubly so because of its unconscious component. As for anti-Semitism in its more mundane varieties, from the charge of being aliens in Europe to the

Protocols of the Elders of Zion, there are passages in *Moses and Monotheism* that could have been written by the Anti-Defamation League or its German precursor, the Verein zur Abwehr des Antisemitismus.[50]

And if the founder of the Jewish religion and creator of the Jewish people was an Egyptian? A blow, if you wish, to a certain kind of Jewish narcissism, but neither ambivalence nor hostility toward Freud's own Jewish identity. Monotheism may have originated in Egypt but, as Freud stresses, it never took root among the Egyptians. Conversely, to the Israelites monotheism had come from an alien source, yet the Jews became its bearers throughout history.

Freud fully recognized the paradox he himself had conjured, and at this one point his hitherto relentless rationalism failed him. All he could offer in explanation was a new Jewish mystique:

> The seed of monotheism failed to ripen in Egypt. The same thing might have happened in Israel after the people had thrown off the burdensome and exacting religion. But there constantly arose from the Jewish people men who revived the fading tradition, who renewed the admonitions and demands made by Moses, and who did not rest till what was lost had been established once again. . . . And evidence of *the presence of a peculiar psychical aptitude in the masses who had become the Jewish people* is revealed by the fact that they were able to produce so many individuals prepared to take on the burdens of the religion of Moses.[51]

That Moses was an Egyptian had been the starting point but, indeed, it was not the essential point. If monotheism was genetically Egyptian, it has been historically Jewish. In one of the truly decisive passages of the book Freud declares with austere pride, "It is honor enough for the Jewish people that it has kept alive such a tradition and produced men who lent it their voice, even if the stimulus had first come from the outside, from a great stranger."[52]

I have tried, contextually, to examine three interlocking themes in *Moses and Monotheism* and in Freud's own life—Judaism, Christianity, and the "Jewish national affair." Let no one think that with his flight to England in 1938 after the *Anschluss* Freud felt so secure as to throw all caution to the Britannic winds. There were abiding and new anxieties. Contemplating his departure from Vienna, he wrote to Ernst Freud in London, "I sometimes compare myself with the old Jacob who, when a very old man, was taken by his children to Egypt, as Thomas Mann is to describe in his next novel. Let us hope that it will not be followed by an exodus from Egypt. It is high time that Ahasuerus [the Wandering Jew] comes to rest somewhere."[53] Settled in his new home, he began to put the final touches to the book. He worried about an adverse reaction from the British public, given its widespread reverence for the Bible. He worried about anti-Semitism. To Jacob Meitlis he confided, "Basically all are anti-Semites. They are everywhere. Frequently anti-Semitism is latent and hidden, but it is there. Naturally, there are also exceptions. . . . But the broad masses are anti-Semitic here as everywhere."[54]

Paranoia? Illness and old age? Freud, by his own admission, was not a connoisseur of people (*Menschenkenner*). He seems to have been a better *Antisemitenkenner*. But was it only the broad masses? Was he never aware of the genteel Bloomsbury anti-Semitism of Alix Strachey, James's wife (both had been in analysis with him, and Alix was later analyzed by Abraham in Berlin), as it now surfaces in their published correspondence? What might Freud have thought had he known of James Strachey's grotesque encounter with Joan Riviere and Ernest Jones on the translation of *Das Ich und das Es* described by James to Alix in a letter of October 9, 1924: "They want to call 'das Es' 'the Id'. I said I thought everyone would say 'the Yidd.' So Jones said there was no such word in English: 'There's "Yiddish," you know. And in German "Jude." But there is no such word as Yidd'.—'Pardon me doctor, Yidd is a current word for a Jew.'—'Ah! A slang expression. It cannot be in very widespread use then.' "[55]

In retrospect that dialogue might even seem comic were it not that the English-speaking world has been saddled ever since with the *Ego* and the *Id,* rather than the simple and accurate the *I* and the *It*. More important at the moment is the question of Ernest Jones himself, Freud's hagiographer, always so compliant, useful, and worshipful, capable of joking lightly about his position as *Shabbes-goy* among the Viennese.[56] And yet toward the end of World War II, the amiable disciple delivered himself of a disquisition entitled "The Psychology of the Jewish Question" which advises total assimilation as the solution to anti-Semitism and contains some astonishing passages, including the broad implication that most German-Jewish refugees in England were ungrateful draft-dodgers. Turning to the physical features of the Jews that contribute to unconscious hostility against them, Jones identifies one as circumcision, which, according to Freud himself, arouses castration anxieties. The other is Jones's original contribution: "The second physical feature alluded to is the Hittite nose, so suggestive of deformity, which the Jews unfortunately picked up in their wanderings and which, by an unlucky chance, is associated with a dominant gene."[57]

Although the essay is readily available in Jones's *Essays in Applied Psycho-Analysis,* it seems virtually surrounded by a conspiracy of silence. Freud, of course, never read it, for it was first published in 1945. But he certainly knew of Jones's anti-Jewish bigotry, having been informed of it repeatedly by Rank, Ferenczi, and A. A. Brill. Characteristically, as in the halcyon days with Jung, Jones was too useful for Freud to give vent to his real feelings about this.

Indeed, right down to the final publication of *Moses and Monotheism* Freud's concern that psychoanalysis not be viewed as a "Jewish national affair" seems never to have really subsided, and this will largely explain why the emotionally charged Jewish feelings we have traced throughout his life were not allowed to seep into the book, or are so attenuated as to be felt only in hints and nuances. The tone is deliberately austere, *wissenschaftlich*. Unlike his letters and his talks with fellow-Jews, the book refers to the Jews as "they" rather than "we." By now we should recognize such distancing as strategic and not be misled by it.

The same is true of the title itself. In motivation and content the book might just as well have been called *Moses and Judaism,* but Freud would not have that. As it is, the English reader does not really have even the published German title, for the alliterative translation sounds good but is imprecise. The German equivalent of "Moses and Monotheism" would have been "Moses und der Monotheismus," a perfectly fine title had Freud wanted to use it. Happily for us, the manuscript reveals that Freud had actually considered such a title in both German and English but had ultimately rejected it.[58] Instead of employing the general, abstract term *monotheism,* Freud's final title was, literally, "The Man Moses and the Monotheistic Religion"—*Der Mann Moses und die monotheistische Religion.* The shift is emblematic. On the one hand the title does not explicitly proclaim this to be a Jewish book. Yet "The Monotheistic Religion," with its emphatic specificity, is, in effect, Judaism. Islam is given short shrift.[59] Christianity after Paul is paganism.

Freud's attitude toward Judaism and Christianity can, I think, best be summed up in an archetypal story from the Upper West Side of Manhattan. I cannot vouch entirely for its "material truth," but I think even Freud would have appreciated its "historical truth." It goes as follows:

> West End Avenue. An upper-middle-class Jewish couple. The father, liberal, intense, a vociferously militant atheist. Wanting a superior education for their son, the parents enroll him at Trinity School, which, whatever its denominational origins, is now secular, open to all. One day, after about a month, the boy comes home and says, casually, "By the way, Dad, do you know what *Trinity* means? It means the Father, the Son, and the Holy Ghost."
>
> Whereupon, barely controlling himself, the father seizes the boy by the shoulders and declares, "Danny, I'm going to tell you something now and I want you never to forget it. *There is only one God—and we do not believe in him!*

4

A Case History?

The deeds of the fathers are the sign
for the sons.

—*Hebrew maxim*

Il n'y a pas de bon père; qu'on n'en
tienne pas grief aux hommes mais au
lien de paternité qui est pourri.

[The rule is that there are no good
fathers; it is not the men that are at
fault, but the paternal bond that is
rotten.]

—Jean-Paul Sartre, *Les mots*

On peut s'essayer à l'histoire du com-
portement, c'est à dire à une histoire
psychologique, sans être soi-même ni
psychologue ni psychanalyste et en se
tenant à distance des théories, du vo-
cabulaire et même des méthodes de la
psychologie moderne, et cependant
intéresser ces mêmes psychologues
sur leur terrain. Si on naît historien,
on devient psychologue à sa manière.

[One can make an attempt at the history of behavior, that is to say, at a
psychological history, without being
oneself either a psychologist or a psychoanalyst and while keeping oneself
at a distance from the theories, the
vocabulary and even the methods of
modern psychology, and nevertheless
to engage these very psychologists on
their terrain. If one is born a historian one becomes a psychologist in
one's own fashion.]

—Philippe Ariès, preface to the second edition of *L'enfance et la vie
familiale sous l'Ancien Régime*

The first attempt to psychoanalyze Freud through his own writings came in 1929 in a book published in Munich, entitled *Freuds tragischer Komplex: Eine Analyse der Psychoanalyse* (Freud's tragic complex: An analysis of psychoanalysis). Though a review by Otto Fenichel appeared in the *Internationale Zeitschrift* and the book is mentioned in the Jones biography, it seems otherwise to have been forgotten. Even details about its author, Charles Maylan, are hard to come by. I have been able to ascertain only that Maylan was born in Alameda, California, in 1886 and must at some point have settled permanently in Germany. In a commemorative history of the Ernst Reinhardt Verlag, Maylan's publishers, which appeared in 1974, a footnote describes him as a German-American (*Deutschamerikaner*) who wrote his book in German. This is followed by the cryptic remark that "evil tongues" (*böse Zungen*) alleged that he had originally been called Lehmann.[1]

Freuds tragischer Komplex certainly deserves a full and separate study. I shall describe only its main features. The book displays a striking dichotomy. Maylan hails psychoanalysis as an important discovery with far-reaching consequences for which he gives Freud due credit. At the same time, both psychoanalytic theory and the psychoanalytic movement are deeply flawed. They are characterized by materialism, denial of spirituality, hatred, and resentment both within and beyond the movement. In an ironically phrased "Open Letter" to Freud, Maylan challenges him to respond to what will follow. The thrust of the book is to show that the flaws of psychoanalysis all have their origin in Freud's own father complex, which he has never succeeded in resolving and has most often repressed. Through the uncovering of this "weak point" psychoanalysis can eventually be merged with Nietzsche's thought and brought to its proper philosophical depth. At the root of the shortcomings and perversions of psychoanalysis lie those of its founder, and these include not only his unresolved neuroses, but his Jewish character. The book is therefore also spiced with anti-Semitic allusions, phraseology, and judgments.

Maylan's aim is to turn psychoanalysis back upon itself—that is, to expose its weaknesses by using psychoanalytic methods, at least as he understands them. But in an analysis of psychoanalysis the patient is an abstraction. Freud must therefore serve as its representative. Maylan's sources are Freud's dreams, taken from his *Traumdeutung,* as well as some known incidents from his life.

Psychoanalysis, according to Maylan, was born out of the centuries-old torture, humiliation, and thirst for revenge of a typical ungenial race. Moreover, Freud is insincere concerning his relations with his father. As a Jew he is deeply rooted in faith and superstition and, at the same time, he represses his fear of castration by his father, a fear that is at the root of his *Todesangst,* his anxiety about death.

When Maylan recalls the incident that so upset Freud when he learned of it as a child (that in which Jakob Freud's hat was once tossed into the street by an anti-Semite and he meekly picked it up and went on his way) he entitles the section "Der Jude im Kot" (The Jew in the excrement).[2] Rome and Christendom are still at the center of Freud's thinking, just as they were when his father told him the story. Hannibal remains the symbol of Judaism which wants to destroy Rome, but Freud does not admit that Rome means the Catholic church. His identification with Hannibal expresses his desire to avenge his father's and his own humiliations by anti-Semites. He aims to undermine Christianity by replacing the papacy in Rome with an international papacy of Reason. Freud's associations to his father's anecdote reflect his sadism.

On the other hand, the childhood incident in which Freud urinated in his parents' bedroom is both a reflection of his narcissism and an act of rebellion against his father. Freud's ultimate wish is to acquire his father's power. His impressions of works of art are really psychological self-portraits. His Michelangelo essay really means that for Freud Moses' left hand symbolizes the "sinfully lusting forbidden" hand of the son, his right hand holding the tablets stands for the brutal hand of the father, and the hair between them (Moses' beard) covers the lap of the mother.[3]

Freud's dreams, some of which are analyzed individually, all point to his castration complex and hatred of his father, though he has repressed these feelings and refuses to acknowledge them. Thus even Freud's dream of his sleeping mother and the bird-beaked figures really represents his wish for the death of his father.

Freud is also incapable of real friendship. In reality he hates his friends because he connects them with his father. He feels "hatred against all non-intellectual cultural values (in particular Christian values), which are not accessible to the Jewish spirit."[4] Freud aspires to the rule of reason over passion and spirit, in reality the rule of the son over father and mother. Psychoanalysis can be saved from itself, and Freud die in peace, only if he is ready to analyze his father complexes and if psychoanalysis, purged of the consequences of these complexes, is fused with Nietzschean nihilism. From Freud's correspondence with Stefan Zweig we learn that a poster in Vienna advertising a lecture by Maylan on Freud contained a favorable blurb on Maylan's book by C. G. Jung.[5]

Freud, it would seem, read or at least perused the book. The response which Maylan so eagerly awaited came in the laconic form of a quotation from Caliban in Shakespeare's *The Tempest* and was conveyed through Max Eitingon: "You taught me language; and my profit on't is, I know how to curse."[6] Anyone who proposes to psychoanalyze Freud might do well to keep these words in mind.

I have paused over Maylan's book because it offers a paradigm of the use and abuse of turning psychoanalysis back on Freud and because it is the unwitting predecessor of all the many such attempts to come. Not everything in this bizarre and malicious book is silly or malign. That Freud's self-analysis, however heroic, was far from complete is something we have known or should have known all along. Ferenczi, late in life, had much to say about it.[7] Nor should we forget that it was Freud who first opened the Pandora's box of applied psychoanalysis and that its problems are still very much with us. And yet for many who seek a richer understanding of art, of history, of Freud himself, the temptation to psychoanalyze has been irresistible.

At the outset of this book I proposed that a major factor in the tendency to psychoanalyze and thus subjectivize *Moses and Monotheism* lies in the widely felt embarrassment of taking its historical and ethnological assumptions at face value. But there are other reasons as well. Freud's almost lifelong personal identification with the figure of Moses is well known. There are stigmata in the text—its repetitiveness; the comparison of the distortion of the biblical text to a murder ("the difficulty is not in perpetrating the deed but in getting rid of its traces").[8] There is no mention of Karl Abraham's *Imago* paper on Amenhotep IV, a parapraxis on which Leonard Shengold has written a rich and exemplary psychoanalytic study linking this with Freud's silence over the biblical Abraham and the patriarchal religion.[9] There is Freud's fainting spell during a discussion of Ikhnaton with Carl Jung, and his obsession with the book itself, which tormented him "like an unlaid ghost."[10]

However, except in their terminology and schematic use of Freudian concepts, are the various "psychoanalytic" treatments of *Moses and Monotheism* really psychoanalytic? Apart from the obvious and inevitable lack of a living dynamic interchange with the subject, we have only the most meager data about Freud's childhood, his sexual life, his parents, all vital elements for any genuine case history. "Origins" and "Boyhood and Adolescence" are traversed in a scant twenty-six pages in Jones's three volumes.[11] Freud himself actively suppressed as much as he could about his early life, though the fragments he deliberately revealed in order to explain his theories in *The Interpretation of Dreams, The Psychopathology of Everyday Life,* and elsewhere have made possible some psychoanalytic sleuthing. Even so we are generally deprived of the very facts that might be most useful to us.

What we have, therefore, is an ongoing plethora of psychological inquiries into Freud, legitimate quests in themselves, but often masking illegitimately under the guise of psychoanalysis and further constricting their potential by feeling obliged to invoke Freudian concepts that become static categories.

Since Maylan, all so-called psychoanalytic investigations of Freud have centered around his relations with his father, Jakob. But what do we really know of Jakob Freud? Who was Jakob Freud?

Extensive searches in Moravian and Viennese archives, notably by Josef Sajner, Renée Gicklhorn, and Peter Swales, have yielded a few new facts, the most potentially sensational being that before marrying Sigmund's mother, Amalie, Jakob may have had not one but two wives. Regrettably, the information about the mysterious Rebekka, who appears in a Freiberg register in 1852 and whose name is crossed out in a passport list, is murky and inconclusive. All extant information about Jakob Freud can be found conveniently gathered, though grossly inflated with gratuitous speculation, in Marianne Krüll's *Freud und sein Vater*.[12] In brief, we know that Jakob was born in Tysmenitz, Galicia; grew up in a Hasidic milieu (Sigmund Freud has testified to that); periodically traveled, first with his grandfather and then alone, on business trips into Moravia; settled in Freiberg, where Sigmund was born and had a Catholic nanny; subsequently settled in Vienna; had brothers who were involved in shady affairs with counterfeit money, one of them going to prison. As a result of Jakob's first marriage the family constellation was somewhat unusual, Sigmund having two half-brothers more than twenty years older than he, and being uncle to a nephew who was his senior by a year. A younger brother, Julius, died in infancy.

What, psychoanalytically, does it all amount to? True, Freud claimed to have analyzed Gustav Mahler during an afternoon stroll, but we do not have even this peripatetic advantage. Yet on the slim basis of what we do have, from Maylan (who had even less), to Marthe Robert (for whom Freud's unresolved Oedipal relation to his father is the *clef* to his *roman*), to Marie Balmary (who regards Jakob's attempt to hide his putative marriage to the elusive Rebekka as the "hidden fault of the father" that decisively affected the son),[13] to Marianne Krüll, part of whose thesis parallels Balmary's,[14] but who is also convinced that Jakob Freud was guilt-ridden over his break with Jewish tradition and what she assumes to have been his frequent masturbation during his otherwise sexually deprived journeys away from Galicia, the burden of guilt being transferred to Sigmund—and so on to a host of others too numerous to mention—the temptation to psychoanalyze the relationship between father and son has captivated many but has yielded no consensus. Indeed, it has most often produced conflicting and irreconcilable conclusions. One is almost tempted to turn, for relief, to Turgenev.

Some, indeed, in an effort to fathom Jakob Freud, have felt the serious need to understand his Jewish background and have accordingly made forays into Jewish history. (Conversely, the Jerusalem scholar Ernst Simon, whose extensive Jewish knowledge alerted him to some neglected aspects of Freud's Jewish identity, overstepped his bounds by diagnosing Freud, at least hypothetically, as an "obsessive neurotic," a stock phrase that in this case explains virtually nothing).[15] David Bakan's *Freud and the Jewish Mystical Tradition* (1958) was a pioneering attempt to seriously consider Freud's Jewish background and identity, but it was deeply flawed by his relentless attempt to prove that Freud and psychoanalysis are heirs to the Kabbalah and its heretical offshoots, Sabbatianism and Frankism. I want to stress that there is nothing intrinsically wrong with such a line of investigation, but it must be pursued with a rigor and subtlety that are lacking here. And one is not reassured by Bakan's reliance on secondary sources out of which he can indiscriminately invoke Gershom Scholem, the occultist Arthur E. Waite, and the novelist Joseph Kastein.[16]

Marianne Krüll has diligently read whatever in Jewish historiography seemed relevant and was linguistically accessible to her. Her bibliography bristles with some of the most distinguished names in modern Jewish scholarship: Graetz, Dubnow, Balaban, Raphael Mahler, Filip Friedman. She has read Blond's memorial book on Tysmenitz, Haas on Moravian Jewry, and, inevitably, Zborowski and Herzog's popular sociological study of the shtetl, *Life is with People*.

Like others, Krüll has discovered the Haskalah, the Jewish Enlightenment, and it is the polarity shtetl–Haskalah that she has appropriated as the historical and conceptual framework for her understanding of Jakob Freud's Jewish identity. According to Krüll, on his travels away from his native Galician environment, though perhaps even earlier, Jakob Freud abandoned the orthodoxy of his youth and became—a *Maskil*. What it amounts to is pressing Jakob Freud into a typological mold on no direct but only the most circumstantial evidence. But what is a Maskil and, for that matter, what is Haskalah? Those who have pasted the label on Jakob Freud equate Haskalah simplistically with the abandonment of virtually all Jewish observance, with agnosticism if not outright atheism, with a desire for the most radical, if not total, assimilation.

Now, even if one were to accept the term *Maskil* as a provisionally convenient category for Jakob Freud, what has been missed is the diversity of currents within the Haskalah itself and the essential differences between the Galician Haskalah, with its spectrum of attitudes, and the German Haskalah (itself not a monolith) that had preceded it. The Galician Maskilim were opposed to using Yiddish except as an instrument for popularizing their ideas, but they remained loyal throughout to the Hebrew language and to historical and national values. They waged open war against what they regarded as religious fanaticism, Hasidic superstition, cultural hermeticism, but not against

Judaism per se.[17] Once we are aware of this, even the facts that Krüll dwells upon will be perceived in a different light.

Yes, Jakob Freud married Amalie Nathanson in a Reform temple in Vienna. But Viennese Reform at that time was a tamely liberalized version of traditional Judaism in which the modern elements were largely confined to such externals as decorum in the synagogue and the preaching of sermons in German. Isaac Noah Mannheimer, the rabbi who officiated, was a religious conservative who saw no necessary conflict between adherence to Jewish tradition and a wholehearted acceptance of universal humane and cultural ideals.[18] You may rest assured that at the wedding Jakob was not bareheaded, all seven nuptial blessings were recited in Hebrew, and the glass was dutifully shattered under Jakob's foot in remembrance of the destruction of the ancient Temple in Jerusalem. When Sigmund ("Shelomoh Sigismund") was born, Jakob recorded the event in Hebrew and German in his bible, and it is clear from the text that the circumcision was performed on the eighth day in all its punctilious detail.[19] Later in life, we are told, Jakob in his leisure time would often study the Bible or even a page of Talmud "in the original."[20] Granted that his visible piety may have eroded over the years, and he wanted to be both modern and affluent (the latter wish was denied him). If you want to persist in calling him a Galician Maskil, so be it, so long as you do not turn the term into a cliché. The same caution is necessary in trying to fathom his relationship with his son.

Thus, even if we accept the universality of the Oedipus complex, it is hard to understand the apparent intensity and longevity of Freud's Oedipal conflicts. Aside from the angry "Nothing will come of him!" when the seven- or eight-year-old Sigmund peed on the floor of the parental bedroom[21] and undoubtedly other occasional outbursts of irritation that have not been recorded, Jakob Freud was a loving, devoted, warmhearted father who openly acknowledged his son's precocious brilliance ("My Sigmund has more intelligence in his little toe than I have in my whole head"). Of course he also expected obedience and respect[22] (we are still in the mid-nineteenth century), but he encouraged his son to surpass him and was proud of his achievements.

In these aspects the relationship seems almost to follow an archetype of the relations between immigrant Jewish fathers and their talented sons in modern times. All such sons have been, in a sense, father-slayers. But unlike the fierce Primeval Father of Freudian mythology, these Jewish fathers have been more than willing victims, eager to be slain, doting on their slayers. "Does a Jewish father," Theodor Reik was asked, "resent it when his son becomes better than he?" "On the contrary," Reik replied, "he enjoys it. . . . Whereas a non-Jew would say: 'What is good enough for me is good enough for him.' "[23] What Reik did not say, and what should be added, is that despite

the acquiescence of the Jewish father the son has often felt an innate, sometimes only half-acknowledged guilt at the very fact that he has gone so far
beyond the father (see Freud's letter of 1936 to Romain Rolland).[24] Whether
such guilt, which seems to be independent of any desire for the mother, can
properly be considered Oedipal is, I think, open to discussion.

It is when we turn to Freud's own pronouncements concerning his early Jewish
background that matters become ever more curious. In essence Freud projected three images in his adult life which became, and have largely remained,
part of his public persona. First—that he had received only the most meager
Jewish religious education. Second—that there had been only the most minimal and perfunctory Jewish observance in his parents' home. Third—that he
does not know and, by implication, never really knew Hebrew or Yiddish.
Now, I am not trying to turn Freud, or even his father, into pious Jews or
Jewish scholars, but even in light of the fragmentary information at our disposal each of these assertions is problematic, to say the least.

Though he obviously did not have the intensive traditional Jewish education
to which his father had been exposed, Freud certainly received a Jewish education that was far from trivial. Up to and after the age of seven he studied
exclusively at home, where Jakob Freud was his teacher. Though we are not
privy to the details of what they studied together, it is certain that Jakob initiated him into the study of the Bible, using Ludwig Philippsohn's bilingual
illustrated edition. It should be noted that this bible was not, as is often
thought, modern in any heretical sense. The modernity of Philippsohn's extensive German commentary lay in its quest for the larger ethical and humanistic implications of the biblical text and in its marshaling of historical
and archaeological information to render the background more vivid and concrete. But the attitude of the commentary toward biblical and later Jewish
tradition is nothing if not reverent, indeed conservative. The integrity of the
sacred text is never questioned, the text is never emended, the central findings
of the Higher Criticism are rejected, and the creation of the world in six days,
as well as the traditional Mosaic authorship of the entire Pentateuch, de-
fended. Contrary to Marianne Krüll's typically rash judgment, the illustra-
tions would not necessarily be seen by all traditional Jews as a violation of
the prohibition of images, and there is no reason to suppose that there were
not even some enlightened orthodox Jews who read the Philippsohn Bible with
interest.

In light of what we shall yet see as Jakob Freud's commitment to the Hebrew language, we may safely assume that he taught the child Sigmund to
read the Hebrew text. Would it not be interesting if, concomitantly, he also
taught him to read German from the parallel translation in the same Phi-

lippsohn Bible? I do not insist on it. The more important question would be in what spirit he taught him the Bible, and here the simplest answer would be—in the spirit of Philippsohn's commentary. Certainly, whatever his interpretations, Jakob was teaching him the Bible not as a collection of fairy tales but as a holy book to be studied with the utmost reverence. A tiny but very revealing glimpse into the way the Bible was presented to him in the home of his childhood is provided by Freud himself, in a fleeting recollection concerning his mother, Amalie, who has always been portrayed as far more radically alienated from Jewish tradition than Jakob ever was. Perhaps it was so, though the portrayal is based exclusively on her behavior in old age, long after Jakob's death; in any case it is irrelevant to the precious anecdote Freud recounts in *The Interpretation of Dreams*:

> When I was six years old and was given my first lessons by my mother, I was expected to believe that we were all made of earth and must therefore return to earth. This did not suit me and I expressed doubts of the doctrine. My mother thereupon rubbed the palms of her hands together—just as she did when making dumplings, except that there was no dough between them—and showed me the blackish scales of *epidermis* produced by the friction as proof that we were made of earth. My astonishment at this ocular demonstration knew no bounds and I acquiesced in the belief which I was later to hear expressed in the words: "*Du bist der Natur einen Tod schuldig*" [Thou owest Nature a death].[25]

The debt to a personified Nature, as Freud admits, came later. Primary was the mother's astonishing "ocular demonstration" that the story of the creation of Man in Genesis 2:7 was literally true. How lasting an influence the Bible had on Freud has been closely explored by Théo Pfrimmer in his *Freud, lecteur de la Bible,* and the evidence remains powerful even if one does not necessarily agree with Pfrimmer's specifically psychoanalytic conclusions.[26]

I shall give only one telling example. In a letter of July 23, 1880, to his friend Carl Koller, Freud describes his anxieties over the material he had not yet reviewed the day before he was to face his professors in the oral examination in medicine known as the *rigorosum*:

> So I decided to forget about pharmacology . . . and to repeat this worthy subject quietly after vacation. But on Wednesday afternoon, twenty-four hours before the decision, I thought it over again; the fiendish laughter of Hell yelled in my ears, the clamor in Israel was great, and my best friends sang the dirge, "Tell it not in Askalon, publish it not in the streets of Gath" [*Erzählet es nicht in Askalon, verkundet es nicht in den Strassen von Gad*], which was sung at the

death of Saul and Jonathan. So I decided to delve for twelve more hours into the depths of pharmacology."[27]

One is struck immediately by the ease and naturalness with which Freud summons up the biblical verse (II Samuel 1:20), by his awareness of the original context, and by the fact that he is quoting from memory (hence the reversed order of the two Philistine cities mentioned). But he was to paraphrase the same verse seventeen years later in a far more significant letter sent to Wilhelm Fliess on September 21, 1897. Here, at a turning point in the history of psychoanalysis, Freud told Fliess that he was in the process of giving up the seduction theory in the etiology of neurosis and added the following observation:

> Can it be that this doubt represents an episode in the advance toward further insight?
> It is strange, too, that no feeling of shame appeared—for which, after all, there could well be occasion. *Of course I shall not tell it in Dan, nor speak of it in Askelon, in the land of the Philistines,* but in your eyes and my own, I have more the feeling of a victory than a defeat (which is surely not right).[28]

Here, if we read closely, the verse has taken on a multiplicity of meanings. On a literal level Freud is using the verse in what has become its proverbial sense of not revealing a secret to others (even in modern Hebrew we sometimes say, "Do not tell it in Gath"). But, as we saw from the letter to Koller, he was fully aware of the original context. In the Bible the verse appears in David's great elegy at the death of Saul and Jonathan. That there should be an unconscious link to mourning is not surprising. Despite his brave words, Freud must also have been saddened by the collapse of his prior theoretical structure with, as yet, nothing firm to replace it. At the same time he was still literally in mourning over his father, who had died less than a year before. And yet he has "more the feeling of a victory than a defeat." This too echoes the biblical context, for in the narrative of the Book of Samuel, immediately after his lament David is acclaimed king of Judah. "Which is surely not right," Freud has added parenthetically, a sign of his inner conflict over the abandonment of the seduction theory and, if you wish, over his father's death. But there is more.

In reprinting this important letter in the *Standard Edition* James Strachey notes the fact that Freud is "misquoting" the biblical verse but says nothing further. The fact is, however, that "I shall not tell it in Dan" is more than misquoting (in the sense that Freud misquoted the verse to Koller by reversing the order of Gath and Askelon). It is a genuine "Freudian slip," for *Dan* does not even appear in the original verse; here Freud has substituted Dan for Gath.

Why Dan, which was not a Philistine city but an Israelite tribe and territory? The answer lies once more in a return to a biblical context which, as we shall see further on, is confirmed also by Jakob Freud's own words to his son. The association is to Samson, who, like Saul, Jonathan, and David after him, fought the Philistines, but was himself a member of the tribe of Dan. Thus the meaning of the slip may be that, unconsciously, in abandoning the seduction theory Freud fleetingly identified not only with David but with Samson, whose hair had been cut off (I need not tell you what *that* means). Yet even Samson had his victory. Though he perished in the effort, he did, after all, pull their temple down over the heads of the Philistines.

But the Bible, of course, is not yet Judaism. What Jewish observances, if any, could Freud have witnessed as a child at home? Freud does not tell us. We do have firm testimony, however, that Jakob Freud would impressively recite the entire text of the Passover Haggadah by heart at the annual Seder.[29] Presumably that text was sufficiently familiar to Sigmund that he could glibly parody its final line in a letter to Fliess on April 16, 1900: "If I closed with 'Next Easter in Rome' I would feel like a pious Jew."[30] We learn too that at some point his siblings, and perhaps he as well, were costumed for a *Purimspiel*.[31] Thus Passover and Purim. Was there nothing else? We should pay closer attention to a very important letter Freud sent to Martha in 1882, describing his encounter in Hamburg with an old Jewish stationer who had been an ardent disciple of her grandfather, Haham Isaac Bernays:[32] "The man from whom I ordered this despotic paper on Friday could supply it only on Sunday; 'for on Saturday,' said he, 'we are not here. It is one of our ancient customs' (Oh, I know that ancient custom!)." How did Freud know? From Martha's family or from his own childhood? We cannot yet be certain. But let us listen further:

> His beard was shaggy. Yesterday they were not allowed to be shaved. "You know, of course, which Fast Day is upon us?" *I knew all right.* Just because years ago at this season (owing to a miscalculation) Jerusalem had been destroyed I was to be prevented from speaking to my girl on the last day of my stay. But what's Hecuba to me? Jerusalem is destroyed and Marty and I are alive and happy. And the historians say that if Jerusalem had not been destroyed, we Jews would have perished like so many races before and after us. According to them the invisible edifice of Judaism became possible only after the collapse of the visible Temple. So, said my old Jew, nine days before Tisha B'Av we deny ourselves every pleasure.

So Freud "knew all right" about the Fast of the Ninth of Av, and the force with which he says it somehow conveys a knowledge that has been there all along, since childhood, derived from the father.[33] Moreover, he knows not only the practice but the why of it, and one is startled to realize that the notion of the invisible structure of Judaism being revealed only after the destruction of the visible Temple will resonate more than half a century later in *Moses and Monotheism* in the section entitled "The Progress in Spirituality."[34]

Bereft as we are of solid information about the inner life of Jakob Freud's household, I do not claim to have demonstrated how much of Jewish tradition was to be found there. My only purpose is to point out that at every turn there are hints and fragments that challenge the images Freud publicly projected. To the same order belongs a sentence in the letter of 1880 to Koller which I cited earlier. "So I sat in travail," Freud wrote, "with the fateful eve of examination approaching (*eref* examination as they said in olden times) and noticed that I still had all the material in front of me."[35] *Eref*, of course, is nothing but the Hebrew-Yiddish *Erev* with a German accent. But no one had ever said "*erev* examination" in "olden times." Traditionally and universally the word was used for the eve of a holy day, all such days in the Jewish calendar beginning in the evening. What Freud must have heard in his childhood was "*Erev Shabbes*," "*Erev Pesach*," "*Erev Yomtev*," and it was so natural to him that he could conjure it up with ease and wittily apply it to the eve of the *rigorosum*.

Beyond any detail, the very violence of Freud's recoil against Jewish religious belief and ritual must arouse our deepest suspicion. It displays an aggressive intensity that normally accompanies a rebellion against an equally intense former attachment, more typical of a former Yeshiva student in revolt against Judaism than of one who had received a minimal Jewish education and whose father, we are assured, had become a freethinker by the time he settled in Vienna. Why not, as seems to have been the case with Ferenczi, Karl Abraham, Hanns Sachs, and others, simple indifference? Yes, there was the Catholic nanny in Freiberg who took him to church and who seems, literally, to have frightened the hell out of him.[36] But nutricide cannot suffice us; we demand a patricide, and a Jewish one at that. One is reminded of the "Yom Kippur Balls" held in the 1890s in New York by the Jewish anarchists, themselves East European Jews who had known traditional Jewish life personally and intimately and now, having broken with all that, set out to publicly desecrate the Day of Atonement. At which point the *Forward*, the leading Socialist Yiddish newspaper, editorialized gently, "*Ateistn, zeit nisht fanatiker* [Atheists, do not be fanatics]."

Finally, Freud's ignorance of Hebrew and Yiddish. In 1930 he writes to the American A. A. Roback, who had sent him an inscribed copy of his *Jewish Influences in Modern Thought*, "My education was so un-Jewish that today I cannot even read your dedication, which is evidently written in Hebrew. In later life I have often regretted this lack in my education."[37]

His education was "so un-Jewish"? After being tutored by his father he studied Bible, Jewish history and religion, as well as Hebrew throughout his Gymnasium years with Samuel Hammerschlag, whom he hails as a wonderful teacher and to whom he remained almost filially devoted for the rest of his life.[38] Granted that the time allotted to religion classes in the Gymnasium was too limited for intensive study of Hebrew as a language and that by this time he may have forgotten most of what he had known. But to the degree that he could no longer distinguish between Hebrew and Yiddish?

I have casually counted thirteen Yiddish words in the portions of Freud's correspondence published to date. Significantly, perhaps, most of them crop up in the letters to Fliess, where Freud is at his most uninhibited. True, some of the words, such as *Schammes, Schnorrer, Meschugge,* even *Parnosse,* were common coinage even for those who didn't know the language (like *Chutzpah* in current American idiom). But was that the case with words like *Knetcher* (wrinkles), *Stuss* (nonsense), *Dalles* (poverty), or *tomer dokh* (perhaps, after all?)?[39]

Theodor Reik has stated that Freud's mother did not speak to him in High German but in Galician Yiddish.[40] If this be so, even though Amalie Freud had grown up in Vienna, what shall we say of Jakob Freud, who grew up in Galicia? Even granting that German was spoken in the home that Freud did not leave until he was twenty-seven, is it not reasonable to suppose that Yiddish was a lingua franca alongside it and that he could speak or at least understand it as well?

In analyzing his "My Son the Myops" dream, Freud deliberately gives the impression that he had to rely on others for the meaning of the word *geseres:* "According to information I have received from philologists, '*Geseres*' is a genuine Hebrew word derived from a verb '*goiser*', and is best translated by 'imposed sufferings' or 'doom.' The use of the term in slang would incline one to suppose that it meant 'weeping and wailing.'"[41]

Yet I find it difficult to believe that Freud had not known the meaning of the word. Like the Yiddish *Rishes* (Hebrew: *Rish'ut* [wickedness]), the term used by German-speaking Jews to connote anti-Semitism, *Geseres* was commonly known, even among assimilated Jews, to mean anti-Jewish decrees and persecution. The context of the dream itself, which is precisely one of impending anti-Jewish persecution ("*On account of certain events which had occurred in the city of Rome, it had become necessary to remove the children to safety . . .*"), and Freud's immediate associations to Herzl's *Das neue Ghetto* and to "the Jewish problem, concern about the future of one's children, to whom one cannot give a country of their own," demonstrate that on some level at least Freud knew it. Moreover, as Freud himself pointed out, the word had acquired a secondary "slang" meaning that "would incline one to suppose that it meant 'weeping and wailing'"—that is, the reaction to persecution—or simply making a lot of noise and fuss (further on, Freud recalls the doctor who shouted at the anxious mother of the son with the infected eye, "Why are you making such a *Geseres*?"). But Strachey's translation of *Jargon* as "slang" is only technically adequate. It misses the other, equally valid and far more interesting meaning. For *Jargon* to cultivated German-speaking Jews was also the common deprecatory synonym for Yiddish. And that is not all. The secondary meaning of making an uproar found its way as a loanword into the German language itself. You will find it in the 1897 edition of the *Deutsches Wörterbuch* of the brothers Grimm under *Geseier*. Ironically, you will also find it in *Mein Kampf* in connection with Hitler's attack on the alleged excesses of the Jewish press in Germany.[42]

But let me try your patience once more.

On June 9, 1936, Arnold Zweig wrote Freud that he had been sent a copy of the *Wiener Illustrierte* "with a picture of you with Zofie's puppies at your feet." To which Freud responded, "My Jofie is a stickler for accuracy and does not like being called Zofie by you; Jo as in Jew."[43] But the pronunciation of the chow's name comes through only in German: "Meine Jofie hält auf Exaktheit und will nicht von Ihnen Zofie gennant werden; *Jo wie Jud.*"[44] Of all the languages Freud knew or could have known there is only one in which the name makes sense. In Hebrew *Yofi* means—Beauty.

Thus, you will say, my efforts to retrieve an elusive reality have reached the anticlimax of this petty canine clue. Frankly, at this point I myself share your sense of frustration. But God, it has been said, dwells in the details, and I would not forgo this one, paltry, exotic, perhaps absurd though it may be. It is at least as plausible as the notion of the young Jakob Freud guiltily masturbating his way through Moravia, which is unalloyed guesswork without even circumstantial evidence. What I have been trying to show you is that so far as the Jewish identity of Jakob Freud is concerned, and so by extension his relationship with his son, nothing is closed and everything remains problematic. Even if we accept the possibility of psychoanalysis in absentia, it cannot be persuasive until we have some hard, historical facts at our disposal. Is there any way out of this conundrum? Who, I must ask again, was Jakob Freud?

There is one crucial episode involving Jakob and Sigmund Freud which has not yet been properly assessed, not least because it involves a Hebrew text which has never been properly transcribed (the handwriting is admittedly difficult), let alone adequately glossed.[45] But it is, in effect, the one canonical text of Jakob Freud at our disposal. In what follows I neither presume to dignify my reconstruction as "psychoanalytic" (though it is no less so than others that pretend to be) nor, given the limitations of a single text, do I claim more than a partial insight. But for those intent on understanding *Moses and Monothe-*

ism in terms of Freud's inner life, I propose that a proper exegesis of Jakob Freud's text can point to a more viable psychological interpretation of the meaning of the book than those currently available.

In 1891, on Freud's thirty-fifth birthday, his father presented him with an unusual gift. He had rebound in leather the Philippsohn Bible that Sigmund had studied in his childhood and now gave it to him with an elaborate Hebrew inscription that he had composed (for the original Hebrew text see appendix II).

Those with an intimate acquaintance of Hebrew texts will recognize immediately that this one is written entirely in *melitzah,* a mosaic of fragments and phrases from the Hebrew Bible as well as from rabbinic literature or the liturgy, fitted together to form a new statement of what the author intends to express at the moment. Melitzah, in effect, recalls Walter Benjamin's desire to someday write a work composed entirely of quotations. At any rate, it was a literary device employed widely in medieval Hebrew poetry and prose, then through the Haskalah, and even among nineteenth-century writers both modern and traditional. But before analyzing Jakob Freud's text, let me offer a deliberately literal, and hence abrasively unliterary, translation:

> Son who is dear to me, Shelomoh. In the seventh in the days of the years of your life the Spirit of the Lord began to move you and spoke within you: Go, read in my Book that I have written and there will burst open for you the wellsprings of understanding, knowledge, and wisdom. Behold, it is the Book of Books, from which sages have excavated and lawmakers learned knowledge and judgement. A vision of the Almighty did you see; you heard and strove to do, and you soared on the wings of the Spirit.
>
> Since then the book has been stored like the fragments of the tablets in an ark with me. For the day on which your years were filled to five and thirty I have put upon it a cover of new skin and have called it: "Spring up, O well, sing ye unto it!" And I have presented it to you as a memorial and as a reminder of love from your father, who loves you with everlasting love.
>
> Jakob Son of R. Shelomoh Freid [*sic*]
> In the capital city Vienna 29 Nisan [5]651 6 May [1]891

The question that immediately leaps at us is, why, if Sigmund Freud knew no Hebrew, did Jakob write this elaborate Hebrew inscription to him on his thirty-fifth birthday? Jakob Freud was certainly capable of writing in German.[46] Did he read the inscription to his son and then translate it for him orally? It is possible, of course, but such a circuitous method does not seem likely. Is it not more plausible to assume that one writes important dedications in languages that the recipient is expected to understand, in this case even if it involved a little help along the way? But I shall not pursue this.

The Hebrew inscription is central because of its content and doubly precious for having been written in melitzah. You must understand that in writing it Jakob Freud had not been searching for appropriate words and phrases in a biblical or talmudic concordance. Because of his background, the texts from which he drew he knew intimately, by heart. He was drawing freely from this memory, and each phrase had associations to the original from which it was drawn. In *melitzah* the sentences compounded out of quotations mean what they say; but below and beyond the surface they reverberate with associations to the original texts, and this is what makes them psychologically so interesting and valuable. In the transposition of a quotation from the original (in this case canonical) text to a new one, the meaning of the original context may be retained, altered, or subverted. In any case the original context trails along as an invisible interlinear presence, and the readers, like the writer, must be aware of these associations if they are to savor the new text to the full. A partial analogy may be found in Eliot's use of quotations in *The Waste Land*.

I will not now detain you with a detailed list of every source from which Jakob Freud's dedication quotes or to which it alludes (that will be found in a critical apparatus to the Hebrew text which is printed here as an appendix). I will content myself with the highlights. Opting for caution, I do not want to exaggerate the extent of Jakob Freud's Jewish scholarship. From the sources that can be traced and the facility of his use of melitzah, the profile of Jakob Freud that emerges is one of a learned Jewish layman who has a total command of the Pentateuch, of the rest of the Bible at least in the prophetic portions read in the synagogue as *haftarot*, of the Jewish liturgy. One allusion, as we shall soon see, is to the Talmud, but it is impossible to gauge from this just how much Talmud he knew. What of the general impression? According to Thornton Wilder, Freud once told him that his father had been a "Voltairian."[47] Make of that what you will, there is certainly no Voltairian here. Even if we take the references to the Lord metaphorically, the entire dedication, in content and spirit, is the utterance of a tradition-minded Jew, whatever the degree or detail of his piety. But let us examine some specifics.

The dedication is framed symmetrically, in the first line and the last, by expressions of love, each taken from the thirty-first chapter of Jeremiah: "Son who is dear to me, Shelomoh" (*ben yakir li Shelomoh*) obviously derives from Jeremiah 31:19—"Truly, Ephraim is a dear son to Me" (*ha-ben yakir li Efrayim*)—while [your father] "who loves you with everlasting love" (*'ohavkha 'ahavat 'olam*) is based on Jeremiah 31:2—"with everlasting love have I loved thee" (*ve-'ahavat 'olam 'ahavtikha*). Let it be noted, however, that in Jeremiah the beloved son is Ephraim, symbol of the so-called Lost Tribes of Israel.

Ephraim is depicted as wandering in exile, and the prophetic text holds forth the prospect of return and reconciliation with God the Father. Surely we are entitled to assume that these contexts were not far from Jakob Freud's mind when he used these words. And why not, when the essence of the inscription is a call for Sigmund's return and reconciliation?

When he was seven years old, Jakob points out, "the Spirit of the Lord began to move you" (hehel ru'ah Adonay le-fa'amkha), as in Judges 13:25, speaking of Samson—"And the spirit of the Lord began to move him in the encampment of Dan" (va-tahel ru'ah Adonay le-fa'amo be-mahaneh Dan). Here we may recall, in passing, Freud's slip of substituting Dan for Gath in his letter to Fliess on the abandonment of the seduction theory. But on a manifest level Jakob is referring to the beginning of Sigmund's biblical studies with him at age seven. Recollected here is a promise made at that time, ascribed to the "Spirit of the Lord" but these may have been Jakob's actual words when he began to teach his son the "Book of Books"—that "there will burst open for you the wellsprings of understanding, knowledge and wisdom" (binah, de'ah vehaskel [from the eighteen benedictions of the daily liturgy]). This promise was amply fulfilled, and Jakob is full of praise for Sigmund, who "heard and strove to do" (Exodus 24:7—"All that the Lord has spoken will we do and hear") and as a result "soared upon the wings of the Spirit" (Psalms 18:11—"He soared upon the wings of the wind"), ru'ah in Hebrew meaning both "wind" and "spirit."

However, at some unspecified point since then, Sigmund abandoned the Book. It has been, in Jakob's striking simile, "stored like the fragments of the Tablets in an ark with me." On the surface the statement seems simple enough. The Philippsohn Bible was left behind in the father's home where, in shabby condition, like broken tablets, it was kept in an ark (the word 'aron "ark" in Hebrew, has the meaning both of a bookcase and the ancient Ark of the Covenant). Now, having newly rebound the book in leather ("I have put upon it a cover of new skin"), the father returns it to his son with an implicit plea that he return to its study. As it was his source of inspiration long ago, it will now be a source of renewal: hence Jakob calls it by the words of the Song of the Well—"Spring up, O well! Sing ye unto it" (Numbers 21:17), an allusion to the well that rose miraculously for the Israelites as they wandered through the desert. But one can probe deeper than that.

Jakob Freud's fundamental simile of the broken tablets in the ark is not biblical. In the biblical narrative, when Moses descends from Sinai with the Tablets of the Law and sees his people around the Golden Calf, he smashes the tablets, and nothing more is heard of them. Later, after Israel repents, he receives a second pair of tablets. The notion that the fragments of the first tablets were preserved and kept in the Ark of the Covenant is talmudic. It is to be found in three talmudic tractates—Berakhot, Baba Bathra, and Mena-

ḥot— and it is the context in the latter which is, for our purposes, the most interesting. The text in *Menaḥot* is a midrashic exposition of the beginning of Deuteronomy, chapter 10, in which Moses is told to hew two new tablets of stone similar to the first and to make an ark of wood. "And I will write on the tablets the words which were on the first tablets which thou didst break, and thou shalt put them in the ark" (Deuteronomy 10:2). With midrashic liberty, the Talmud purposefully misreads the syntax and refers the word "them" also to the broken tablets. The passage in *Menaḥot* reads:

> *Which thou didst break and thou shalt put them in the ark.* R. Joseph learnt: This teaches us that both the [new] tablets and the fragments of the [original, broken] tablets were deposited in the ark. Hence [we also learn that] a scholar who has forgotten his learning by reason of his misfortune [that is, through no fault of his own] must not be treated with disrespect [that is, even broken tablets are holy].[48]

Did Jakob Freud have this particular passage in mind, consciously or unconsciously, when he coined his simile? Did he identify with the scholar who had forgotten his learning through circumstances beyond his control? Did he sense disrespect in his son? We cannot answer for certain. But there is more.

The book, Jakob writes, "was stored . . . with me"—in Hebrew "*kamus 'imadi*"—a usage found only once in the Bible, in Deuteronomy 32:34 ("Is it not laid up in store with me [*ha-lo hu kamus 'imadi*], sealed in my treasuries?"). But there what is stored up is the wrath of the Lord against Israel for worshiping strange gods!

Jakob Freud's gift to Sigmund on his thirty-fifth birthday meant that he was giving him the Bible for the second time, a parallel to the two sets of the Tablets of the Law, the first of which had been shattered by Moses. Moses is therefore already implicated in the inscription, which, overflowing with love, also contains an underlying rebuke, even suppressed anger. If, as Marianne Krüll has it, Jakob Freud left a "mandate" to his son, it was neither to assimilate nor to cover up Jakob's alleged guilt. The mandate lies here, in the Hebrew inscription, the dramatic call to return to the Bible, to the originally shared values with the father, a "memorial and a reminder of love." And it is this Hebrew text of Jakob's alone that offers even the possibility of reaching a psychological understanding of Freud's involvement with Moses, from the *Moses* of Michelangelo to the culminating *Moses and Monotheism*. What follows is only a sketch of developments as we can now attempt to reconstruct them.

Jakob Freud died on October 23, 1896. In the next five years, beginning with Sigmund Freud's self-analysis, psychoanalysis is born, and such seminal works as *The Interpretation of Dreams* and *The Psychopathology of Everyday Life* are published. In the very same period he repeatedly expresses intense desires and concrete plans to visit Rome, but although he travels several times to Italy some inner block prevents him from reaching his goal. It will serve no present purpose for us to examine the numerous psychoanalytic attempts to explain these failures to attain his goal. What is important for the moment is the fact that in 1901 he finally made it to Rome with his brother Alexander. There, in the church of San Pietro in Vincoli, he was confronted for the first time with Michelangelo's statue of Moses and became virtually obsessed with it, contemplating it for hours on end, returning to it repeatedly on each subsequent visit to the Eternal City, drawing sketches of its details. In 1914, after an initial reluctance and without signing his name, he published his essay "The Moses of Michelangelo" in the journal *Imago*.

That essay, we should note, is not psychoanalytical. Freud does not attempt to analyze either Michelangelo or Moses. The whole revolves around Freud's strong feeling that he has discovered Michelangelo's conscious intention in depicting Moses the way he did, especially the manner in which Moses is holding the tablets under his right arm. The conventional interpretation of the statue was of an angry Moses about to rise in his wrath and let the tablets fall and shatter. Freud's audacious reinterpretation discovers a radical Michelangelo, who, as we noted in chapter 2, violates the plain sense of Scripture and creates a Moses in the moment of conquering and suppressing his anger, clutching and preserving the tablets just as they are about to fall.

Since, in the two or three years immediately preceding this essay, Freud had suffered the defections of Stekel, Adler, and especially Jung, it has been natural enough for most commentators to posit that Freud's preoccupation with the statue points to his deep identification with Michelangelo's *Moses* as he now understood it. He himself was struggling with his feelings of rage at the betrayals. He was like Moses, who (these are Freud's own words) "remembered his mission and for its sake renounced an indulgence of his feelings" and who accomplished "the highest mental achievement that is possible in a man, that of struggling successfully against an inward passion for the sake of a cause to which he has devoted himself."[49]

That, in itself, seems plausible enough. The only problem is that it does not suffice to explain another vital, indeed explicitly personal aspect of the essay.

One of the salient characteristics of Freud's personality was his lifelong need and extraordinary psychological talent for symbolic identifications, both of himself and of others, with outstanding figures in history and mythology. Indeed, an important book remains to be written about the convoluted inner world of Freud's personae and the psychological needs they fulfilled. Constant vigilance is required, however, so that we do not perceive these identifications as static. Freud was always shifting his personae, and symbolic identifications are always multivalent. In happier days Freud was Moses and Jung was Joshua, because he was choosing a successor and would not himself enter the Promised Land. He is certainly Moses in *Moses and Monotheism,* not because he is an Egyptian and not a Jew, but because just as Moses the Egyptian was a "great stranger" who brought monotheism to the Jews, so Freud the Jew is a great stranger bringing psychoanalysis to the world.

In the Michelangelo essay Moses may be Freud on one level, but in the most emotionally charged passage in that essay Moses must be someone else:

> For no piece of statuary has ever made a stronger impression on me than this. How often have I mounted the steep steps from the unlovely Corso Cavour to the lonely piazza where the deserted church stands, and have essayed to support the angry scorn of the hero's glance! Sometimes I have crept cautiously out of the half-gloom of the interior as though I myself belonged to the mob upon whom his eye is turned—the mob which can hold fast no conviction, which has neither faith nor patience, and which rejoices when it has regained its illusory idols.[50]

If, in this extraordinary, almost hallucinatory statement, Freud is part of the idolatrous mob, guilty, at least for the moment, over his inconstancy, lack of faith, false gods, then at that moment who can Michelangelo's Moses be if not his father Jakob? What on earth could make a man like Freud, who was on a quest for a new science of the human mind and who was rightly proud of not having followed the "compact majority," feel such guilt—if it were not literally Jewish guilt?[51] We are brought back immediately to the Hebrew inscription in the Philippsohn Bible in which Jakob, having given him the second tablets, is indeed Moses (if not God himself). But since that day in 1891 Freud had not fulfilled the mandate that the inscription represents. He had not returned to the Bible and the teachings of the father. He feels guilty, singled out under the rebuking stare of the statue. Unable to bear the full weight of it, he suddenly sees something no one else had ever seen—that Moses-Jakob contains his anger, that the wrath will not burst forth upon him. And is this not what we found in the inscription itself, where Jakob's anger is not expressed on the surface but remains contained in the invisible *ur*-texts from which the melitzot are drawn?

From the time of the break with Jung, Freud had allowed his Jewish feelings to emerge ever more intensely, but they were expressed, as we have seen, largely in private correspondence, not publicly in his works. I believe that he was still worried about the "Jewish national affair." Be that as it may, in 1933 Hitler came to power in Germany and the Nazi onslaught on Jews and psychoanalysis had begun. By the end of 1934 the first draft of *Moses and Monotheism* had been written. I have already explored the nexus between the historical events and the manifest content of the book, which I continue to consider primary. Why, on the manifest level, was Freud so intensely obsessed with it? It seems to me that those who would reduce the book entirely to psychoanalytic autobiography have failed to appreciate how great a role the passion for explanation and the excitement of discovery played in Freud's life. We can only try to imagine what it must have meant to him when, having once solved the riddle of the Sphinx, he felt that he had now, so to speak, solved the enigma of Sinai as well, and this without surrendering his prior thought along the way. Nothing had been lost; there were only new gains. With the Oedipus complex and the "return of the repressed" Freud had the integrative principles through which, in a way he had not foreseen, all pieces of the puzzle seemed wondrously to come together and even reinforce one another—from individual to mass psychology, from psychology to history, from Jewish history back into prehistory and on into the origins of Christianity and the dynamics of anti-Semitism.

In all this the question of "how the Jews have come to be what they are" remained central, and of course it had not only a general but a personal relevance. Here again Jakob Freud's Hebrew inscription offers a key to an alternative psychological explanation of *Moses and Monotheism*, different from those currently in vogue. We have only to tie the threads together.

Under the impact of the triumph of Nazism, in 1934 Freud decides the time has come to write his first and only Jewish book, to attempt to answer the hitherto unanswerable question of what makes him a Jew. In order to do so, at the age of seventy-eight he does what his father mandated to him when he was thirty-five—he returns to the study of the Bible. The point is a major one. In 1924 Freud wrote his so-called *Autobiographical Study,* in which, describing his early intellectual development, we read,

> I was moved . . . by a sort of curiosity, which was, however, directed more toward human concerns than toward natural objects; nor had I grasped the importance of observation as one of the best means of gratifying it. *My deep engrossment in the Bible story (almost as soon as I had learned the art of reading) had, as I recognized much later, an enduring effect upon the direction of my interest.*[52]

Significantly, the last sentence did not appear in the first edition. It was added only in 1935, the year after the completion of the manuscript draft of *Moses.* Only now, in retrospect, did Freud realize the full impact of the study of the Bible on his life, and only now did he fully acknowledge it. In this sense *Moses and Monotheism* represents, at last, a fulfillment of Jakob Freud's mandate or—should I finally allow myself the luxury of a technical psychoanalytic term—an example of "deferred obedience." The concept appears several times in Freud's works, notably in *Totem and Taboo,* where we read, "The dead father became stronger than the living one . . . in accordance with the psychological procedure so familiar to us in psycho-analysis under the name of deferred obedience." And again: "Totemic religion arose from the filial sense of guilt, in an attempt to allay that feeling and to appease the father by deferred obedience to him."[53]

If there is any merit to what I am proposing, then Freud's resolution of the guilt he felt in San Pietro in Vincoli (and certainly not there alone) was a psychological victory. In writing *Moses and Monotheism* he belatedly obeys the father and fulfills his mandate by returning to the intensive study of the Bible, but at the same time he maintains his independence from his father through his interpretation. He rejects the "material truth" of the biblical narrative but rejoices in his discovery of its "historical truth."

Where does this leave us?

When, decades earlier, Oskar Pfister had dismissed Freud's description of himself as a "godless Jew" Freud, so far as we know, did not reply; what he felt at that time about his Jewish identity was, as we have seen repeatedly, almost ineffable. In *Moses and Monotheism* Freud could feel he finally had an answer to that which had so long eluded him—why, godless though he was, he was still so Jewish and what, out of the Jewish past, was inalienably his. The point bears emphasis. In 1935, when he sent a summary of the work to Lou Andreas-Salomé, she responded with an excitement that matched his own:

> What particularly fascinated *me* in your present view of things is a specific characteristic of the "return of the repressed," namely, the way in which noble and precious elements return despite long inter-mixture with every conceivable kind of material. . . . Hitherto we have usually understood the term "return of the repressed" in the context of neurotic processes: all kinds of material which had been wrongly repressed afflicted the neurotic mysteriously with phantoms out of the past . . . which he felt bound to ward off. But in this case we are pre-sented with examples of the survival of the most triumphant vital elements of the past as the truest possession in the present, despite all the destructive elements and counter-forces they have endured.[54]

I wonder if Frau Lou had not intuitively grasped an essential aspect of *Moses and Monotheism* that has largely escaped Freud's commentators. In Freud's scenario the return of the repressed explained not only the compulsive character of religious tradition, but also the retrieval of the purest teachings of Moses after they had been forgotten. Thus the past not only subjugates; it also nourishes. The point is important, not only for a fuller comprehension of the book as Freudian history, but even for those who would exploit it only for the purposes of psychobiography.

Marthe Robert, for example, attributes the preoccupation of the aged Freud with the "return of the repressed" to his feeling of an alarmingly growing resemblance to his father, which he must ward off by identifying himself with an Egyptian Moses.[55] But, even in psychoanalytic terms, would such a solution represent anything but a puerile victory? The fantasy of the family romance is viewed in Freudian theory as a stage of childhood, not of maturity, and, so far as I am aware, after a successful analysis one does not write home to declare, "You are not my father, and I never want to see you again." The Freudian integration of the personality demands the return of the repressed for the sake of new insight, as a result of which we do not have to deny our fathers but can at least attempt to reestablish our relationship on a different plane. *Spring up, O well, sing ye unto it,* Jakob Freud had written in 1891. From 1934 almost to his death the son drank from that well and sang to it. His song was one that the father would surely not have recognized and would perhaps have found discordant. Yet somehow, in the balance, I feel he would not have been displeased.

1. Jakob Freud's bilingual inscription in Hebrew and German in the family Bible, recording Sigmund's birth and circumcision.

2. Jakob Freud's Hebrew dedication in the family Bible, written to Sigmund on his thirty-fifth birthday.

3. "Moses coming from Mount Sinai throws the tablets of the Ten Commandments to the ground," engraved by Kruger in 1770 after a painting by Rembrandt. From Freud's private collection.

4. Rembrandt van Rijn, *The Jews in the Synagogue,* etching, 1648. From Freud's private collection.

5. Antiquities and two kiddush cups in Freud's consulting room at Berggasse 19, photographed in 1938 prior to his flight to England.

6. The kiddush cups (detail).

7. Bronze Hanukkah menorah, thirteenth century, 12.07 × 16.81 × 5.23 cm. The Hebrew inscription reads, "For the commandment is a lamp and the Teaching is light" (Proverbs 6:23). From Freud's private collection.

8. Picture postcard sent by Freud from Rome to Karl Abraham, September 13, 1913, showing the Arch of Titus, which commemorates the Roman destruction of Jerusalem in 70 C.E. (Within the arch are two friezes, one depicting the Romans carrying off the spoils of the Temple, including the Menorah.) Freud has written over the picture: "Der Jude übersteht's! Herzlichen Gruss und Coraggio Kasimiro!" (The Jew survives it! Cordial greetings and courage Kasimiro!).

9. Reverse of postcard to Karl Abraham.

5

Monologue with Freud

Let me speak, then, and find relief.

—*Job* 32:20

Dear and most highly esteemed Professor Freud:

Four lectures on your *Moses,* but for what remains I feel an inner need to speak to you directly and to have the audience eavesdrop, as it were. Whence this compulsion (for it is not merely a caprice) I cannot fully articulate even to myself. I know only that this fiction which I somehow do not feel to be fictitious enables me à mode of speech which has hitherto not been possible, but which now becomes imperative because we have reached a time of reckoning. All this will probably strike you as impudence, but you will indulge me. The notion of speaking to someone who is not there is not entirely alien to you, as *The Future of an Illusion* attests, and there your interlocutor was pure invention, whereas you are real and, for me, curiously present. Though I shall occasionally invite you to respond, unlike you I shall not pretend that what follows does not remain essentially a monologue. But it is a monologue addressed directly to you. In what is at issue here, indeed has been so all along, we both have, as Jews, an equal stake. Therefore in speaking of the Jews I shall not say "they." I shall say "we." The distinction is familiar to you.

Dear Professor Freud, I have done my best with the *Moses* book, and I know it is not adequate, at most a prolegomenon, perhaps a "historical novel," at worst—a series of wrong tracks. Lest you think me falsely modest, let me add immediately that where I have failed or missed I am far from accepting the entire blame. Once, in discussing the difficulty of psychoanalyzing Goethe, you observed, "This is because Goethe was not only as a poet, a great self-revealer, but also, in spite of the abundance of autobiographical records, a careful concealer."[1] As a concealer you have, of course, outstripped your hero, and as for the records, some of your more zealous epigoni have stationed themselves, like gnostic archons, to bar the way to the hidden knowledge. None of this has made it easy for the serious student of your work (I emphasize your *work*; your life—only to the degree that it is implicated in your work. The rest is of concern to your biographers).

You have noticed, I trust, that I have not tried to pry any of your secrets out of mere curiosity. If I have at times attempted to recover fragments of your life, especially those that relate to your Jewish identity and some of which I believe you suppressed, it has been only for the sake of a better understanding of the conscious intention of your work, thinking that you yourself would want it that way. I have not rummaged through your life in search of flaws. Those uncovered by others in recent years have not affected my engrossment in your uncommon achievement, which continues to pursue me "like an unlaid ghost."

In 1939, shortly after the complete *Moses and Monotheism* appeared, my teacher Salo Baron published a review in which, after a calm perusal of your historical premises, he concluded by exchanging your "statue on a base of clay" for a more architectural metaphor, calling the book a "magnificent castle in the air."[2] Others, less charitable, have made the point that if the book had been written by someone else it would have been ignored. This is, I think, both correct and irrelevant. Correct, because if *Moses* were merely an essay in biblical history written by some adventurous academic, it would long have gathered dust on the more tenebrous shelves of theological libraries. Irrelevant because, after all, it was not written by someone else but by you. Baron himself, who occasionally attended your lectures in Vienna, makes the point at the outset: "If a thinker of Sigmund Freud's stature takes a stand on a problem of vital interest to him, the world is bound to listen." Just so.

But in our present encounter I shall not conduct my inquiry along the conventional lines. I shall not harp on the historical weaknesses that others have laid bare in detail and which you yourself worried about (though the gaffe in the equation of Aton with "Adonay" is almost unforgivable). I have nothing to add to the anthropological critiques (the Totem theory is, to put it bluntly, *kaputt*). I shall not elaborate on the scientific status of your phylogenetic assumptions, for that too has been done by those more qualified in the matter than I, though I may yet return to this matter from a different perspective.

True, you were aware of all the pitfalls, and in your anxiety you tried, on several occasions, to cover yourself. Already in *Totem and Taboo* you had written,

> There are no grounds for fearing that psychoanalysis, which first discovered that psychical acts and structures are invariably overdetermined, will be tempted to trace the origin of anything as complicated as religion to a single source. If psychoanalysis is compelled—and is, indeed, duty bound— to lay all the emphasis upon one particular source, that does not mean it is claiming either that that source is the only one or that it occupies first place among the contributory factors.[3]

That was well said, and the thought is echoed in *Moses and Monotheism*: "It is enough for our need to discover causes (which, to be sure, is imperative) if each event has *one* demonstrable cause. But in the reality lying outside us that is scarcely the case; on the contrary, each event seems to be overdetermined and proves to be the effect of several converging causes."[4] Yet between such pronouncements and the actual course of your argument there is so wide a gap as to make one think the pronouncements are no more than formal concessions. In any case, this too is not the direction I want to take.

Nor, for the purposes of our discussion, am I really disturbed by your cavalier rejection of the findings of specialists in other disciplines when they threatened your own. Thus, after showing your full awareness that Robertson Smith's totemic theories have been utterly repudiated, you write, "A denial is not a refutation, an innovation is not necessarily an advance. Above all, however, I am not an ethnologist but a psychoanalyst. I had a right to take out of ethnological literature what I might need for the work of analysis."[5] It is said that when someone once told you that Sellin had abandoned his theory that Moses had been murdered by the Hebrews, you merely replied, "He was right the first time." There is something both awful and awesome in such Olympian obstinacies. On the one hand they are repellent. At the same time it cannot be ruled out that because of your very ability to ignore the "facts" when they stood in your way, you were able to leap over them and find your own way to certain truths. But let it be. Ours will be a different kind of discourse.

In the first paragraph of part II of *Moses* you make a conventionally invidious allusion to "the schoolmen and the Talmudists who delight in exhibiting their ingenuity without regard to how remote from reality their thesis may be," and you brusquely dissociate yourself from such presumably arid scholasticism. But, as you well know, Talmudists have other qualities as well. Rabbi Yochanan ben Zakkai, whom you so admired and with whom you identified, was, after all, one of the architects of the Talmud. And when, in 1908, Karl Abraham expressed his feeling of intellectual kinship with you, writing that "after all, our Talmudic way of thinking cannot disappear just like that," and even adding that your book on *Jokes* was "in the technique of apposition and in its whole structure . . . completely Talmudic," you did not object but took it for the compliment it was meant to be.[6] So you will not take it amiss if now, dispensing with any remaining preliminaries, I begin talmudically.

▬▬

I open, then, with a talmudic *terminus technicus,* with the Aramaic word *ledidakh,* which means "according to you." More amply, it signifies that for the sake of the discussion and its effort to ascertain the truth, one party will provisionally accept the assumptions of the other, and they will go on from there. It is, of course, a universal tactic of debate, only in Talmudic-Aramaic garb. I use the term symbolically, as it were, precisely for that reason, for we shall yet come to the question of the universal and the particular. But in terms of our discourse it means that I intend to ignore the historical, ethnological, and biological critiques that have been leveled against *Moses and Monotheism* and to which I have alluded, because in the end none of them strikes at the heart of the matter. And so, initially, let it be *le-didakh,* according to you: Moses was not a Hebrew but an Egyptian. He learned his monotheism from Ikhnaton. He gave the new religion to our forefathers, who subsequently rebelled and killed him.

The critical question—because it affects the very core of your analogy between the development of religious tradition and that of individual neurosis—is not whether these things happened but, if indeed they really did happen, whether they would have been repressed and forgotten.' The pivot of your entire construction is the initial repression of Moses' murder, for without it there could obviously have been no "return of the repressed," the very element which, according to you, endowed the Jewish religious tradition with its neurotic power over its adherents.

You took it for granted, of course, that Moses' Egyptian origin and especially the trauma of his murder were repressed, forgotten, except as latent memories in the unconscious of the group, and it is here that you went astray. What eluded you was the most singular aspect of Jewish tradition from the Bible onward, to wit—its almost maddening refusal to conceal the misdeeds of the Jews. A fundamentalist approach to the Bible is not at issue here. No doubt the ancient Israelites forgot much, and the biblical chroniclers and editors concealed and distorted many things. The vital question remains whether, if Moses had been murdered in the wilderness, *this* would have been forgotten or concealed. And here we must not merely speculate but contemplate directly, if briefly, some relevant aspects of Jewish tradition itself.

No ancient scripture, epic, or chronicle known to me exposes the people that is its subject to the vilifications heaped repeatedly on Israel, the "Chosen People," in the Hebrew Bible. The biblical narratives of the sojourn in the wilderness do not hesitate to tell of constant rebellion by a stiff-necked and ungrateful people which, at one point, seems fully prepared to stone both Moses and Aaron to death (Numbers 14:10). The prophets are, by the irritating nature of their mission, always at risk. Jeremiah (chapter 26) is almost lynched in the Temple for treason and is rescued only in the nick of time. Zechariah son of Yehoiada the priest is stoned by order of King Joash (II Chronicles 24:21). Elijah cries out to the Lord (I Kings 19:10): "The children of Israel have forsaken Thy covenant, thrown down Thine altars, and slain thy prophets with the sword, and I, even I only, am left; and they seek my life to take it away." All this is told unabashedly, without any sign of reticence. Classical rabbinic literature goes still farther in elaborating and expanding on the theme of murdered prophets, even when the alleged events have little or no basis in the biblical text. Thus, to come back to the journey through the wilderness: "When Israel did that deed [the Golden Calf], at first they went to Hur [Hur is identified as a prophet]. They said to him: *Arise, make us a god* (Exodus 32:1). Because he did not obey them, they stood over him and killed him.''[8] In another Midrash we read,

> And the Holy One reproved them through Jeremiah, peace unto him, who was stoned to death by the Jews in Egypt and the Egyptians buried him. . . . And not only this prophet did [the Jews] kill, but many others did they kill. Hur. And [king] Baasha killed the prophet Shemaiah, and [king] Abiah killed Ahiyah the Shilonite, and [king] Joash killed Zechariah son of Yehoiada in the Temple Court and sprinkled his blood on the wall. . . . And the prophet Isaiah was killed by [king] Manasseh son of Hezekiah, who sawed him apart with a saw.[9]

Indeed the rabbis in the Midrash are fully persuaded that an attempt was made on the life of Moses, and they make this more explicit than does the biblical text:

> *And the entire community threatened to stone them with stones* (Numbers 14:10). And who were they? Moses and Aaron. [But the verse continues] *when the glory of the Lord appeared [in the tent of meeting unto all the children of Israel].* This teaches us that they [the Israelites] were throwing stones and the Cloud [of the Lord's Glory] would intercept them.[10]

What it all amounts to, Professor Freud, can be stated succinctly. If Moses had actually been killed by our forefathers, not only would the murder not have been repressed but—on the contrary—it would have been remembered and recorded, eagerly and implacably, in the most vivid detail, the quintessential and ultimate exemplum of the sin of Israel's disobedience. The meaning of chosenness in Jewish tradition is expressed in one biblical verse (Amos 3:2): *You only have I known of all the families of the earth; therefore will I visit upon you all your iniquities.* And to this day, as you may possibly remember from your childhood, the great collective confession of sins on the Day of Atonement is recited in the form of an acrostic, for such a confession must exhaust all the twenty-two letters of the Hebrew alphabet and, symbolically, all the resources of language.

As for Moses being an Egyptian, what's in a name? Both Philo and Josephus knew that the name Moses is etymologically Egyptian, but they did not conclude from this that he was of Egyptian stock. Had there been felt the slightest need to obliterate Moses' Egyptian origin we would not read in the report by Jethro's daughters of their first encounter with him (Exodus 2:19): *An Egyptian delivered us out of the hand of the shepherds,* which simply means that in speech, dress, and manner, he appeared to them to be an Egyptian. The narrator is obviously unconcerned that anyone might infer from this that

Moses was born an Egyptian and not a Hebrew. That the Israelites were culturally assimilated while in Egypt is not only natural, but understood as a matter of course. And in a wonderful jeu d'esprit, the Midrash will unselfconsciously have God begin the Ten Commandments in Egyptian "because *'anokhi* [the first word "I" in "I am the Lord your God"] is an Egyptian word, and He wanted to use the language they had used in Egypt."[11]

Now of course, Professor, you might reply that Moses is an exception, since he was, according to you, the founder of the Jewish religion and, by Jewish consensus, the greatest of the prophets. All the other murders of prophets might be remembered and still the murder of Moses be repressed. But such a reply would have a strained, somewhat desperate quality, don't you think? You may also try to turn the tables on me and even welcome the texts I have brought forward, regarding them as "screen memories" that merely mask the actual origin and fate of Moses. That, of course, is your prerogative. But in so doing you would be ignoring the essential character of Jewish tradition and the contexts in which these things make perfect sense, and we shall have reached an impasse. Let us, then, move on, for it is my purpose not merely to criticize, but to interrogate you on deep and weighty matters in which the stances you have taken are not clear to me, or are susceptible of alternative approaches which were available to you but which you did not choose to take.

For me the abiding significance of *Moses and Monotheism* lies, not in the specific answers you have given to the question of "how the Jews have come to be as they are," but in your uniquely powerful formulation of the question and its problematics. In addressing the matter, you have raised issues from which ordinary historians have tended to shy away—the phenomenology of religious tradition, the Jewish in particular; of collective memory, forgetting, anamnesis; of the psychological, rather than theological, relationships between Judaism and Christianity. And, presiding invisibly, the fiercely Jewish "godless Jew" who emerges and persists out of what seems to be a final and irreparable rupture in the tradition, and who seems himself without tradition in any traditional sense, in short—yourself, but hardly you alone.

Late in the *Moses* book you make a rather splendid statement that suddenly lifts the problem of the history of Judaism out of the realm of the banal. You write,

> There is an element of grandeur about everything to do with the origin of a religion, certainly including the Jewish one, and this is not matched by the explanations we have hitherto given. Some other factor must be involved to which there is little that is analogous and nothing that is of the same kind, something unique and something of

the same order of magnitude as what has come out of it, as religion itself.[12]

It is a statement to be applauded, for it says what had to be said—that with all the exertions of historians of religion, theologians, and scholars in other disciplines, whatever the gains in more than a century of intensive effort, the essential still remains beyond our grasp—the uncanny power of a religion to command and sustain the allegiance of men and women over centuries, even millennia. It is therefore not only the "origin" of a religion that should engage us, but "what has come out of it" *(was daraus geworden ist)*. "The religion of Moses," you write, "only carried through its effect on the Jewish people as a tradition."[13] Thus not only *Ursprung* is important but, equally if not more so, *Tradition* (I even prefer the synonymous *Überlieferung*, with its more vivid sense, for those who do not know the Latin root of the former, of transmission, handing over). And just as origin cannot be explained merely by reference to impersonal socioeconomics in which the impact of the "great man" is ignored (a point you insist upon), so the workings of tradition cannot be grasped, as again you emphasize, merely as verbal transmission. Which is to say that the force and longevity of religious tradition cannot be apprehended if tradition is presented essentially in terms of the history of ideas, or the history of education, or even as a system of symbols whose mythical, material, and social referents can be decoded, while its psychological dimensions are ignored. It is precisely here that psychoanalysis may be of help. The question is how to apply it.

Tantalizing though it may be, your notion of a tradition transmitted through the unconscious of the group, even if only during a period of "latency," is impossible to accept, and not only because of modern genetics or molecular biology. There are differences between individual and collective memory so fundamental as to be unbridgeable by the analogy you have proposed. It is not that there is anything intrinsically wrong with analogic thinking, a venerable and valid mode of thought that often enables a leap of creative insight. Indeed, certain analogies can fruitfully be drawn between the individual and the group. But you insisted on pressing the analogy to the point of *identity* (your own word), which is a very different matter.

Though it is composed of individuals, the group does not possess the organic unity and continuity of the least of its members, who can remember, forget, and recall his or her personal experiences. I have written elsewhere that as the "life of a people" is a biological metaphor, so the "memory of a people" is a psychological metaphor, useful, but not to be literalized.[14]

Peoples, groups, at any given time or in any generation, can only "remember" a past that has been actively transmitted to them, and which they have accepted as meaningful. Conversely, a people "forgets" when the generation that currently possesses the past does not convey it to the next or when the latter rejects what it has received and does not pass it onward. The break in transmission can occur abruptly or by a gradual process of erosion. In either case the process is rarely, if ever, simultaneous for the entire group, for the group has neither the biological nor psychological homogeneity of the individual. Many and mighty things have been truly and totally forgotten in the course of human history, and these are irretrievable. Other things *seem* to have been forgotten over long periods (which you call latency), only to resurface. But these do not reemerge from some collective unconscious. When such a reemergence takes place other factors must account for it. For even when most "forget," there remain those, be they only individuals, who "remember"; or—to put it in your terms—even after most have repressed, some have not, and at certain historical junctures those few to whom they have actively transmitted what they know may play a key role in the anamnesis (or what you would call the return of the repressed) among the group as a whole.

In fact, at one point in part II of *Moses* you yourself wavered and assigned this role to the Levites, who, even after Moses' murder "remained loyal to their master, preserved his memory and carried out the tradition of his doctrines." Such a conception of collective forgetting and anamnesis would have found an echo, structurally at least, in Jewish tradition itself. In the talmudic tractate *Sukkah* (20a) we read,

> In ancient times when the Torah was forgotten from Israel, Ezra came from Babylon and established it. [Some of it] was again forgotten and Hillel the Babylonian came up and established it. Yet again was [some of it] forgotten, and R. Hiyya and his sons came up and established it.

Perhaps even better for our purposes is the epiphany at the Burning Bush in Exodus, chapter 3, where a reluctant Moses asks God,

> When I come to the Israelites and say to them, "The God of your fathers has sent me to you," and they ask me, "What is His name?" what shall I say to them? And God said to Moses, "*I am that I am*." And He said: "Thus shall you say to the Israelites: *I am* sent me to you." And God said further to Moses, "Thus shall you speak to the Israelites: The Lord, the God of your fathers, the God of Abraham, the God of Isaac, and the God of Jacob has sent me to you."

This text, it seems to me, should suit us both. The fact that God must introduce himself to the Hebrew slaves through a new name indicates that indeed there was something very novel in the religion that Moses forged. But the fact that Moses can also appeal to them in the name of the God of the Fathers indicates a dimension of the familiar, a linkage. It presupposes that the God worshiped by the patriarchs had not entirely been forgotten. In the narrative Moses thus appears both as an innovator and as an agent of anamnesis. You, of course, would have nothing whatever to do with the God of the Fathers, nor, as I have noted, did most biblical scholars at the time. But I cannot resist telling you, mischievously and en passant, that in his fourth and final *Joseph* novel, which you did not have the chance to read, Thomas Mann, otherwise your great admirer (the admiration was mutual), committed a minor heresy. Although he was thoroughly familiar with *Moses and Monotheism,* here Ikhnaton is not the founder of monotheism. Rather, it is the Hebrew Joseph who, according to Mann, inducts Ikhnaton into the true and higher monotheistic belief which he had inherited from his fathers, the patriarchs.[15]

Mann, of course, was a novelist. You became a historian. What is of genuine moment is the fact that later, in the more decisive part of your *Moses,* you abandoned your clandestinely loyal Levitical transmitters in favor of the "archaic heritage," which "comprises not only dispositions but also subject matter—memory-traces of the experience of earlier generations," and even more explicitly—"memory-traces of the experience of our ancestors, independently of direct communication and of education by example," and you added: "When I spoke of the survival of a tradition among a people or of the formation of a people's character, I had mostly in mind an inherited tradition of this kind and not one transmitted by communication."[16]

It seems to me, however, that the potential value of psychoanalysis to the understanding of religious tradition does not reside in such precarious postulates. One cannot explain the transmission of a tradition at any time as a totally unconscious process. Though much of the process of transmission may be nonverbal, that is not tantamount to its being unconscious. The basic modalities in the continuity of a religious tradition are precept and example, narrative, gesture, ritual, and certainly all of these act upon, and are interpreted by, not only consciousness but the unconscious. The true challenge for psychoanalysis is not to plunge the entire history of tradition into a hypothetical group unconscious, but to help clarify, in a nonreductive way, what unconscious needs are being satisfied at any given time by living within a given religious tradition, by believing its myths and performing its rites. And that task, which would also help us to understand the changes in the evolution of tradition, has hardly begun.

Nevertheless, the very fact that you chose to take your stand upon the reality of an archaic unconscious inheritance forged out of the historical experience of our ancestors and transmitted "independently of direct communication and education by example" is for me of superlative interest. I am convinced that you really believed it; it can be traced from at least the Fliess period to the end of your life. But I am almost equally persuaded that it also served a powerful inner personal need. For if a "national character" (those are your words) can indeed be transmitted "independently of direct communication and education by example," then that means that "Jewishness" can be transmitted independently of "Judaism," that the former is intermin- able even if the latter be terminated. And thus the puzzle that so plagued you about your own Jewish identity would seem to be resolved (and the subtitle of this book incidentally explained).

Far more fruitful was your application of psychoanalytic concepts to the relationship between Judaism and Christianity. Here, for me, it is not so much a matter of disagreement as of untapped possibilities, and le-didakh—"according to you"—becomes not so much a mode of disputation as a means of following up on your own leads.

For example, in attempting to understand the biblical narrative of the birth and rescue of Moses, you invoked the ubiquitous presence of the "family romance" in the myths of the birth of heroes. (Curiously, you did not quite explain the unique reversal of the pattern in the Moses narrative, where our hero, if your interpretation be correct, was actually of noble birth, and it is only the fantasy that gives him his humble Hebrew origins). Be that as it may, there is a strong element of the "family romance" also in the early development of Christianity, especially in relation to Judaism, which you have ignored. For illustration we will turn, by your leave, from the Hebrew to the Christian Scriptures and from the Rabbis of the Talmud to the Fathers of the Church.

I wonder if it ever occurred to you that the very opening of Christian Scripture (chapter 1 of Matthew) is a "family romance" far more blatant than the one you perceived in the Book of Exodus, and that this was to have untold consequences for both Christians and Jews through ages to come. Here, in a transparently retroactive attempt to legitimize the messiahship of Jesus, he is given a mythical genealogy as a direct descendant of King David, this royal pedigree being a sine qua non for the Messiah in Jewish tradition itself. But the fateful role of the family romance in Christianity does not stop there.

In their passion for the new, most moderns are unaware that one of the important obstacles that Christianity encountered in its early missionary efforts lay precisely in the fact that it was a new religion, one that no one had heard of before. Novelty, in the pagan Roman world, was not an attribute to validate a religion or render it attractive. Even if newly imported, religions, like wine, should not be of recent vintage. Ironically, whatever its other handicaps, Judaism had the advantageous cachet of antiquity and venerability, whereas Christianity, by its very suddenness and newness, was exposed to both Jewish and pagan taunts of illegitimacy. The efforts of early Christianity to legitimize itself, already fully worked out in the Christian Scriptures, display the characteristics of the family romance precisely because they required the mythic adoption of a noble and venerable lineage. This it could accomplish only by appropriating the history and hence the antiquity of Judaism itself. It was a need that was felt as late as the fourth century of the Christian era, when Eusebius of Caesarea wrote his *Ecclesiastical History*. One of the dominant motivations of the work was to demonstrate "the real antiquity and divine character of Christianity . . . to those who suppose that it is recent and foreign, appearing no earlier than yesterday." Eusebius desires that "no one might think of our Savior and Lord, Jesus Christ, as a novelty because of the date of his ministry in the flesh," and that "no one may suppose that his teaching either was new and strange." According to Eusebius all the heroes and good folk of Hebrew Scripture were already, in effect, Christians or proto-Christians. In a characteristic typological reading he asserts that Moses himself was the first to recognize the glory of the name of Christ because he applied this title (in Greek as in the Hebrew, *mashiah* means simply "the anointed one") to the High Priest. Through such assumptions and exegetical devices Eusebius concludes that "it must clearly be held that the announcement to all the gentiles, recently made through the teaching of Christ, is the very first and most ancient and antique discovery of Abraham and those lovers of God who followed him."[17]

Some decades later John Chrysostom, he of the "golden mouth," though more virulent in his hatred of Jews and Judaism, is also more frank than Eusebius. In his sermons against the Judaizers in Antioch he freely admits, as did Paul, a discontinuity of origins. Most Christians were, after all, descended from pagans, while the Jews had once been God's chosen people. Now, however, the positions are reversed, and on this score the very violence of Chrysostom's language is revelatory:

> Although those Jews had been called to the adoption of sons, they fell
> to kinship with dogs; we who were dogs received the strength,
> through God's grace, to put aside the irrational nature which was
> ours and to rise to the honor of sons. How do I prove this? Christ
> said: "It is not fair to take the children's bread and to cast it to the
> dogs" [Matthew 15:26]. Christ was speaking to the Canaanite
> woman when he called the Jews children and the gentiles dogs. But
> see how thereafter the order was changed about: they became dogs,
> and we became the children."[18]

Here we have not only a "family romance" of the most radical kind, but a clear implication, easily demonstrable from other Christian sources, that this exaltation of the former "dogs" to the status of children of God goes beyond the mere projection of a new lineage that we find in the ordinary family romance. The Christian appropriation of the sacred history and chosenness of the Jews involves, necessarily, an aggressive displacement of the Jews themselves with all the intensity of a fierce struggle over a royal succession or a bitter contest over an inheritance. This dimension seems to have eluded you.

In your *Moses* you provided a creative and stimulating application of the Oedipus complex to the problem of Judaism and Christianity, both as repetitions of the primeval patricide and as emblematic of the character of each of the two religions. But I think you did not carry your Oedipal analysis far enough. Christianity is a "Son-Religion," to use your apt phrase, not only because it deified the Son but because, both historically and theologically, it is an offspring of Judaism and therefore stands in an Oedipal relationship to Judaism itself. Thus, despite the figurative Christian claim to spiritual antiquity, the Jews are the "Old" Israel, the Christians the "New," the former possess the "Old Testament," the latter the "New." In each instance the "New" supplants the "Old" just as the Son usurps the Father.

At the same time, in their relationship to God the Father, Judaism and Christianity are both son-religions, each inevitably claiming its exclusive legitimacy at the expense of the other, for if one be true the other must be false. Hence, if it is to serve as a useful analytic tool in probing the deeper meaning of Judaism vis-à-vis Christianity, we must further complicate the Oedipus complex. We should take into account not only the rivalry of the son with the father, but the rivalry between the sons. "Over whom?" you may well ask. (Curiously, desire for the mother, so significant in your account of the Oedipal conflict of the individual, disappears along with the wives of the Primeval Father in your account of the history of religion.) Who, then, at the juncture we have reached, is the mother? I would simply and brazenly answer—the Torah, the Teaching, the revelation, the Torah which in Hebrew is grammatically feminine and which is midrashically compared to a bride. It is over possession of her that Christianity, the younger son, came to challenge, not so much the Father as Judaism, the elder son. For this struggle "sibling rivalry" is perhaps too tame a phrase. Psychologically (and alas, all too often even historically) we are talking about fratricide.

Why it is that throughout your work you have concentrated so exclusively on patricide, why only the Oedipus complex and not a "Cain complex," has remained an enigma to me, especially since you yourself were able to admit your murderous fantasies toward your infant brother Julius, whose actual death, therefore, so burdened you subsequently with guilt. The first crime in the biblical narrative was not a patricide but, precisely, a fratricide. You knew this, of course, but did nothing with it. Augustine knew it as well but perhaps more profoundly. Whereas you took Oedipus as your paradigm for our malaise, Augustine found his in Cain, and in *The City of God* he universalized him by making him the founder of the earthly city:

The first founder of the earthly city was consequently a fratricide; for overcome by envy, he slew his own brother, who was a citizen of the eternal city sojourning upon this earth. No wonder then that this example or, as the Greeks call it, archetype, was followed by a copy of its own likeness long afterwards at the foundation of the city that was destined to be the capital of this earthly city . . . and to rule over so many nations. For here too, as one of their poets [Lucan] put it when he recorded this crime: "In blood fraternal were the first walls steeped." This is indeed the way that Rome was founded when Remus, as the history of Rome tells us, was slain by his brother Romulus.[19]

Though it lacks your sophisticated notion of the return of the repressed, Augustine's view of the first fratricide as an archetype seems to me not that far removed in spirit from your own view of the repetition of the murder of the primeval father. But I shall not linger over this. Of immediate concern is the vastly influential Augustinian typology, which made Cain and Abel into figures of the Jewish people and Jesus. In his *Reply to Faustus the Manichaean* he writes,

Abel, the younger brother, is killed by the elder brother; Christ, head of the younger people, is killed by the elder people of the Jews; Abel dies in the field; Christ dies on Calvary. . . .
   Then God says to Cain, "What have you done? The voice of your brother's blood cries out unto me from the ground." So the voice in the Holy Scriptures accuses the Jews. . . .
   Then God says to Cain: "You are cursed from the earth, which has opened its mouth to receive your brother's blood at your hand. . . ." It is not 'Cursed is the earth,' but, 'Cursed are you from the earth. . . .' So the unbelieving people of the Jews is cursed from the earth, that is, from the Church which, in the confession of sins, has opened its mouth to receive the blood shed for the remission of sins by the hand of the people that would not be under grace, but under the law.[20]

Will you still maintain, as you wrote, that the core of the Christian accusation against our people—"You killed our God"—is merely translatable into the unconscious taunt "You will not *admit* that you murdered God. . . . We did the same thing, to be sure, but we have *admitted* it and since then we have been absolved"? Even if it were so, why should such an unconscious perception inspire hatred rather than pity? Granted that this hatred is itself "overdetermined," at least historically, surely one cannot even begin to fathom it psychologically without taking into account an element of Christian guilt toward Judaism and the Jews.

This guilt, repressed and denied, is a fratricidal one, the guilt of having usurped the birthright of which Christianity is never completely secure so long as the Jews, obstinately refusing to acknowledge the usurpation, remain as a witness and a reproach. This lingering uncertainty over the legitimacy of its own triumph will explain the particular intensity of the age-old Christian attempt to convert the Jews and its frustration at not having achieved it. It will also go far in explaining the intrinsic and perennial conflict within the Church which, for all its anti-Jewish animus, has never wavered in its conviction that the Jews must be preserved until the issue of the birthright is settled eschatologically, at the end of history.

To my contention that Cain provides as potent an explanation as Oedipus, you will undoubtedly reply that while fratricide may play some role, patricide remains primary, that even I have pointed out the filial relationship of the "New Israel" to the "Old," and that this should be viewed as more decisive than the sibling one. I also expect you to say that my own citation of the Augustinian text in which the Church "has opened its mouth to receive the blood shed for the remission of sins" only reconfirms your Oedipal interpretation of the unconscious meaning of the doctrine of Original Sin and the ritual of the Eucharist.

Let it be so. But even then you will not have explained, as you yourself admit toward the end of *Moses*, why "only a portion of the Jewish people accepted the new doctrine," why so many Jews, then and later, remained Jews and did not become Christians; or, in analytic terms, why they were capable of achieving only a partial return of the repressed, recollecting the teachings of the father figure Moses, but without the further "forward step" of recalling his murder as well. Well, perhaps, as I argued at the beginning, because there had been no murder to repress and therefore, on this score, nothing to remember? No, you will turn your back on something so simplistic. Perhaps, then, something else. Perhaps because they actually preferred the rigorous imperatives of the Law to the subjective consolations of Grace? Perhaps, as Franz Rosenzweig once suggested, because, already so close to the Father, they felt no need for the Son? And—forgive the personal intrusion again, Professor—if we could translate these terms into the language of the unconscious, perhaps they were among the reasons that you yourself, as you once boasted, always remained "*in der jüdischen Konfession*"? But as you have indicated, "a special enquiry would be called for to discover why it has been impossible for the Jews to join in this forward step."

Dear, esteemed Professor Freud, despite my fumblings and gropings, have patience and please do not misunderstand me. Not for a moment do I doubt the significance of the Oedipus complex for our understanding of the psychology of the individual human being. It is only in relation to the view you have elaborated of human history as a whole, beginning with *Totem and Taboo* and culminating in the analysis of Jewish history in *Moses,* that I must press the interrogation one step farther. I ask once more in the spirit of *le-didakh.* Let us assume it all happened as you say, from the slaying of the Primeval Father to the death of Jesus and its interpretation by Paul. I pose my question metaphorically: Is Oedipus immortal?

In your psychoanalysis of history you have presented us with a haunting vision of Eternal Return more seductive, because so much more subtle, than that of Friedrich Nietzsche. Beneath the dizzying multiplicity of events and phenomena that history throws up to the surface you have discerned a pulsating repetition: patricide, repression, return of the repressed, followed by reenactment of the entire cycle, though disguised under different forms, in a seemingly endless spiral. Like Sisyphus pushing his rock, Oedipus and Laius must contend forever. At one point of the cycle the Father must be slain by the son, at another, that of the return of the repressed, the Father returns, but his return is only partial, illusory, temporary, for the cycle will begin again.

In chapter 2 I pointed to the affinities between your mode of historical thinking and that of the biblical historians, who also focus on an invisible history with a pattern of archetype and repetition. Please do not protest that your historiography is scientific while theirs, being sacred history, was based to begin with on illusion. If the God of Israel was an unconscious projection of the retrieved memory of the Primeval Father, your concept of the latter was no more empirical, but only a conscious and deliberate projection into history of what you had learned from your study of the individual psyche.

Indeed, the charm of it all is that Oedipus is far from alien to the Bible itself, where the entire relationship between God and Man and especially between God and Israel is always the tense agon of Father and son. The dramatic difference lies not in the perception of past and present, but in the anticipation of a specific hope for the future. There is a remarkable verse in the last of the prophets (Malachi 3:24) which expresses a unique vision that is not to be found—at least not explicitly—in the messianic prophecies of any of his predecessors. All the others, we might say, posit an ultimate resolution of the Oedipal conflict between Israel and God; Malachi does so also on the level of the purely human: "*Ve-heshiv lev avot 'al banim ve-lev banim 'al avotam*" (He shall reconcile the heart of fathers with sons and the heart of sons with their fathers).

Le-didakh. Let it be according to you that religion, the great illusion, has no future. But what is the future of Laius and Oedipus? We read to the end of your *Moses,* and you do not say. But should you tell me that, indeed, they have no hope, I shall simply reply—you may very well be right. But it is on this question of hope or hopelessness, even more than on God or godlessness, that your teaching may be at its most un-Jewish.

hopeless

Dear Professor Freud, I am drawing to a close in the sense of the old Hebrew phrase *tam ve-lo nishlam* (it is finished but not completed). Among the myriad matters that I would still long to discuss with you, one must take precedence. I come, in the end, to the "Jewish national affair."

Throughout the preceding lectures I have tried in every way to understand and empathize with your positions and strategies in regard to the problem. When psychoanalysis was struggling for recognition your concern that, along with the other hostilities it had to overcome, it should not have to bear the additional burden of being stigmatized as "Jewish" seemed to me fully comprehensible. Even your tendency to present a public persona of the universal European scientist in which many aspects of your Jewish formation and feelings were withheld, finding their expression only in private communications, did not disturb me. Under the circumstances, I find it remarkable that, even so, you did on occasion publicly affirm the basic fact of your Jewish identity and that you did so with pride.

I am therefore not among those who would judge you for having courted Jung for so long or for urging Abraham to endure a bit of "masochism" in face of the Swiss, all for the sake of the "cause," just as I believe you had learned by then not to condemn your father for having quietly picked his hat out of the mud. I cannot join those who accuse you of valuing psychoanalysis more than your fellow Jews because in 1938 you would not publish part III of *Moses* in Vienna for fear of upsetting the Catholic church, but once in England you had no compunctions about upsetting the Jews. The two situations are not comparable and the conclusion demonstrably unwarranted.

To be sure, some of what you otherwise did or did not do along the way is, at least initially, open to question. From some of your unpublished correspondence I learn that you had certain contacts with your disciples and admirers in Poland and Lithuania. In 1930, for example, you accepted, along with Albert Einstein, Simeon Dubnow, Edward Sapir, and a few others, membership in the honorary Praesidium of the Vilna Yiddish Scientific Institute (YIVO), for which you were warmly thanked by S. Raisin and Max Weinreich (in 1936 the latter would undertake the translation of your *Introductory Lectures* into Yiddish).[21] In July of 1938 you were visited in London by a Polish-Jewish psychologist, Dr. Samuel Stendig.[22] Less than six months later, on January 6, 1939, he wrote to you from Cracow. He asked you for a copy of *Moses,* of which he wanted to write a review. But the crux of the letter concerned a Polish-Jewish encyclopedia (*Encyklopedii Zydów Polskich*) with which he was involved and of which two volumes had already appeared. Now he informed you that a special section had been reserved for "the most prominent Jewish savants," and for this he requested from you a brief article to be entitled either "My Teachings in Poland" or "My Jewish Disciples in Poland"; a signed photograph; and a letter to the editorial committee with "a couple of sentences concerning Polish Jewry." Einstein had apparently agreed to send such materials. As to the reason for all this, I quote Stendig's words to remind you: "We have in Poland a difficult struggle for existence [*einen harten Daseinskampf*] and we want in this Encyclopedia to demonstrate our achievements, and if our achievements, our great savants."

In your reply of January 21, you refused. You cannot, you said, even manage your correspondence, you have no inclination for writing anything, you don't even have a suitable photograph, those you had having been destroyed when you left Vienna. In a key sentence you stated, "I am also sick and tired of propaganda, would readily hand all such things over to younger powers." And although at first glance your response to so poignant a request seems rather callous (Polish Jewry was indeed in a *Daseinskampf* even though the German invasion would not come until September, the month of your death), I am prepared to give you every benefit of the doubt and to believe you. You were suffering terribly from the disease that was finally killing you. You had reached the conclusion years ago that anti-defamation activities and replies by Jews to anti-Semitism were absolutely useless. You had made the same point even when you picked up your pen in November 1938 to publish your somewhat cryptic "Ein Wort zum Antisemitismus" in the periodical *Die Zukunft* and the brief note on "Anti-Semitism in England" in *Time and Tide*: It is not Jews but non-Jews who should reply to anti-Semitism. So now again you were true to your principles, but you were also, if you will allow me, missing the point. The utility of all anti-defamation literature, from Josephus's *Contra Apionem* down to this day, has been not its negligible effect on anti-Semites, but the solace it brings to the Jews who are its readers. But then, you never were strong on consolation, and if you even refused sedatives for your own physical pain lest they impair your clarity of thought, you were, at least, stoically consistent to the last.

Let it be. The past cannot be undone though I could wish (I see your brow grow even sterner at that word) that some aspects had been different. When, after the break with Jung, you wrote those brave and potent words to Sabina Spielrein—remember?—"We are and remain Jews . . ."—that juncture could have marked the public emergence of the full Jew within you. With all the talk of German science and French science, neither of which implied that its contents are not universally accessible or applicable, why not Jewish science, especially in the case of psychoanalysis? Why not say, with psychoanalysis in mind, "*Judaeus sum, nihil humani a me alienam puto*," which is, in effect, what you privately wrote in different words to Ferenczi when he asked you about "Jewish" and "Aryan"? There was, in short, an opportunity to finally lay to rest the false and insidious dichotomy between the "parochial" and the "universal," that canard of the Enlightenment which became and remains a major neurosis of modern Jewish intellectuals. But you could not overcome your initial anxieties, and publicly you retained your inhibitions and your tactical restraints.

I repeat: I do not blame you. You acted as you did because you could not do otherwise. I have come only to inform you that it was all in vain; it made no difference. History made psychoanalysis a "Jewish science." It continued to be attacked as such. It was destroyed in Germany, Italy, and Austria and exiled to the four winds, as such. It continues even now to be perceived as such by enemies and friends alike. Of course there are by now distinguished analysts who are not Jews, and in some countries a majority may not be Jews. France and Lacan (have you heard of him?) are a separate and complicated story. But the vanguard of the movement over the last fifty years has remained predominantly Jewish, as it was from the beginning. You acted cautiously, as you felt you had to. But in so doing you unwittingly left some legacies, or precedents at least, which many of your followers have characteristically frozen into unspoken dogmas.

You left us, Professor Freud, at the outbreak of a war whose full horror and whose devastation of a third of the Jewish people you could not have anticipated. You also felt that "folk psychoses are immune to arguments." But there are moments in history when protest, even if ineffectual (we have perhaps since learned otherwise), is an ethical imperative. So far as I am aware, from 1939, when there was already nothing left to lose, to the end of the Second World War, no official body of any official psychoanalytic organization ever raised its voice, not only over the destruction of Jews, but over the destruction of psychoanalysis itself, the one being part of the other, in Nazi Germany and the lands it occupied. It was almost as though any overt linking of Jews and psychoanalysis were under a taboo.

Matters were not much different, with a few recent exceptions but even now, in the psychoanalytic institutes and within the orthodox analytic process itself. Oh, to be sure, when analysts gather convivially, even in groups of Jews and non-Jews, there will always be Jewish jokes (after all, you have made Jewish humor psychoanalytically de rigueur), and there has never been a lack of reductive monographs on the psychoanalytic meaning (or meaninglessness) of Jewish religious myths and rituals. But as a serious problem with implications for the origin and history of psychoanalysis, and even for its clinical aspects, Jewishness and Judaism were, at least until recently, as though by tacit agreement, beyond the pale.

But why should the Jewish identity of a prospective analyst be shunted aside or glossed over, as I know occurs, in so many training analyses? Would it not be valuable for a gentile analyst to analyze his unconscious feelings at being

perpetually surrounded by Jewish colleagues? How much does it matter to a
patient whether he or she chooses a Jewish or gentile analyst? How many men
and women still lie on couches wondering whether the analyst is or is not
Jewish because the name does not reveal the identity, but who will never ask
directly because the topic seems far more sensitive and threatening than sex?
How much anti-Semitic feeling may be not only repressed but consciously
suppressed in the transference to a Jewish analyst, and how much else may
be missed as a result?[23]

I will leave it to those in clinical practice to decide whether such questions
are in order and, if so, to attempt to answer them. To you, Professor Freud,
I confess to a thought that I have withheld all along because I cannot sub-
stantiate it. I have tried to understand your *Moses* within its stated framework
of the history of religion, of Judaism, and of Jewish identity without reading
it as an allegory of psychoanalysis. What I have done, whether well or not,
stands by itself. But I carry within me a pent-up feeling, an intuition, that you
yourself implied something more, something that you felt deeply but would
never dare to say. So I will take the risk of saying it. I think that in your
innermost heart you believed that psychoanalysis is itself a further, if not final,
metamorphosed extension of Judaism, divested of its illusory religious forms
but retaining its essential monotheistic characteristics, at least as you understood and described them. In short, I think you believed that just as you are
a godless Jew, psychoanalysis is a godless Judaism. But I don't think you intended us to know this. Absurd? Possibly. But *tomer dokh*—perhaps, after
all . . . ?

The psychoanalytic movement, I have said, is historically Jewish. On March
8, 1934, your daughter Anna wrote to Ernest Jones, concerning the flight of
the psychoanalysts from Germany, that it is "a new form of diaspora," and I
am fascinated to discover that she found it necessary to add, "You surely know
what this word means: the dispersion of the Jews throughout the world after
the destruction of Jerusalem."[24]

In 1977 the Sigmund Freud Professorship was created at the Hebrew University in Jerusalem. On the occasion of the establishment of the chair, for the
first time the International Association of Psychoanalysis held its congress in
Jerusalem, though it had refused an Israeli offer to do so twenty years earlier.
Anna, your Antigone, was invited to attend but could not come in person.
Instead she sent a paper which was read on her behalf to the assembled analysts. It was a sober and clear review of the possible future directions of
psychoanalysis and its potential place within a university setting. In all, it was
an eminently suitable paper for the academic event. It was the abrupt and
unexpected ending, in total discontinuity with what had come before, that
sent a shock of amazement through the eminent audience. I quote her
words:

During the era of its existence, psychoanalysis has entered into con-
nexion with various academic institutions, not always with satisfactory results. . . . It has also, repeatedly, experienced rejection by them,
been criticized for its methods being imprecise, its findings not open
to proof by experiment, for being unscientific, even for being a 'Jewish science.' However the other derogatory comments may be evalu-
ated, it is, I believe, the last-mentioned connotation which, under
present circumstances, can serve as a title of honour.[25]

Nothing that your daughter said or wrote publicly during her long life had
prepared anyone for this statement. But what did she mean by "under present
circumstances"? Was her statement merely a rhetorical flourish? Did she mean
that "a Jewish science" is a "title of honour" for psychoanalysis in Jerusalem
but not elsewhere? Or was she saying that after all that had transpired the
time had finally arrived, heightened by the symbolism of this occasion, when
one was at last liberated to affirm what had earlier been so strenuously denied,
to turn Balaam's curse into a blessing?[26]

In 1926 you wrote privately to Enrico Morselli that you were not sure that
his notion that psychoanalysis is a direct product of the Jewish mind is correct,
but that if it is, you "wouldn't be ashamed."[27] Professor Freud, at this point
I find it futile to ask whether, genetically or structurally, psychoanalysis is
really a Jewish science; that we shall know, if it is at all knowable, only when
much future work has been done. Much will depend, of course, on how the
very terms *Jewish* and *science* are to be defined. Right now, leaving the se-
mantic and epistemological questions aside, I want only to know whether *you*
ultimately came to believe it to be so.

In fact, I will limit myself even further and be content if you answer only
one question: When your daughter conveyed those words to the congress in
Jerusalem, *was she speaking in your name?*

Please tell me, Professor. I promise I won't reveal your answer to anyone.

Appendix I
Freud's Introduction
to the
Manuscript Draft
(1934) of *Der*
Mann Moses

[For an English translation see above, p. 17]:[1]

9.8.34   *Der Mann Moses*
                     Ein historischer Roman

[1] Wie die geschlechtliche Vereinigung von Pferd und Esel zwei
verschiedenen Hybriden den Ursprung giebt, dem Maulthier und dem
Maulesel, so läßt auch die Vermengung von Geschichts-
schreibung und freier Erfindung verschiedene
Produkte entstehen, die unter der gemein-
samen Bezeichnung "historischer Roman" bald als Historien, bald als
Romane gewürdigt werden wollen—die einen von ihnen handeln
von Personen und Begebenheiten, die historisch bekannt sind, aber
sie legen es nicht darauf an, deren Eigenart getreu wiederzugeben.
Sie entlehnen zwar das Interesse von der Historie,
aber ihre Absicht ist die des Romans; sie wollen
auf die Affekte wirken.[2] eindrucksvolle
Schilderungen entwerfen, und Andere
dieser literarischen Schöpfungen benehmen sich
grade entgegengesetzt. Sie tragen kein Be-
denken, Personen und selbst Begebenheiten
zu erfinden, wenn sie hoffen den eigentüm-
lichen Charakter einer historischen Epoche durch

---

1. First published in Bori (1979); Yerushalmi (1989), 392f.
2. The phrase is transposed in this manner in the manuscript.

diese Hilfsmittel besonders zutreffend beschreiben
zu können. Was sie anstreben ist also in erster
Linie geschichtliche Wahrheit trotz der einge-
standenen Erdichtung. Anderen noch gelingt es, die
Ansprüche der Kunstschöpfung mit denen der
historischen Treue ein Stück weit oder
weitgehend zu versöhnen. Wieviel Dichtung
sich noch gegen die Absicht des Ge-
schichtsschreibers in seine Darstellung ein-
schleicht bedarf nur einer leisen Andeutung!
Wenn aber ich, der weder Geschichtsforscher noch
Künstler ist, eine meiner Arbeiten als
"historischen Roman" einführe, so muß dieser
Name noch eine andere Hinwendung zu-
lassen. Ich bin zur sorgsamen Beobachtung
eines gewissen Erscheinungsgebietes erzogen,
an Erdichtung und Erfindung knüpft sich
für mich leicht der Makel des Irrtums.
[2] Meine nächste Absicht war eine Kenntnis der Person
des Moses zu gewinnen, mein entfernteres Ziel
auf solche Art zur Lösung eines noch heute aktu-
ellen Problems beizutragen, das erst späterhin
genannt werden kann. Eine Charakterstudie er-
fordert zu ihrer Begründung zuverlässiges
Material, aber nichts was über den Mann
Moses zu Gebote steht, kann zuverlässig
genannt werden. Es ist eine Tradition
aus einer einzigen Quelle, von keiner anderen
Seite bestätigt, wahrscheinlich zu spät schriftlich
fixiert, in sich widerspruchsvoll, sicherlich
mehrfach überarbeitet und durch den Ein-
fluß neuer Tendenzen entstellt, und den
religiösen und nationalen Mythen eines
Volkes innig verwoben. Man wäre
berechtigt den Versuch als hoffnungslos abzu-
brechen, würde nicht die Großartigkeit
der Gestalt ihrer Entlegenheit ein Gegen-
gewicht bieten und zu erneuter Bemühung auffordern. Man unternimmt es also,
jede einzelne der im Material gegebenen
Möglichkeiten als Anhaltspunkt zu behandeln
und die Lücken zwischen einem Stück und

dem nächsten, sozusagen, nach dem Gesetz des
kleinsten Widerstandes auszufüllen, das
heißt, jene Annahme zu bevorzugen, der
man die grössere Wahrscheinlichkeit zu-
schreiben darf. Was man mit Hilfe dieser
Technik erhält, kann man auch als eine
Art von "historischem Roman" auffassen,
es hat keinen oder nur einen unbestimm-
baren Wirklichkeitswert, denn eine
noch so große Wahrscheinlichkeit fällt
nicht mit der Wahrheit zusammen,
die Wahrheit ist oftmals sehr unwahr-
scheinlich und tatsächliche Beweismittel
sind auch in kärglichem Ausmaß durch
Ableitungen und Erwägungen zu er-
setzen.

Appendix II
Jakob Freud's
Hebrew Inscription

1 בן יקיר לי שלמה

2 בשבע בימי שני חייך החל רוח ד' לפעמך

3 ודבר בך לך קרא בספרי אשר כתבתי

4 ויבקעו לך מעינות בינה דעה והשכל

5 ספר הספרים חנהו ממנו חפרו חכמים

6 ומחוקקים למדו דעת ומשפט

7 מחזה שדי חזית שמעת ונסית עשות

8 ותדא על כנפי הרוח

9 מן אז היה הספר כמוס כשברי לוחות

10 בארון עמדי

11 ליום נמלאו שנותיך לחמשה ושלשים

12 נתחי עליו מכסה עור חדש

13 וקראתי לו "עלי באר ענו לה"

14 ואקריבנו לפניך לזכרון

15 ולמזכרת אהבה מאביך

16 אוהבך אהבת עולם   יעקב ברש' פרייד

17 בעיר הבירה ווען כ"ט ניסן תרנא 6 מאי 891

(1) <u>בן יקיר לי</u>: ירמ' לא:יט — הבן יקיר לי אפרים (גם בשמונה עשרה של ר"ח). (2) <u>בשבע בימי שני חייך</u>: בר' מז:ח — ויאמר פרעה אל יעקב כמה ימי שני חייך. והש' בר' מא:לד — בשבע שני השבע; <u>החל רוח ד' לפעמך</u>: שופ' יג:כה — ותחל רוח ד' לפעמו במחנה דן. (3) <u>ודבר בך</u>: הש' דב' ו:ז — ודברת בם (גם בקריאת שמע). <u>בספרי אשר כתבתי</u>: הש' שמ' לב:לב — מחני נא מספרך אשר כתבת. (4) <u>ויבקעו לך מעינות</u>: בר' ז:יא — נבקעו כל מעינות תהום רבה: בינה דעה והשכל: ראה שמונה עשרה נוסח ספרד. (6-5) <u>ממנו חפרו חכמים ומחוקקים למדו</u>: הש' במ' כא:יח — באר חפרוה שרים כרוה נדיבי עם במחקק במשענתם. והש' שופ' ה:יד — מני מכיר ירדו מחקקים. (7) <u>מחזה שדי חזית</u>: במ' כד:ד, טז — מחזה שדי יחזה; <u>שמעת ונסית עשות</u>: הש' שמ' כד:ז — ויאמרו כל אשר דבר ד' נעשה ונשמע. (8) <u>ותדא על כנפי הרוח</u>: תה' יח:יא — וידא על כנפי רוח. (10-9) <u>מן אז</u>: יר' מד:יח — ומן אז חדלנו לקטר; <u>כמוס . . . עמדי</u>: דב' לב:לד — הלא הוא כמוס עמדי; <u>כשברי לוחות בארון</u>: ברכות ח; בבא בתרא יד:, תרי' במיוחד מנחות צט. — "אשר שברת ושמתם בארון" (דב' י:ב). תני רב יוסף: מלמד שהלוחות ושברי לוחות מונחין בארון. מכאן לתלמיד חכם ששכח תלמודו מחמת אונסו שאין נוהגין בו מנהג בזיון. (12) <u>נתחי עליו מכסה עור חדש</u>: במ' ד:י — ונתנו אותה . . . אל מכסה עור תחש (והש' שם, ו, יא, יב, יד): (13) <u>"עלי באר ענו לה"</u>: במ' כא:יז — אז ישיר ישראל את השירה הזאת עלי באר ענו לה. (14) <u>ואקריבנו</u>: אולי ע"ש איוב לא:לו — כמו נגיד אקרבנו. <u>לזכרון</u>: שמ' יג:ט — ולזכרון בין עיניך. (16) <u>אהבת עולם</u>: יר' לא:ב — ואהבת עולם אהבתיך.

Jakob Freud Inscription (Translation)

[Line numbers refer to the Hebrew text]
1 Son who is dear to me, Shelomoh,
2 In the seventh in the days of the years of your life the Spirit of the Lord
    began to move you
3 and spoke within you: Go, read in my Book that I have written
4 and there will burst open for you the wellsprings of understanding,
    knowledge, and wisdom.
5 Behold, it is the Book of Books, from which sages have excavated
6 and lawmakers learned knowledge and justice.
7 A vision of the Almighty did you see; you heard and strove to do,
8 and you soared upon the wings of the Spirit.
9 Since then the Book has been stored like the fragments of the Tablets
10 in an ark with me.
11 For the day on which your years were filled to five and thirty
12 I have put upon it a cover of new skin
13 and have called it: "Spring up, O well, sing ye unto it!"
14 and I have presented it to you as a memorial
15 and as a reminder of love from your father,
16 who loves you with everlasting love. Jakob son of R' Sh[elomoh] Freid [*sic*]
17 In the capital city Vienna 29 Nisan [5]651 6 May [1]891

Sources

(1) *Son who is dear to me*: Jeremiah 31:19 (also in Eighteen Benedictions of Rosh Ha-shanah). (2) *the days of the years of your life*: Genesis 47:8; cf. Genesis 41:34; *the Spirit of the Lord began to move you*: Judges 13:25. (3) *and spoke within you*: cf. Deuteronomy 6:7; *my Book that I have written*: cf. Exodus 32:32. (4) *and there will burst open for you the wellsprings*: Genesis 7:11; *understanding, knowledge, and wisdom*: Eighteen Benedictions of the daily liturgy, Sephardic rite. (5–6) *from which sages have excavated and lawmakers learned*: cf. Numbers 21:18 and Judges 5:14. (7) *A vision of the Almighty did you see*: Numbers 24:4,16; *you heard and strove to do*: cf. Exodus 24:7. (8) *and you soared upon the wings of the Spirit*: Psalms 18:11. (9–10) *Since then*: Jeremiah 44:18; *stored . . . with me*: Deuteronomy 32:34; *like the fragments of the Tablets in an ark*: see Babylonian Talmud, Berakhot, 8b;

Baba Bathra, 14b; and especially Menaḥot, 99a. (12) *put upon it a cover of new skin*: Numbers 4:10; cf. also Numbers 4:6, 11, 12, 14. (13) *Spring up, O well, sing ye unto it*: Numbers 21:17. (14) *and I have presented it*: perhaps on basis of Job 31:37; *as a memorial*: Exodus 13:9; *everlasting love*: Jeremiah 31:2.

Appendix III
Unpublished Freud
Correspondence

1. Freud to Theodor Herzl, September 28, 1902

[see above, p. 12]:

> 28 Sept. 1902
> IX., Berggasse 19

Hochgeehrter Herr Doktor

Über Anregung Ihres Redaktionskollegen, des Herrn Max Nordau habe ich mir erlaubt, Ihnen durch die Buchhandlung Fr. Deuticke ein Exemplar meines 1900 publizierten Buches über die Traumdeutung sowie einen kleinen, dasselbe Thema behandelnden Vortrag zuzusenden. Ich kann nicht wissen, ob Sie den Eindruck empfangen werden, daß das Buch sich für die Verwendung eigne, die Herr Nordau im Auge gehabt hat, aber ich [2] bitte Sie, es für alle Fälle als ein Zeichen der Hochachtung zu behalten, die ich—wie so viele Andere—seit Jahren dem Dichter und dem Kämpfer für die Menschenrechte unseres Volkes entgegenbringe.

> Ergebenst Ihr
> Prof. Dr. Freud

2. Freud to the Executive Committee of the Yiddish Scientific Institute [YIVO] in Vilna, December 29, 1929

[see above, p. 96]:

> 29.XII.1929
> Wien, IX., Berggasse 19

Sehr geehrte Herren,

Wenn Sie meinen Namen noch für Ihr Praesidium brauchen können, bedienen Sie sich seiner. Ich wünsche Ihrer Bemühung besten Erfolg.

> Ihr ergebener
> Freud

3. Reply of the Executive Committee of YIVO [January 7, 1930]:

Wilno, den 7. Januar 1930.

Herrn
Professor Dr. Siegmund (*sic*) Freud,
Wien.

Sehr verehrter Herr Professor,
  mit herzlichem Dank bestätigen wir das Eintreffen Ihres Schreibens, in dem
Sie Ihre Bereitwilligkeit aussprechen, dem Ehrenpräsidium des Kuratoriums
des Jiddischen Wissenschaftlichen Instituts beizutreten. Es wird uns ein Verg-
nügen und eine Ehre sein, diese Zustimmung der Oeffentlichkeit zu unter-
breiten.

> In ausgezeichneter Hochachtung
> ergebenst
> DER EXEKUTIVAUSSCHUSS
> I.A.
> [Initialed] MW (Max Weinreich)
> SR (S. Raisin)

4. Dr. Samuel Stendig (Cracow) to Freud, January 6, 1939

[see above, pp. 96–97]:

Prof. Dr. Samuel Stendig
Przewodniczacy Komitetu Redakcyjnego
Encyklopedii Zydów Polskich
W. Krakowie

> Kraków, dnia, 6. Januar 1939
> Starowisina 86

Hochverehrter und Liebenswuerdiger Herr Professor,
  Am 13. Juli 1938 hatte ich die Ehre Sie, hochgeschätzter Herr Professor
und Meister, in Ihrer Wohnung in London zu besuchen. Ich lege hier einen
Ausschnitt aus einer Zeitung bei, in dem ich es mir erlaube etwas aus Ihrem
Leben und unserem Gespräch mitzuteilen. Da Herr Sachs aus Johannesburg
zugegen war, schicke ich auch ihm die Zeitung ein.
  Ich erlaube mir zu ersuchen mir gefälligst zu berichten, wie es Ihnen, lieber
Herr Professor, jetzt zugeht und wie es mit Ihren Sachen steht, die Sie aus Wien
zu bekommen hatten.
  Die Aufnahme, die ich während meines Besuches machte, kann ich leider
nicht einschicken, da mir an der deutschen Grenze sämtliche Photographien
durchlichtet wurden. Man hat naemlich eine so gründliche Revision durch-

geführt, dass mir selbst in die Klischees hineingesehen wurde. Der ganze Film ging mir so kaput. Welch Schaden. Als Redakteur der Enzyklopoedie des polnischen Judentums ersuche ich Sie, geehrter und lieber Herr Professor, um einen kurzen Artikel aufs Thema: Meine Lehre in Polen, oder meine. Jüdischen Anhänger in Polen/die Schreibenden/. Dann eine Photographie mit Ihrer eigenhändigen Unterschrift. Sollten Sie das nicht machen können, dann bitte ich um Ihre Photographie mit Handschrift und um einen Brief für die Redaktion mit ein paar Sätzen in Betreff des polnischen Judentums. In der Enzyklopoedie, deren zwei Bände bereits erschienen sind, ist ein spezieller Raum bestimmt für die prominentesten jüdischen Gelehrten. So haben wir auch von Prof. Einstein dasselbe.

Bei dieser Gelegenheit gestatte ich mir sie aufs Höflichste zu bitten mir Ihre letzte Arbeit schenken zu wollen, die Sie gerade beendet haben, als ich Sie in London besuchte, die Arbeit über Moses. Ich will sie auch besprechen, wie ich es in der Presse getan habe mit dem Buche von Th. Mann, das mir der Bermann-Fischer Verlag eingeschickt hatte. Sollte ich das Buch erhalten, würde ich um Ihre gef. Dedikation ersuchen.

Wie Sie bereits wissen, aus meinem Bericht, leite ich die Krakauer Psychologische Gesellschaft, wo Ihre Lehre propagiert und gelehrt wird. Meine jüngste Arbeit, Sie betreffend, habe [ich] Ihnen persönlich gegeben. Die neue, Sie betreffend, kommt in die Enzyklopoedie, und zu diesem Zwecke bitte ich eben um Ihre Mitarbeit, wie oben.

Wir haben in Polen einen harten Daseinskampf und wir wollen in dieser Enzyklopoedie unsere Leistungen ausweisen und wenn Leistungen, dann unserer grossen Gelehrten. Es hat also einen tiefen Grund, wenn wir unsere Gelehrten hier der Welt vorzeigen wollen.

Indem ich hoffe recht gut verstanden zu sein, erlaube ich mir Sie wie auch Ihre w. Frau Gemahlin herzlich zu grüssen.

> Ihr ganz ergebener
> Stendig

5. Freud to Stendig, January 21, 1939:

> 21.I.1939
> 20 Maresfield Gardens
> London N. W. 3

Geehrter Herr Professor

bitte erwarten Sie keinen Beitrag von mir. Ich befinde mich nicht sehr wohl, kann kaum meine Korrespondenz bewältigen, wie Sie auch aus der Verspätung meiner Antwort ersehen, und habe gar keine Neigung irgend etwas zu schreiben. Ich bin auch der Propaganda ziemlich überdrüssig, möchte alles ähnliche gern jüngeren Kräften überlassen und—ich besitze keine Photographie, die ich Ihnen schicken könnte. Meine früheren Bilder sind in Wien vernichtet worden. Wenn Sie nach all diesen unfreundlichen Belehrungen noch fortfahren, [2] meine Lehren in Polen zu vertreten, werde ich es Ihnen hoch anrechnen müssen.

Mit herzlichem Gruss
Ihr Freud

Provisional postscript (July 22, 1990)

Only a week after I had sent off the manuscript of this book to the publisher I received a very kind and totally unexpected letter from Dr. Lynn Gamwell, director of the University Art Museum, State University of New York at Binghamton. Her name was known to me as the organizer of the traveling exhibition of Freud's collection of antiquities, of which a sumptuously illustrated and detailed catalogue had been published (Gamwell and Wells [1989]). None of the items displayed in the collection was Jewish, and I had assumed, as must have others, that Freud did not possess any specifically Jewish objects.

I must confess that I found this a bit odd but accepted it as a fact. Stranger than this was a sentence in a letter from Rome sent by Freud to his wife Martha on September 21, 1907, describing a visit to the catacombs, in which he states: "In the Jewish ones the inscriptions are Greek, the candelabrum—I think it's called Menorah [*Menora, glaube ich, heisst er*]—can be seen on many tablets" (Freud [1960], no. 129, p. 261; [1980], p. 278). What perplexed me all along was the apparent uncertainty about the word *Menorah*. I find it almost impossible to believe that the term was not part of Freud's vocabulary or that he had not seen a Menorah in his father's house. In the Philippsohn Bible there is a fine engraving of a seven-branched Menorah at the end of the section (Exodus 25:31–40) which describes the making of the Menorah for the Tabernacle. On September 13, 1913, Freud sent a picture-postcard from Rome to Karl Abraham which depicted the Arch of Titus. There, as is well known, the spoils of the Temple in Jerusalem are shown being carried away by Roman soldiers, and the most prominent object is the Menorah. Freud's message on the card was: "Der Jude übersteht's!"—"the Jew survives it!" (Freud/Abraham [1965], p. 146; [1980], p. 145) (see photo gallery above, following p. 80).

The news that Dr. Gamwell now brought me was that at the Freud Museum in London objects have been found "which are related to Freud's Jewishness" and "which have evidently gone unnoticed until now." These items, of which she generously supplied me with photographs, include Rembrandt's "The Synagogue" (original etching); Rembrandt's Moses Lifting the Tablets of the Law (engraved by Kruger, 1770); two Kiddush cups shown standing in front of a group of Egyptian statuettes on a table, in a photograph taken at Freud's house in Vienna by Edmund Engelmann in 1938 (at least one of the cups shows the Tablets of the Law); and, finally, a bronze or brass Hannukah Menorah of the type that hangs on the wall and is lighted by oil and wicks (see photo gallery above, following p. 80). According to Dr. Gamwell there is "irrefutable evidence that these were in Freud's study during his lifetime." Strangely enough, the actual Kiddush cups have not been found, though the photographs of 1938 attest to their existence. At the time of this writing Dr.

Gamwell is preparing to go to London to examine the objects at first hand and, hopefully, to find the cups as well.

As for the Menorah, which does exist, I shall only add a few details that I am able to discern from the photograph. There are three (heraldic?) animal devices, each within a circle on the triangular surface, one large and two small. Running across the bottom of the triangle there is a Hebrew inscription which I could recognize as "Ki ner mitzvah ve-Torah 'or" (For the commandment is a lamp and the Teaching is light) (Proverbs 6:23).

After scrutinizing the pictures, I turned to consult the well-known publication of Edmund Engelman's photographs of Freud's home and offices entitled *Berggasse 19* (1976). The photograph of the Kiddush cups and the Egyptian statuettes is there (plate 15), but it is harder to identify them as such because the tablets on the one cup are less clear than in the photograph sent to me. The cups reappear, in fact, in plate 17. But since neither the text of the book nor the captions to plates 15 and 17 make any allusion to them, they are easily glossed over.

I offer these observations for what they are worth. I do not know if Freud bought these ritual objects or inherited them from his parents. I do not claim for a moment that the fact that Freud owned two kiddush cups and a Menorah means that he ever used them for the purposes for which they were intended, any more than I would think he necessarily worshipped his Egyptian deities. That the Jewish objects were part of his most private ambiance seems, for the moment, sufficiently noteworthy and (such are the surprising vicissitudes in the unfolding story of Freud) may, with the discovery of further facts, even prove significant. I would very much like to know why the aforementioned Jewish objects were not made available for the original exhibition and catalogue and "have evidently gone unnoticed until now." Happily, I learn from Dr. Gamwell that they will be on view, along with the rest of Freud's collection, at the Jewish Museum in New York beginning November 7, 1991.

Notes

Chapter 1. The Fourth Humiliation

1. Reik (1954), p. 18. No date is given, but according to Reik the conversation took place before the publication in 1909 of Otto Rank's *Der Mythus von der Geburt des Helden*. Rank, however, had already presented a summary of the book at a meeting of the Vienna Psychoanalytic Society on November 25, 1908; see Nunberg and Federn (1962–75), vol. 2, no. 60, pp. 65–72; (1976–81), vol. 2, pp. 59–65. A slightly different version of the joke appears in Freud (1916–17), p. 161.

2. Ricoeur (1965), pp. 40 ff.; (1970), pp. 32ff.

3. Sellin (1922). On Freud and Sellin see below, ch. 2.

4. On the inaccuracy of the standard English title and its implications, see below, ch. 3. I have retained it only because it has become a fixed convention in the English-speaking world.

5. One of the most sweeping and bitter contemporaneous Jewish responses was that of Trude Weiss-Rosmarin (1939), who, while offering some astute criticisms, interpreted the entire work as an expression of Freud's "Jewish self-hatred." Cf. A. S. Yahuda's Hebrew review (1946), begun shortly before Freud's death and written more in sorrow than in anger (Yahuda had tried personally to convince Freud not to publish the book). Yahuda had high praise for Freud and for psychoanalysis but attributed the writing of *Moses and Monotheism* [hereafter *M.M.*] to Freud's assimilation and to his consequent acceptance of the anti-Jewish biases implicit in much of modern German biblical criticism. Among the sporadic but ultimately futile attempts to defend *M.M.* as history see Blum (1956) and Chandler (1962).

6. The curt dismissal of *M.M.* by the eminent biblical scholar W. F. Albright (1940), pp. 74f., is representative of the general reaction of most of his colleagues. For the anthropologists the central question has naturally been the validity of the Totem theory, on which the argument of *M.M.* hinges. A balanced overview is provided by Wallace (1983), ch. 4 ("History of the Criticism of *Totem and Taboo*"), and passim. Cf. the devastating critique of the Totem theory by C. Lévi-Strauss, *Le totémisme aujourd'hui* (1962), English tr. (1963). A selection of contemporary reviews of *M.M.*, unfortunately omitting some of the most important ones, is now available in Kiell (1988), pp. 623–54.

7. See Yerushalmi (1982), ch. 4.

8. The manuscript (hereafter MS 1934) is in the Freud Archives at the Library of Congress, Washington, D.C. It is listed in the typescript catalogue, *Library of Congress, Manuscript Division: The Sigmund Freud Collection*, p. 18, under Series B: Unrestricted Portion, Container no. B 18. Curiously, the catalogue records in brackets only the dates of *publication* [1937–39], without any indication that the first page of the manuscript is dated 9 August, 1934 in Freud's own hand.

9. Klein (1985), p. 130. For Rank's text in English translation see ibid., Appendix C, pp. 170–73.

10. For the three "blows" see Freud (1917), pp. 139–43. See also the similar statement in Freud (1916–17), pp. 285f.

11. "Israel in der Wüste," in Goethe (1888), vol. 7, pp. 170f. A similar notion crops up in Bin-Gorion (1926), pp. 420, 512, based on Hirsch (1873), pp. 162–64.

12. Breasted (1933), pp. 22, 145, 369, and passim. Flinders Petrie (1906), p. 193; (1924), p. 95. A more sophisticated view, stressing the qualitative differences between Israelite and Egyptian "monotheism," is presented by Kaufmann (1954), vol. 2, pp. 42–45; (1960), p. 226 n. 6. For a lucid argument by an Egyptologist that Ikhnaton's religion cannot be regarded as genuine·monotheism, see Wilson (1951), pp. 224ff.

13. Weber (1952), p. 122; Chamberlain (1977), p. 442; Popper-Linkeus (1899), pt. 2, pp. 127–29.

14. Josephus, *Antiquities*, II.228 ([1978], vol. 4, pp. 262f.). Although correct in his surmise that the name Moses is of Egyptian derivation, the specific etymology Josephus offers ("the Egyptians call water *moû* and those who are saved *esês*") is, of course, his own fancy.

15. All the texts are conveniently assembled with copious annotations, in the original Greek and in English translation, in Stern (1976–80), vol. 1, pp. 83, 299, 394; vol. 2, p. 277. For further discussion see Gager (1972), pp. 38–47, 92–94, 113–18, 122–24.

16. On all these see Rossi (1984), ch. 17: "The Egyptian Culture of Moses." The quotation from Toland is on p. 128.

17. "Die Sendung Moses," in Schiller (1962), vol. 4, pp. 783–804. It is highly probable that Freud had read the essay. See Blum (1956), pp. 373–75. On Freud and Schiller see also Brandt (1959).

18. Popper-Linkeus provides a relevant instance of a different kind. In his "Josef Popper-Linkeus and the Theory of Dreams" (1923) Freud acknowledged that in the latter's *Phantasieen eines Realisten*, published a year before *The Interpretation of Dreams*, elements of his own dream theory had been anticipated, but he insisted that each had arrived at his notions independently. See also Freud (1932), where he returns to the same theme. In 1938, however, after parts I and II of *M.M.* had appeared, Israel Doryon wrote to Freud from Jerusalem pointing out that in the sketch entitled "Der Sohn des Königs von Egypten" (Popper-Linkeus [1899], pt. 2, pp. 127–29) Moses is depicted as the son of Pharaoh and therefore an Egyptian. In a letter of October 7, 1938, Freud replied that "it would not bother me at all if my assertion that Moses was an Egyptian could be traced back to his suggestion. I have often experienced manifestations of cryptomnesia which have clarified the sources of seemingly original ideas." The letter (along with three others from Freud to Doryon) is in the Schwadron Collection of the Jewish National and University Library in Jerusalem. English and Hebrew translation in the exhibition catalogue *Freudiana* (1973), no. 25. Doryon's Hebrew book (1940) on Popper-Linkeus contains a short preface by Freud (and one by Einstein). Cf. *Freudiana*, no. 28.

19. Freud (1939), p. 10. Freud's "Family Romances" first appeared, with minor variations, as part of Rank's book (1909), pp. 64–68; (1959), pp. 67–71. See Strachey's note to Freud (1909), p. 236. It was first published under his own name as "Der Familienroman der Neurotiker" in Freud (1931), pp. 300–04.

20. "Amenhotep IV (Ichnaton). Psychoanalytische Beiträge zum Verständnis seiner Persönlichkeit und des monotheistischen Atonkultes," *Imago*, 1 (1912), pp. 334–60. English translation in *Psychoanalytic Quarterly*, 4 (1935), pp. 537–

69, reprinted in Abraham (1955), pp. 262–90. Oddly enough, although mentioning Abraham's paper, James Strachey's "Preliminary Notes Upon the Problem of Akhenaten" (1939) makes no reference to Freud's *M.M.*

21. For details on the various publications see Strachey's "Editor's Note" in Freud (1939), p. 3. I have in my possession an apparently unrecorded issue of the first German edition dated 1939 and identical in every respect with the one published by Allert de Lange in Amsterdam, including the latter's copyright on the verso of the title page, except that the title page itself has as the publisher Longman's Green and Co., Alliance Book Corporation, New York/Toronto. Autopsy reveals that the original sheets and covers were used, only the title page was changed. I am informed by John Gach, the erudite dealer in rare psychoanalytica, that he has seldom seen a copy. It remains, for me at least, a bibliographical enigma. The first American edition of *M.M.* was published by Knopf in 1939, but in English translation and with the copyright assigned to Freud himself.

22. See Jones (1953–57), vol. 3, pp. 234f. Further details in Gay (1988), p. 637.

23. Freud (1960), no. 294 (January 17, 1938), p. 440, and Freud (1939), p. 7. See also Gay (1988), p. 633. In a postscript to a letter to Max Eitingon on March 5, 1939, Freud wrote, "Martin Buber's pious phrases won't do much harm to *The Interpretation of Dreams*. The *Moses* is much more vulnerable, and I am prepared for an onslaught by the Jews on it" (Schur [1972], pp. 520, 566).

24. Writing about *M.M.* to Charles Singer on October 31, 1938, Freud had exclaimed characteristically, "Needless to say, I don't like offending my own people, either. But what can I do about it? I have spent my whole life standing up for what I considered to be the scientific truth, even when it was uncomfortable and unpleasant for my fellow man. I cannot end up with an act of disavowal. Your letter contains the assurance which testifies to your superior intelligence, that everything I write is bound to cause misunderstanding and—may I add—indignation. Well, we Jews have been reproached for growing cowardly in the course of the centuries. (Once upon a time we were a valiant nation). In this transformation I had no share. So I must risk it" (Freud [1960], no. 307, pp. 453f.; [1980], pp. 469f.).

25. Robert (1974), p. 278; (1976), p. 167. Ricoeur (1965), p. 239; (1970), p. 244. Even more radically, Oring (1984), p. 101: "*Moses and Monotheism* would seem to be the work of a modern apostle, a new gospel with a perhaps not-so-new *Epistle to the Hebrews*. . . . If Moses was not a Jew then neither was Freud. If anti-Semitism were to disappear, then the Jews must be prepared to acknowledge the underlying message of the Christ myth as preached by a psychoanalytic prophet." Equally extreme, and much more elaborate, is the recent "revisionist" attempt by Vitz (1988) to prove a lifelong attraction to Christianity in Freud's "Christian Unconscious." Such a thesis is in itself hardly novel (see, inter alia, Velikovsky [1941], Oehlschlegel [1943], Puner [1947], pp. 243f.).

The list of those who claim that, at least unconsciously, Freud resented, denied, or repressed his Jewishness, and who interpret *M.M.* accordingly, is considerable. Partial references in Rainey (1975), pp. 86f. n. 95. A judicious overview of some "Interpretations of Freud's Jewishness, 1924–1974" is provided by Miller (1981). Further bibliography in Gay (1988), pp. 777f., and in this book.

Peter Gay's approach requires some special comment. In a series of works (1978, 1982, 1987) culminating in his magisterial biography of Freud (1988), he has consistently maintained that although Freud's Jewish identity may have been personally important to him, it had no relevance to his creation of psychoanalysis. The intellectual and spiritual pedigrees of psychoanalysis are to be sought exclusively in the legacy of the Enlightenment *philosophes* and the scientific positivism of such teachers as Meinert and Brucke. Gay is equally firm in rejecting any alleged influence of Austrian politics (a thesis advanced by Schorske [1973] and elaborated in different ways by McGrath [1986]) or even of the Viennese milieu in which Freud reached maturity. "In truth," Gay writes ([1988], p. 10), "Freud could have developed his ideas in any city endowed with a first-rate medical school and an educated public large and affluent enough to furnish him with patients." This hyperbole might be apt for Freud's preanalytic work on the nerve cells of crayfish or the gonads of eels, but surely not on the interpretation of dreams or on human sexuality. In effect Gay has thrown a *cordon sanitaire,* if not around Freud then around psychoanalysis, shielding it from any taint of historical or cultural conditioning. To find such an essentially ahistorical approach in an eminent social and intellectual historian is curious. Surely "science," "art" or "imposture" (the alternatives mentioned in the preface to Gay's biography) are not the only options available when discussing psychoanalysis. If science, then surely of the softer kind, always malleable by personal and social factors. Nor am I in accord with other propositions advanced in the aforementioned works. That religious faith (as distinct from particular religious institutions) is incompatible with scientific discovery is a bias which, although shared by Freud himself, has been increasingly repudiated among historians of science. That Freud described himself as a "godless Jew" (cf. Gay [1987]) means, as I hope to show, that the noun must be taken at least as seriously as the adjective. That Freud did not name his six children after deceased relatives but after his own teachers and culture-heroes (Gay [1982]) is interesting but shows at best a normal and superficial onomastic assimilation, common enough among Jews of all stripes. We have only to note that at certain points in Jewish history Marduk became Mordecai, Ishtar became Esther, and so quintessentially Yiddish a name as Feibush had once been Phoebus. Ironically, as Freud did with "Moses," Gay loads too great an exegetical burden on these names (it would be equally perilous to deduce from Freud's naming two daughters Sophie and Anna after the niece and daughter of his religious teacher Hammerschlag that he shared the latter's religious convictions). Finally, that artistic and scientific creations may have the most unlikely psychological and cultural roots is an idea of which Freud himself made us keenly aware. In principle, therefore, the possibility that Freud's Jewishness was somehow implicated in the formation of psychoanalysis should not be foreclosed. To pursue a running polemic with Professor Gay beyond this excursus would only swell this book immoderately and serve no real purpose. Happily, his works are sufficiently well known for the reader to form an independent opinion.

26. See Ernest Jones's report of the meeting of the board of directors of the Vienna Society on March 13, 1938 (Jones [1953–57], vol. 3, p. 221); Freud's letter to Jacob Meitlis on November 30, 1938 (Meitlis [1951], p. 21), and the passage in *M.M.* itself (Freud [1939], p. 115).

27. "Einem Volkstum den Mann abzusprechen, den es als den grössten unter seinen Söhnen rühmt, ist nichts, was man gern oder leichthin unternehmen wird, *zumal wenn man selbst diesem Volke angehört*" (Freud [1939b], p. 9; my italics).

28. "Man wird sich nicht leicht dazu entschliessen, einer Nation ihren groessten Mann abzuerkennen *einer Namensdeutung wegen*" (MS 1934, p. 5; my italics). It

is also interesting that in the published version Freud attenuated the word *Nation* to *Volkstum,* yet another instance of the different nuances in Freud's public and private expressions of his Jewish identity with which we shall be concerned all along.

29. Schur (1972), p. 468 (in German on p. 563). Freud's reference to Moses as an "anti-Semite" is, of course, meant ironically and refers, as Schur properly observes, to Moses' wrath against the Israelites at the making of the Golden Calf. In the same sense all the Hebrew prophets could be called anti-Semites as well.

30. Freud/Zweig (1968), p. 109; (1970), p. 98.

31. Robert (1974), p. 251; (1976), p. 150.

32. Freud/Pfister (1963a), p. 63; (1963), p. 64.

33. On Lessing and Mendelssohn see Altmann (1973), passim; on *Nathan the Wise*, pp. 569–73.

34. *Vom Geist der ebräischen Poesie,* in Herder (1903), p. 267.

35. Rieff (1959), pp. 258f. (on Freud as "psychological Jew"), and ch. 10: "The Emergence of Psychological Man" (ibid., pp. 329–57).

36. I owe this suggestion to an as yet unpublished lecture by Peter Swales entitled "Freud, His Origins and Family History: The Freuds, the Nathansons and the Bernayses," presented at the Center for Israel and Jewish Studies, Columbia University, on January 26, 1987.

37. Jones (1953–57), vol. 1, pp. 116, 119, 125, 167. "He [Freud] once went to a Jewish wedding when his friend Paneth married Sophie Schwab. He gazed at the scene with a fascinated horror and then wrote a letter of sixteen pages describing all the odious detail in a spirit of malign mockery" (ibid., p. 140, based on an unpublished letter, dated May 16, 1884, to Martha Bernays). Jones's summary notwithstanding, one would very much like to read this letter, presumably still sealed in the Freud Archives, to know precisely which features of the wedding Freud found so distasteful. It should be noted that when Freud described the death and funeral of his friend Nathan Weiss in a long letter to Martha on September 16, 1883, he did not mention the ritual at all but was outraged only by the loud, bitter family feud that erupted in the presence of the corpse, and this largely because "we were all petrified with horror and shame in the presence of the Christians among us. It seemed as though we had given them reason to believe that we worship the God of Revenge, not the God of Love" (Freud [1960], no. 22, p. 65; [1980], p. 72).

38. Freud (1960), no. 7, p. 22; (1980), p. 32.

39. See below, ch. 3.

40. The essential point has been grasped, though perhaps a bit overstated, by Chasseguet-Smirgel (1988), p. 19; (1988a), p. 256: "A Jew of the diaspora, living under the conditions that reigned at the end of the nineteenth century and the first half of the twentieth century, as Freud did, who would not be ambivalent with regard to his Jewishness, would simply have escaped the laws governing the human psyche."

41. Freud (1925a), p. 291.

42. Freud (1960), no. 219, p. 365; (1980), p. 380.

43. Freud (1941 [1926]), pp. 273f.; (1960), no. 220, pp. 366f.; (1980), p. 381.

44. Freud/Fliess (1985), p. 293; (1986), p. 319.

45. Freud (1900), p. 442.

46. Loewenberg (1970), esp. pp. 130f.

47. See Goldhammer (1937, 1958), quoting the relevant line. A photocopy of the original letter, now in the Central Zionist Archives in Jerusalem, was generously given to me by Ernst Pawel, who had rediscovered it while working on his biography of Herzl. The full text now appears in English translation in Pawel ([1989], p. 456). From this it turns out that the person who suggested to Freud that he send the book for review was Max Nordau, whom Freud had first met in Paris in 1885 (Jones [1953–57], vol. 1, p. 188). For the German text of Freud's letter see below, appendix III.

48. Martin Freud (1983), pp. 164f. One wonders what is meant by the phrase "and I may say now." Could this not be said before? For a recent psychoanalytically oriented attempt at a comprehensive study of Freud and Zionism see Chemouni (1988).

49. *Freudiana* (1973), no. 19, and Ernst Simon's comments (ibid., pp. xvii–xviii) on the historical background. Gay ([1988], p. 598n.) cites an almost identical letter to Einstein. Simon's observations on Freud himself, based on his "Sigmund Freud the Jew" (Simon [1957]), are less pertinent. The positions Freud adopted in this letter were hardly peculiar to him. Jewish "territorialists" and many "cultural Zionists" doubted the desirability or possibility of a Jewish State in Palestine. Committed Zionists like Simon himself, Martin Buber, Gershom Scholem, and Judah Magnes, thought that only a binational state was feasible.

50. *Freudiana* (1973), no. 20.

51. Freud (1934 [1930]), p. xv. First published in German in 1934 and in Hebrew not until 1939, when the Hebrew translation of *Totem and Taboo* finally appeared.

52. Freud (1960), no. 282 (April 19, 1936), p. 428. The letter was written originally in English.

53. Graf (1942), p. 473.

54. Freud (1941 [1926]), p. 274; cf. Freud (1925), p. 9.

55. Freud/Zweig (1968), p. 11; (1970), p. 3.

56. Freud/Zweig (1968), p. 14; (1970), pp. 5 f.

57. Freud/Zweig (1968), pp. 51f.; (1970), p. 40.

58. See, in general, Jones (1953–57), vol. 3, pp. 181–88. On the Göring Institute and psychotherapy in the Third Reich see Cocks (1985). Writing under the influence of the "new social history" in German historiography, Cocks argues reasonably for an awareness of greater continuities, complexities, even advances (e.g., the recognition and professionalization of psychotherapy alongside psychiatry) than have hitherto been assumed for Nazi Germany. Such revisionism, akin to the larger tendency to "historicize" the Nazi period represented by the German historian Martin Broszat (see Cocks's theoretical essay [1988]), may have its positive aspects. However, by shifting the focus of attention to the broader category of "psychotherapy," the specific fate of *psychoanalysis* is lost in the shuffle. Cocks's attempts to show lingering psychoanalytic influences in Nazi Germany are, in my opinion, not convincing and, in any case, largely irrelevant. The central fact remains that psychoanalysis as a creative and institutionally independent force was destroyed in Germany under the Nazis, and a comprehensive study of that phe-

nomenon is still a desideratum. For recent studies of particular aspects see the essays in Lohmann (1984) and in Timms and Segal (1988) as well as Hermanns (1988); Brecht (1988); and the vividly documented exhibition catalogue compiled by Brecht et al. (1985).

59. Freud/Zweig (1968), p. 102; (1970), p. 91.

60. MS 1934, pp. 1f. The German original is given below, appendix I. For other ramifications of Freud's use of the term "historical novel" see Yerushalmi (1989).

[*Addendum*, September 10, 1990]: This entire book was already in the hands of the publisher when I recently returned from Paris to find a letter sent to me from Bologna, Italy, on July 13, 1990. The writer, previously unknown to me, was Professor Pier Cesare Bori of the University of Bologna. In the most cordial and encouraging terms he told me that after reading my "Freud on the 'Historical Novel'" he simply wanted to inform me that he had already seen Freud's manuscript draft when it was still in Anna Freud's possession. Indeed, with the permission of Freud Copyrights, he had published a transcription of the introduction in an article (Bori [1979], reprinted in Bori [1989]). In light of this new information I gladly yield priority for publishing Freud's introduction to Professor Bori. For myself I can only add that Professor Bori's article, not cited in any of the literature I read, remained unknown to me until now. In fact, neither Freud Copyrights nor the editors of the International Journal of Psycho-Analysis gave me any indication that they were aware of a publication of this particular text prior to my own.

61. In a passage on Moses and the Jews that did not find its way into the published version of *M.M.*, Freud wrote (MS 1934, p. 20): "Ja eine eigentümliche Reaktion dieses Volkes, die sich wiederholt in seiner Geschichte zeigt, und der es zum guten Teil seiner Fortbestand verdankt, scheint bereits im Charakterbilde Moses, wie wir es zu erraten versuchen, vorgezeichnet. Ich meine die Bemühung durch einen Schicksalsschlag das Verlorene auf anderem Boden, mit neuen Mitteln wiederaufzubauen." An echo of this appears in Freud's letter of January 17, 1938, to his son Ernst, who had established himself in England: "It is typically Jewish not to renounce anything that has been lost. Moses, who in my opinion left a lasting imprint on the Jewish character, was the first to set the example" (Freud [1960], no. 294, p. 440; [1980], p. 456).

62. Letter of November 13, 1934, quoted by Jones (1953–57), vol. 3, p. 194.

63. Freud (1960), no. 294, p. 440; (1980), p. 456.

Chapter 2. Sigmund Freud: Jewish Historian

1. See Freud (1960), no. 293, p. 439; (1980), pp. 454f., written on December 14, 1937, to an unidentified "Herr Doktor." Despite a pronounced anti-Freudian bias, Eliade (1969) provides an illuminating background to Freud's enterprise by discussing the general quest for the "origins" of religion.

2. Freud/Fliess (1985), p. 272; (1986), p. 293.

3. Freud (1901), pp. 258f. (italics in the original).

4. Nunberg and Federn (1962–75), vol. 1, no. 17, p. 151; (1976–81), vol. 1, p. 143.

5. Freud (1907), pp. 126f.

6. Freud/Zweig (1968), p. 108; (1970), p. 97.

7. Freud/Zweig (1968), p. 109; (1970), p. 98.

8. Freud/Zweig (1968), p. 117; (1970), p. 106.

9. Freud (1939), p. 17.

10. Before approaching the material that would eventually become part III of
M.M., Freud presents a short summary of his historical reconstruction and states
(MS 1934, p. 26), "Hiemit kann ich abschliessen, was ich als den historischen Ro-
man um den Mann Moses angekündigt habe."

11. Freud (1914), p. 230.

12. See the surveys of biblical scholarship on Moses by Smend (1959) and
Thompson (1970). The "historical Jesus" fared no better, indeed often worse, in
New Testament criticism (see Schweitzer [1954]).

13. See Delitzsch (1902). Freud's lecture, whose text has not survived, is mentioned by Knoepfmacher (1979), p. 444, and Klein (1985), pp. 159f. The brief eyewitness account, extremely hostile to Freud and the Jewish audience that
applauded him, is in Grunwald (1952), p. 242.

14. Freud (1900), p. 514 (where Strachey mistranslates the German phrase as
"Holy Writ").

15. See Meyer (1906); Beer (1912); Gressmann (1913).

16. MS 1934, p. 29.

17. MS 1934, p. 33.

18. Freud (1939), p. 58.

19. Sellin (1922), pp. 52f.

20. Ibid., pp. 155f.

21. It was rejected not only by "Jewish" scholars, as implied by Jones (1953–
57), vol. 3, p. 373. However, Jones is right in questioning whether, as has often
been reported, Sellin ever explicitly retracted his views. To Jones's evidence that he
did not do so, at least in print, add Sellin's article "Hosea und das Martyrium des
Mose" (1928) and the third edition of his Hosea commentary (1929), pp. 16, 95,
97, 127.

22. Freud (1939), pp. 55, 57. Cf. his letter describing his work on Moses to
Lou Andreas-Salomé on January 6, 1935: "And now you see, Lou, this formula,
which holds so great a fascination for me, cannot be publicly expressed in Austria
today, without bringing down upon us a state prohibition of analysis on the part
of the ruling Catholic authority. And it is only this Catholicism which protects us
from the Nazis. And furthermore the historical foundations of the Moses story are
not solid enough to serve as a basis for these invaluable conclusions of mine. And
so I remain silent" (Freud/Salomé [1980], p. 224; [1972], p. 205).

23. Freud/Zweig (1968), p. 102; (1970), p. 70.

24. An exception is Wolfgang Huber, who has written on Schmidt within the
context of the history of psychoanalysis in Austria and Catholic attitudes toward it.
See Huber (1977), pp. 40–46 and (1978), pp. 79f. P. Vitz's "discovery" ([1988],
p. 197) that Schmidt was not a minor figure but a famous ethnologist is belated to
say the least, and his enthusiasm for the latter's thesis of a universal primitive
monotheism, uncritical. See, in this connection, the strictures of Eliade (1969) and
Petazzoni (1958). More seriously, having stumbled onto Schmidt, Vitz has not
bothered to seek out and read those of Schmidt's writings that might have really
offended or alarmed Freud. He can therefore write blandly (p. 198), "Schmidt's
other contribution, *his research on the nature of primitive religion*, did lead him

occasionally to cross swords with Freud. But for Freud to call him his 'chief enemy' was certainly a curious overstatement" [my italics]. Wallace (1983), pp. 141f., cites only Schmidt's manual of comparative religion (see below, n. 26) and in dealing specifically with M.M. discusses only psychodynamic factors (pp. 258ff. and passim; see also Wallace [1977]).

25. On Schmidt (1868–1954), see the entry in the *International Encyclopedia of the Social Sciences,* vol. 14, pp. 56ff., and the further references cited there. A complete bibliography of Schmidt's vast output has been compiled by Bornemann (1954). The final two volumes (11 and 12) of Schmidt's *Ursprung* appeared posthumously in 1954–55.

26. See Schmidt (1930), English translation (1931), pp. 109–15. Cf. Kroeber (1920). Kroeber later (1939) reformulated and somewhat softened the tone of his critique of *Totem and Taboo.*

27. E.g., "Eine wissenschaftliche Abrechnung mit der Psychoanalyse" (Schmidt [1928–29]) and "Prof. Dr. Freuds psychologische (psychoanalytische) Theorie zum Ursprung der Familie und der Religion" (Schmidt [1928–29a]). Schmidt's 1928 Vienna lecture was reported shortly afterward with extensive commentary in the Vatican newspaper *Osservatore Romano* on January 9, 1929. See David (1970), p. 116 n. 42).

28. Schmidt (1929), p. 411: "Auf diesem Gipfelpunkt der Atrocität angelangt, fühlt Freud selbst die Notwendigkeit sich zu entschuldigen, indem er die Anmerkung beifugt: 'Niemand, der mit der Literatur des Gegenstandes vertraut ist, wird annehmen, dass die Zurückführung der christlichen Kommunion auf die Totemmahlzeit eine Idee des Schreibers dieser Zeilen sei.' Nein, in dieser Torheit hat er tatsächlich bereits Vorgänger; aber jeder, der diese Vertrautheit mit der einschlägigen Literatur besitzt, wird bestätigen müssen, dass es einzig der Begründer der Psychoanalyse war, der durch die Herstellung der Verbindung mit dem Ödipus-Komplex und seinem Vatermord jene an sich schon reichlich irritierende Zurückführung der christlichen Kommunion bis zur intellektuellen und affektiven Unerträglichkeit übersteigert hat."

29. Schmidt (1929), pp. 417–21. It is only fair to note that unlike others who shared these prejudices, Schmidt never attacked Freud as a Jew nor psychoanalysis as "Jewish." He was not an anti-Semite, and his repeatedly outspoken stance, on both Catholic and anthropological grounds, against Nazi racial theory and "Aryan" Christianity, forced him in 1938 to leave Vienna for Switzerland, where he held a professorship at Fribourg until 1952. Even before Hitler's rise to power, in an article entitled "Das Rassenprinzip des Nazionalsozialismus" (Schmidt [1931–32]), he denied any fundamental racial difference between the Jews and Aryan peoples, while granting a difference in "psychic structure" (seelische Struktur), due to long historical and cultural conditioning, between them and Christian peoples. In general he concluded that it is "inconceivable that a really thinking and living Catholic could be a National Socialist." In another article devoted specifically "Zur Judenfrage" (Schmidt [1933–34), he acknowledged a serious problem in Austria arising from the disproportion of Jews in culture, the press, and the professions and warned that some solution should be found lest later on it prove a violent one. He was even more concerned, however, over racial discrimination against Jewish converts to Catholicism. Again, in a published lecture entitled "Blut-Rasse-Volk," he spoke of the Nazis' treatment of the Jews in Germany: "What a tragic mistake it is that this chosen people [the Germans] should now severely persecute another

chosen people [the Jews] by appealing to the racial principle, when the Jews, through the Mediterranean basic element of the Semito-Hamitic peoples stand racially closer to the Germans than the Magyars, Finns, Japanese, who have resolutely and successfully kept away from themselves the stigma of racial inferiority in Berlin" (Schmidt [1936], pp. 79f.).

30. I owe the suggestion concerning Father Gemelli to Dr. Anna Maria Accerboni Pavanello of Trieste (letters of June 29 and November 10, 1989). She bases it on an unpublished letter of Edoardo Weiss to Ernest Jones but stresses that, however probable, this must remain a hypothesis until direct research is undertaken in the Vatican archives.

31. See Freud (1939), p. 66.

32. Monotheism as the essence of Judaism was already an axiom in Imanuel Wolf's celebrated essay of 1822 heralding the new "scientific" study of Judaism (*Wissenschaft des Judentums*) and was espoused by leading Jewish thinkers and scholars throughout the nineteenth century. See Ismar Schorsch's introduction to Graetz (1975), pp. 13ff. It was this prevalent notion that the young Heinrich Graetz assailed, arguing that "the monotheistic idea is not even the primary principle of Judaism, as has been widely believed until now. . . . Therefore, the idea of monotheism in no way exhausts the entire content of Judaism; the latter is infinitely richer, infinitely deeper" (ibid., pp. 40, 69).

33. E.g., Freud (1939), p. 36. On February 13, 1935, Freud wrote to Arnold Zweig, "I shall send you back your *Schöpfungsgedicht* since you have just one copy. It seems to me to pay too much respect to the barbarous god of volcanoes and wildernesses whom I grew to dislike very much in the course of my studies in Moses and who was quite alien to my Jewish consciousness" (Freud/Zweig [1968], pp. 112f.; [1970], p. 102).

34. Freud (1939), p. 52.

35. On the "Chain of Tradition" see Yerushalmi (1982), pp. 31f., 114 n. 2.

36. Freud (1912–13), p. 158. Cf. ibid., p. 31.

37. Freud (1939), p. 101.

38. Ibid., p. 94. I have preferred here the Katherine Jones translation (Freud [1939a], p. 120). Cf. Freud (1939), p. 72: "The only satisfactory analogy to the remarkable course of events that we have found in the history of the Jewish religion lies in an apparently remote field; but it is very complete and approaches identity [*sie kommt der Identität nahe*]."

39. Freud (1987), giving both the German text and English translation.

40. Freud (1940 [1938]), esp. pp. 167, 190 n. 1, 200f., 207.

41. Freud (1987), p. 83 (quoted by Ilse Grubrich-Simitis from an unpublished letter to Ferenczi in 1915).

42. On the question as to whether the slaying of the primeval father was a singular or ubiquitous event Freud in *M.M.* remains ambiguous and elusive. Thus (Freud [1939], p. 81): "An essential part of the construction is the hypothesis that the events I am about to describe occurred to all primitive men. The story is told in an enormously condensed form, as though it had happened on a single occasion, while in fact it covered thousands of years and was repeated countless times during that long period." But later on (p. 101): "After this discussion I have no hesitation

in declaring that men have always known (in this special way) that they once possessed a primal father and killed him." And once again (p. 129): "We do not believe that there is a single great god today, but that in primaeval times there was a single person who was bound to appear huge at that time and who afterwards returned to men's memory elevated to divinity."

43. Ibid., p. 99.

44. Grubrich-Simitis in Freud (1987), pp. 99ff. Her essay "Metapsychology and Metabiology" (pp. 75–107) also contains an enlightening general discussion of Freud's and Ferenczi's Lamarckism. See further the stimulating approach to Freud's Lamarckism by Edelheit (1978), arguing that although human evolution is "Darwinian via the genes" it is "Lamarckian via language and culture" (p. 65). Cf. below, n. 52.

45. Freud (1939), p. 30 n. 2.

46. Heine (1982), pp. 398f.

47. Ibn Verga (1947), p. 129.

48. Ibid., p. 38; my italics.

49. For a comparative phenomenology see Yerushalmi (1982a).

50. Freud (1939), p. 100: "If we assume the survival of these memory traces in the archaic heritage, we have bridged the gulf between individual and group psychology. . . . If it is not so, we shall not advance a step further along the path we have entered on, either in analysis or in group psychology. The audacity cannot be avoided."

51. Ibid., p. 132.

52. Yerushalmi (1982), ch. 1. In this context see also Edelheit's interesting suggestion ([1978], pp. 63f.) that while, in common with others, Freud's Lamarckism "was related to a general foreshortening of the evolutionary time scale in the nineteenth century," his "personal compression of evolutionary time . . . suggests that his implicit time-scale was in fact biblical."

53. Freud (1939), pp. 88f.; my italics.

54. Sachs (1944), p. 152.

55. Bergmann (1976), reprinted in Ostow (1982), pp. 134f.

56. Despite a wealth of legend glorifying Moses in rabbinic literature and in Jewish folklore, the major thrust of the biblical narrators as well as the rabbis was to emphasize that, great as he was, Moses was all too human and merely an instrument of God. No aura of divinity or any cult was allowed to develop around him, no descent is claimed from him, and, Sellin's thesis notwithstanding, he plays no discernible role in the messianic vision of the Hebrew prophets. Though the three biblical patriarchs are mentioned in the 'amidah, the core of every Jewish liturgical service, Moses is not. In the Passover Haggadah, whose many-layered recital is orchestrated around the exodus from Egypt, the name of Moses never appears. That there is in all this a conscious attempt to prevent any confusion of the roles of Moses and God has been commented on by many. How deliberate this has been may be seen in the Passover Haggadah itself: "*And the Lord brought us forth out of Egypt* [Deut. 26:8]: not by the hands of an angel, and not by the hands of a seraph, and not by the hands of a messenger, but the Holy One, blessed be He, Himself, in His own glory and in His own person."

Chapter 3. Father-Religion, Son-Religion

1. Freud (1939), pp. 86–89.

2. Ibid., pp. 135f. On Judaism as "fossil" see p. 88.

3. Ibid., p. 129, in the section entitled "The Historical Truth" (*Die historische Wahrheit*). See also Strachey's note, p. 130, observing that the distinction between "historical" and "material" truth is relatively late in Freud and is first stated explicitly in the 1935 "Postscript" to the *Autobiographical Study*. There Freud writes, "In *The Future of an Illusion* I expressed an essentially negative valuation of religion. Later, I found a formula which did better justice to it: while granting that its power lies within the truth it contains, I showed that that truth was not a material [*materielle*] but a historical truth" (Freud [1935], p. 72). The same year, on January 6, 1935, Freud concluded his report to Lou Andreas-Salomé of his work on Moses, "Religions owe their compulsive power to the *return of the repressed*; they are reawakened memories of very ancient, forgotten, highly emotional episodes of human history. I have already said this in *Totem and Taboo*. I express it now in the formula: the strength of religion lies not in its *material* [here Freud uses the German word *reale*], but in its *historical* truth" (Freud/Salomé [1972], p. 205; [1980], p. 224; italics in the original). The phrase "*materielle* [or *reale*] *Wahrheit*" does not yet appear in MS 1934, though "*historische Wahrheit*" does (p. 42).

4. Ibid., p. 101.

5. Ibid., p. 90.

6. For the English and German texts see, respectively, Freud (1960), no. 19, p. 54; (1980), p. 60.

7. Freud (1900), p. 197.

8. Freud (1960), no. 29, pp. 78f.; (1980), pp. 84f. Letter of December 16, 1883.

9. Martin Freud (1983), pp. 70f.

10. Freud (1960), no. 55 (letter to Martha Bernays, January 6, 1885), p. 136. For the background and a contemporary newspaper account of the duel, see Byck (1974), pp. 297–301.

11. Freud (1960), no. 94, p. 203; (1980), pp. 209f.

12. Viereck (1930), p. 30.

13. Karl Kraus and Heinrich Mann were among the few exceptions. For a discussion of the "treason of the intellectuals" see Timms (1986), ch. 16, pp. 285–303.

14. Klein (1985), esp. ch. 3, pp. 69–102. This is not to deny that the socioeconomic profile of Viennese Jewry at the time also made it "a very great statistical probability that Freud's circle would contain a high proportion of Jews," as stressed by Oxaal (1988), pp. 47–51.

15. Freud/Jung (1974), no. 40F, p. 80; (1974a), p. 88.

16. Freud/Abraham (1965), p. 34; (1980), p. 47. On July 20 Freud wrote to him, "On the whole it is easier for us Jews, as we lack the mystical element." This denial, reflected also in Freud's conception in *M.M.* of both Egyptian monotheism and Judaism in contrast to Christianity, must not be interpreted to mean that Freud was ignorant of the existence in Judaism of the Kabbalah or Hasidism, or that he was consciously or unconsciously repressing any personal links to such tra-

ditions. The denial is simply another instance of the pervasive legacy of nineteenth-century Jewish rationalism in which even a historian of the stature of Graetz (see above, ch. 2, n. 32) could recognize the historical extent of Jewish mystical traditions and yet reject them as inauthentic forms of Judaism, the products of superstitious minds, alien influences, or deliberate deceivers. Cf. also below, n. 22.

17. Freud/Abraham (1965), pp. 46f.; (1980), pp. 57f.

18. Freud/Abraham (1965), p. 64; (1980), p. 73.

19. Jones (1953–57), vol. 2, p. 153.

20. Ibid., p. 149. On "Viennese" as a code word for "Jewish" Freud writes with barely controlled rage in *On the History of the Psychoanalytic Movement,* "We have all heard of the interesting attempt to explain psychoanalysis as a product of the peculiar character of Vienna as a city . . . but this theory about psychoanalysis always seems to me quite exceptionally stupid, so stupid in fact, that I have sometimes been inclined to suppose that the reproach of being a citizen of Vienna is only a euphemistic substitute for another reproach which no one would care to put forth openly" (Freud [1914a], p. 72).

21. Carotenuto (1982), on which the following summary of events is based.

22. Ibid., chs. 3, 6, 7. For an extensive discussion of Spielrein's paper "Destruction as a Cause of Coming into Being" (1912) in relation to Jung's *Transformation and Symbols of the Libido* and to its alleged influence on Freud's later "death instinct" in *Beyond the Pleasure Principle,* see Kerr (1988).
Spielrein continued to correspond with Jung at least until 1918. Her last extant letter to him, written in January, opens abruptly: "It is not only the Jewish people who murdered their prophet; indeed, it seems to be the fate of prophets that they are never recognized in their own country during their lifetime." Since Jung's letters to her remain unpublished, one is left wondering what Jung had written that provoked this response. Later in the same letter she attempted to set Jung straight on the relation of Jews to mysticism: "You reproach us Jews, including Freud ["excluding" in the printed text seems an obvious *lapsus*], with viewing our most profound spiritual life as infantile wish fulfillment. In response to that I must first counter that there is hardly another people as prone to seeing mystical and prophetic import everywhere as the Jewish people. Freud's clear analytical and empirical spirit contrasts with that inclination" (Carotenuto [1982], p. 83). Cf. above, n. 16.

23. Carotenuto (1982), pp. 116f.

24. Carotenuto (1982), pp. 120f. (the letter is dated August 28, 1913).

25. Blüher (1922), which also offers (pp. 23f.) an attack against Freud that is fairly typical of the time: "Es gibt eine Anzahl korruptiver Gedankengänge des Judentums. Die Juden erzeugen oft grosse Gelehrte, die wichtige Entdeckungen machen . . . Beispiel einer solcher Entdeckung: die des Juden Sigmund Freud. Sie ist richtig und hat grosses Format: sowie aber am Phänomen der Liebe misst, tritt ihr korruptiver Grundcharakter (sie ist reiner Materialismus) unabweisbar zu Tage. Diese Gedankengänge werden erst fruchtbar, wenn sie durch ein deutsches Gehirn gehen, das imstande ist, ihrem tückischen Urgrunde Widerstand zu leisten."

26. Grubel (1979), p. 74. Letter dated July 4, 1923.

27. Dolles (1921), p. 9.

28. Ibid., p. 31: "Sollte es ein Zufall sein, dass die neueste Richtung in der Psy-

chologie, die Psychoanalyse, ihren Ausgang von Studien zur Hysterie nahm und dass diese ganze Richtung zunächst vornehmlich von Juden oder Ärtzten und Psychologen mit jüdischem Einschlag geschaffen und gefördert wurde? Gegenüber der ganzen Denkweise dieser Richtung (wenigstens bei der alten ursprünglichen Freudschen Schule in Wien) kann man sagen: die Juden haben den psychischen Mechanismus der (hysterischen) jüdischen Seele sehr gut herausgearbeitet. Hier ist der Patient (oder auch der Artzt selbst) der characteristische Jude, der immer an sich und andern herumdoktern muss, der ewig mit sich Unzufriedene, Uneinige, der sich stets den Puls fühlen muss und nicht zuletzt derjenige, welche selbst im Seelenleben schachert, Geschäfte macht usw."

29. Freud/Zweig (1970), pp. 43, 45; (1968), pp. 54f., 56.

30. Freud/Zweig (1970), p. 48; (1968), p. 59.

31. For the life of Bernays see Bach (1974). His work on catharsis, *Grundzüge der verlorenen Abhandlung des Aristoteles über die Wirkung der Tragödie* was published in 1857. A second edition appeared in 1880 as *Zwei Abhandlungen über die Aristotelische Theorie des Drama.* For the possible influence on Freud see Dalma (1963).

32. See Fraenkel (1932), pp. 50–57 (Bunsen to Bernays, November 7–14, 1852); pp. 58–60 (Bernays's reply). The latter is also available in Kobler (1935), pp. 290–93 and in Bach (1974), pp. 115f.

33. Freud/Pfister (1963a), p. 140; (1963), p. 152.

34. "An interview on Radio Berlin," in Jung (1977), pp. 59–66.

35. "Editorial [1933]," in Jung (1970), p. 533; "Verschiedenes Geleitwort [1933]," in Jung (1974), p. 581.

36. "The State of Psychotherapy Today" ("Zur gegenwärtigen Lage der Psychotherapie") [1934], in Jung (1970), pp. 165f.; (1974), pp. 190f.

37. Largely through the publication of his correspondence (see below, n. 39). After the war Jung shied away from publicly discussing his personal role. But see his article "After the Catastrophe" ("Nach der Katastrophe") (1945) in Jung (1970), pp. 194–217; (1974), pp. 219–44. Though the need to acknowledge a collective guilt is largely couched by Jung as advice to the Germans, the alert reader will easily detect personal nuances as well. Thus: "While I was working on this article I noticed how churned up one still is in one's own psyche. . . ." On the other hand, any allegation of anti-Semitism was immediately and fiercely rejected as originating from Freud or the "Freudians." See Jung's letter of January 14, 1946, to J. H. van der Hoop (Jung [1973–76], vol. 1, p. 405; [1973–80], vol. 2, p. 10). Similarly in a letter of April 18, 1946, to Michael Fordham, apparently not made available to the editor of Jung's correspondence but described in some detail by Brome (1981), pp. 246f.

38. See Scholem's letter of May 7, 1963, to Aniela Jaffé, published in Jaffé (1989), p. 100.

39. "A Rejoinder to Dr. Bally" ("Zeitgenossisches" [1934]) in Jung (1970), pp. 535–44; (1974), pp. 583–93. Letter to Gerhard Adler, June 9, 1934, in Jung (1973–76), vol. 1, pp. 164f.; (1973–80), vol. 1, pp. 213f. Jung also found it necessary to explain himself to others. See his letters during 1934 to A. Pupato (March 2); B. Cohen (March 26); Max Guggenheim (March 28); E. Beit von Speyer (April 13); James Kirsch (May 26 and September 29); C. E. Benda (June 19: "That psychoanalysis is, so to speak, a Jewish national affair is not my inven-

tion but Freud's"). Another example of the wide reverberations of Jung's pronouncements and how they were perceived may be seen in a letter from Walter
Benjamin to Gershom Scholem, July 2, 1937: "Perhaps you have heard that Jung
recently leaped to the rescue of the Aryan soul with a therapy reserved for it alone.
My study of his essay volumes dating from the beginning of this decade . . .
teaches me that these auxiliary services to National Socialism have been in the
works for some time" (Benjamin/Scholem [1980], no. 93, p. 240; [1989], p. 197).

40. Freud (1939), p. 88. For Freud's "die Hohe der Vergeistigung" Strachey has
"the high level in things of the mind." On the problem of translating German
Geist and its derivatives see below, n. 43.

41. Ibid., p. 136. Cf. Freud's statement at a meeting of the Vienna Psychoanalytic Society, February 7, 1912: "Christianity had its origins not only in the moral
reaction of the Jewish community; other sources include heathen religions which
propagated themselves in the Mysteries. The tendencies of Christianity have their
origin in the Mysteries; Judaism is merely the screen fantasy" (Nunberg and
Federn [1962–75], vol. 4, no. 161, p. 42; [1976–81], vol. 4, p. 38).

42. Freud (1939), p. 134.

43. Ibid., p. 113. Strachey was fully aware of the perils in translating the in-
tractable *Geistigkeit* and opted almost throughout for "intellectuality." In his note
to p. 86 he writes, "The obvious alternative would be 'spirituality,' but in English
this arouses some very different associations," and he refers the reader to Freud's
own discussion of the etymology of the word (p. 114) where, in a further note, he
despairs: "It will have been seen that this last paragraph is untranslatable." Katherine Jones adopted the other alternative ("spirituality"), as have I. The current
French translation (Freud [1986], p. 210) has, as the section title, "Le progrès
dans la vie de l'esprit." The glossary in the programmatic volume intended to set
down guidelines for the new and complete Freud translation undertaken by the
Presses Universitaires de France gives *Geist* as *esprit, Geistigkeit* as *spiritualité,* and
Vergeistigung as *spiritualization* (Bourguignon et al. [1989], p. 243). If this word
has its risks (but even in English it need not carry overtones of religion or "spiri-
tualism"), it seems to me that "intellectuality" is worse, being far too narrow and
cerebral and, in the contexts of *M.M.*, often anachronistic (in an earlier section [p.
47] Strachey himself translated "eine so hoch vergeistigte Religion" as "such a
highly spiritualized religion"). Moreover, Freud's etymology of *Geist*—"from a
breath of wind—'*animus*', '*spiritus*', and the Hebrew '*ruach* (breath)'")—seems to
me sufficient warrant for the choice I have made. Cf. also the passage shortly before this (p. 113) where, discussing the "omnipotence of thoughts," Freud describes it as "an overestimation which our mental [*seelischen*], in this case
intellectual [*intellektuellen*], acts can exercise in altering the external world."

44. K. Jones translation (Freud, 1939a), p. 134. Cf. Freud (1939), p. 105.

45. Freud's positive evaluation of the power of sublimation in Judaism is already
adumbrated in a discussion at the Vienna Psychoanalytic Society on May 24, 1911,
of Werner Sombart's recently published *Die Juden und das Wirtschaftsleben.* In-
voking Freud for support and expressing his admiration for his theories, Sombart
([1911], p. 280) had written that among the Jews there has been a displacement of
sexuality onto money-making. When this was reported at the meeting, Freud replied, "Sombart has neglected a basic difference; otherwise he would have seen
that the old Jewish religion has rendered a great service in the restriction of *per-*

verted sexuality, by guiding all currents into the bed of propagation" (Nunberg and Federn [1962–75], vol. 3, no. 144, p. 272; [1976–81], vol. 3, p. 260).

46. See "Bericht über den XV. Internationalen Psychoanalytischen Kongress," *Internationale Zeitschrift für Psychoanalyse und Imago,* 24 (1939), 360–70, which includes E. Jones's presidential speech on the liquidation of the Vienna Psychoanalytic Society (referred to as "die Katastrophe in Österreich"). The lecture is noted on p. 364: "Professor Sigm. Freud, London (in absentia): Der Fortschritt in der Geistigkeit." The text is printed in full, ibid., pp. 6–9. That Anna Freud read it is noted by Strachey in Freud (1939), p. 3. No issue of the *Internationale Zeitschrift* appeared in 1938 (see the "Vorbemerkung" to the 1939 volume, p. 5; Freud's death in London is announced on p. 371).

47. K. Jones translation (1939a), p. 147. Cf. Freud (1939), p. 115.

48. My translation. Freud (1939), p. 106. Cf. Freud's note (p. 42): "It is historically certain that the Jewish type was finally fixed as a result of the reforms of Ezra and Nehemiah in the fifth century before Christ."

49. Meitlis (1951), p. 21.

50. See Freud (1939), pp. 85, 90–92, 105. There is an occasional psychological twist of Freud's own. Thus the "wishful phantasy" of world domination once attached to the hope of reward in the "religion of the primal father" and "long abandoned by the Jews, still survives among that people's enemies in a belief in a conspiracy by the 'Elders of Zion.'" The notion that a "barbarous polytheism" is still alive under a "thin veneer of Christianity" is at least as old as Heine (see Bieber and Hadas [1956], pp. 331f.). But Freud draws the conclusion that the resentment of the constraints imposed by Christianity has been displaced upon its source, and that in this sense "hatred of Jews is at bottom a hatred of Christians" (for a similar remark attributed to an unspecified lecture by Freud see Zweig [1934], pp. 293f.).

Freud's reply to the charge that the Jews are aliens in Europe—namely, that Jews were present in Roman Cologne before the Germans—contains nothing new. The remark is interesting, however, because in the *Autobiographical Study* (Freud [1925], p. 8) he reports a tradition that his father's family were settled in Cologne "for a long time" until, owing to anti-Jewish persecution, they fled eastward in the fourteenth or fifteenth century.

51. Freud (1939), p. 111.

52. K. Jones translation (1939a), p. 63. Cf. Freud (1939), p. 51.

53. Freud (1960), no. 297, pp. 442f.; (1980), p. 459. Dated May 12, 1938.

54. Meitlis (1951), pp. 20f. See also Freud's letter on anti-Semitism in England (Freud [1938]), published in *Time and Tide* on November 11, 1938, and his "Ein Wort zum Antisemitismus" (Freud [1938a]), published in German and in English in the Paris emigré journal *Die Zukunft* on November 25. The effort of Richmond (1980) to identify Freud's allegedly "lost" gentile source for the latter as Mark Twain's article "Concerning the Jews" (1899) is valiant but not convincing. The parallels to Twain are very tenuous and can be drawn to Freud's *M.M* as well. Besides, Freud stressed that the text he "came upon" was not only "of very recent date" (p. 291), but that it had been "provoked by the *recent persecutions* of the Jews" (p. 290; my italics). The suggestion (Jones [1953–57], vol. 3, pp. 239f.) that Freud himself invented the text remains the most plausible. Far from indicating a deterioration of memory, such an invention is in harmony with Freud's insistence

in the letter to *Time and Tide* that gentiles, not Jews, should respond publicly to anti-Semitism, while his challenge to the reader to supply the author's name is both ingenious and ironic, unless we fall into the trap and take it seriously. The point is, precisely, that Freud is looking for the hypothetical non-Jew who *should* have written what he himself wrote, but he cannot find him.

55. James and Alix Strachey (1985), p. 83. The editors observe of Alix in Berlin, "Though a reflex anti-Semitism typical of her class shows up with distressing frequency in Alix's letters, she was constantly in Jewish company" (p. 38). On the ramifications of "Ego" and "Id" see Bettelheim (1983), pp. 52–57, who also remarks, "Only the wish to perceive psychoanalysis as a medical specialty can explain why three of Freud's most important new theoretical concepts [ego, id, and superego] were translated not into English but into a language whose most familiar use today may be for writing prescriptions."

56. In a well-known anecdote Jones, of course, applied the Hebrew-Yiddish term to Richard Sterba when he fled Vienna in 1938 ("O weh, unser einziger *Shabbes-Goy* ist fort"). See Jones (1953–57, vol. 2, p. 163, repeated in his autobiography (Jones [1959], p. 210), where his description of himself as "the only gentile" surrounded by Jewish analysts makes it transparently applicable to him as well. The thrust of Jones's remarks is to show how successfully he adapted himself to the Jewish group as well as his insider's knowledge of them ("I am going to prove this to any Jewish readers of this book by an anecdote which I shall not attempt to translate to others"). For any current reader unfamiliar with the term, among traditional Jews *Shabbes-Goy* referred to a non-Jew hired, by prearrangement, to perform certain basic tasks in the house otherwise forbidden to Jews on the Sabbath; hence metaphorically—a gentile among Jews.

57. Jones (1951), vol. 1, p. 293. There is no mention of this essay in the standard biography by Brome (1983) or, for that matter, in any of the literature on Freud or the psychoanalytic movement known to me. The sole exception is the biography of Otto Rank by Lieberman (1985), pp. 407f., who also stresses other instances of Jones's prejudice (pp. 64f., 189f., 217, 220f.).

58. MS 1934, p. 50: "*Der Mann Moses und der Monotheismus*," in which, as the position and handwriting show, "Der Mann" was added to the left of "Moses und der Monotheismus" as a provisional afterthought. Followed by "Drei Abhandlungen / von Sigm. Freud / I Moses ein Aegypter / II Wenn Moses ein Aegypter war. . . . / III Moses, sein Volk und die monotheistische Religion"; on the next three lines: "Moses and Monotheism / by / Sigm. Freud."

59. In part because, lacking the murder of a father-figure, Islam somewhat disturbed Freud's construct. Thus (Freud [1939], pp. 92f.): "The founding of the Mahommedan religion seems to me like an abbreviated repetition of the Jewish one, of which it emerged as an imitation." The "internal development of the new religion soon came to a stop, perhaps because it lacked the depth which had been caused in the Jewish case by the murder of the founder of their religion." Freud then continues with an even more shockingly abrupt dismissal of "the apparently rationalistic religions of the East" which "are in their core ancestor worship and so come to a halt, too, at an early stage of the reconstruction of the past."

Chapter 4. A Case History?

1. Maylan's place and date of birth are given in Kürschner (1931), p. 1889, but with no further information except for the titles of three articles: "Schmerz, Wahrheit, Psychoanalyse," *Deutsche Rundschau* (1929); "Die psychoanalytische Methode," ibid. (1930); and "Neurose als Zeiterscheinung," *Die Säule* (1930). To these can be added: "Rechts und Links. Eine psychoanalytische Betrachtung," *Zeitschrift für Menschenkunde* (1930), as well as "Die Psychoanalyse am Scheidewege," which appeared in 1931 in the *Suddeutsche Monatshefte* (the entire August issue bears the title "Gegen Psychoanalyse"). Maylan concludes the latter article with characteristic bombast: "Mir scheint, als stünden wir heute am Anfang einer solchen Erlösungsmöglichkeit der Erlösungslehre Freuds von der Gebundenheit ihres Ursprungs und ihres Schöpfers. 'Denn noch vom Grösserem, als alle Erlöser waren, müst ihr, meine Brüder, erlöst werden!' ruft uns die Stimme Zarathustras prophetisch zu" (Maylan [1931], p. 776).

From the archives of the Ludwig-Maximilian-Universität in Munich Prof. Dr. Laetitia Boehm has sent me a copy of Maylan's matriculation certificate for 1927–28, which shows him registered for pedagogy and philosophy. Fenichel's review (1930) easily picks out the anti-Semitic current in Maylan's book and, given the circumstances, seems rather restrained. The publisher's note on Maylan appears in *75 Jahre Ernst Reinhardt Verlag, München Basel, 1899–1974*, p. 58. See also below, n. 5.

2. Maylan (1929), pp. 27–36.

3. Ibid., p. 57.

4. Ibid., p. 163.

5. Stefan Zweig (1987), pp. 183, 186ff., letters from Freud to Stefan Zweig dated December 4 and December 7, 1929. In the first letter Freud writes from Vienna that, while taking a walk, he noticed a big poster announcing a lecture by Maylan "against me." He describes Maylan as "a vicious fool, an Aryan fanatic" and claims that he had sought psychoanalytic training in Berlin but was rejected after several months as "abnormal and unsuitable . . . whereupon, probably to avenge himself and become famous quickly, he published a pseudo-analytical book about me." Freud's letter was precipitated by the fact that, in addition to endorsements from Jung and from a Berlin newspaper, the poster carried one by Zweig himself. In view of their "close relationship" Freud wanted to know if Zweig had actually read Maylan's book and whether the favorable opinion expressed on the poster was really his. Shocked, Zweig replied (ibid., 183f.) that Maylan had taken some words from a private letter, out of context and without permission. Freud readily accepted the explanation. In the second letter he writes that "the misuse was just too much like that scoundrel, the betrayal too little like you. Since the American methods of ruthless advertising have reached Europe one cannot exaggerate the [need for] reticence in one's public statements." He then offers to make some materials in the archives of the Vienna Psychoanalytic Society available to Zweig for "the share intended for me in your new book" (presumably Zweig's *Die Heilung durch den Geist* [1931]; Eng. tr. *Mental Healers: Franz Anton Mesmer, Mary Baker Eddy, Sigmund Freud* [1932]).

6. Cited by Jones (1953–57), vol. 3, p. 145.

7. E.g., Ferenczi/Groddek (1982), p. 72; Ferenczi (1988), p. 185.

8. Freud (1939), p. 43.

9. See Shengold (1972).

10. On Freud's fainting see Jones (1953–57), vol. 1, pp. 316f., vol. 2, p. 146; Jung (1961), pp. 156f. "An unlaid ghost," Freud (1939), p. 103. Cf. Freud/Salomé (1972), p. 205; (1980), p. 224: "It suffices me that I myself can believe in the solution of the problem. It has pursued me through the whole of my life."

11. This is, of course, not meant as a criticism. Comparable space on these matters in the biographies by Clark (1980) and Gay (1988).

12. Krüll (1979, 1986), esp. chs. 2 ("Prehistory: Kallaman Jacob Freud") and 3 ("The Trauma: Sigmund Freud's Childhood and Youth").

13. Balmary (1979), (1982).

14. Though differing as to the specific nature and details of Jakob Freud's transgressions, both Balmary and Krüll attribute Freud's abandonment of the seduction theory as well as the formulation of the Oedipus complex to his inability to fully confront his father's guilt and his need to continue to hide it from himself. The affinity of views is recognized by Krüll (1986), p. 270 n. 34. The result, in either case, is to totally subjectivize and explain away two key elements in Freudian theory and thus, by implication, to discard them.

15. Simon (1957), pp. 294–97, taking his cue from Freud's statement to Jung (Jones [1953–57], vol. 2, p. 423) that "were he ever to suffer from a neurosis it would be of an obsessional type." To this well-known and often cited essay add Simon (1962), esp. pp. 449–65, and his essay on Freud and Moses (1980).

16. E.g., Bakan (1958), pp. 70, 95. The recent attempt by Lévi-Valensi (1984) to argue that both the notion of Moses as an Egyptian as well as his murder came to Freud from the *Zohar* via Joseph Popper-Linkeus is ingenious but unconvincing. As she herself realizes, the Zoharic texts she cites neither state, nor do they really imply, that Moses was an Egyptian by birth or that he was murdered by the Jews. Moreover, there is no evidence that Popper-Linkeus knew the *Zohar*. That through him Freud retained a kind of "screen memory" for these texts which triggered his own thinking decades later remains, therefore, a gratuitous assumption.

17. It will suffice to turn to Raphael Mahler's study of Hasidism and Haskalah in Galicia, whose original Yiddish edition (1942) is cited in Krüll's bibliography. A Hebrew edition, expanded to include Poland, appeared in 1961 and is now available in English. In a section devoted to "The Vein of Rationalism in the Haskalah" he writes, "The Haskalah, which to some extent is correctly designated as Jewish rationalism, was very far from western European rationalism in its attitude toward religion. Even [Judah Leyb] Mieses, the most radical rationalist of all the Galician Maskilim of his time, published *Tekhunat ha-Rabbanim,* in which [David] Caro railed against those who believed 'that Voltaire and Mirabeau represent the last word in wisdom and progress and scoff at God and his Torah, without comprehending what is the truth.' But within the camp of the radical Maskilim there were those—and Mieses fell within this camp as well—who, though their attitude toward the Talmud was one of respect, obliquely but unmistakably rejected the absolute authority of the Talmud as the source of Jewish law. The majority of the Maskilim, however, not only did not tamper with the holiness of the Talmud but also sanctified the very essence of the rabbinic tradition. Most of them did not go beyond expressing opposition to Hasidism, to its faith in zaddikim and to the superstitions that were widespread among the people" (Mahler [1985], pp. 40f.).

18. On Mannheimer's Judaism and Viennese Reform at the time, see Rainey (1975), pp. 13–16, and Meyer (1988), pp. 144–51, who shows how Viennese conditions curbed Mannheimer's earlier radicalism.

19. Jakob Freud's "Gedenkblatt" first records the death and burial of his own father in February 1856. "Shelomoh Sigismund" (so in the Hebrew) was born on May 6. No one seems to have noticed that the German reads "Schelome *Sigmund,*" and that it was therefore Jakob who first used this form, long before Freud himself made the change. Facsimile of the Hebrew text of the birth and circumcision, with English translations, in Aron (1956–57), p. 288; Roback (1957), p. 89. Facsimile of the entire "Gedenkblatt" in Hebrew and German, with transcription of the latter (but erroneously transcribing "Sigmund" as "Sigismund"!), in E. Freud et al. (1976), p. 46.

20. Heller (1956), p. 419.

21. Freud (1900), p. 216.

22. Jones (1953–57), vol. 1, pp. 19f.: "but he would never dare to contradict me."

23. Freeman (1971), p. 156.

24. Freud (1936), p. 247: "It must be that a sense of guilt was attached to the satisfaction in having gone such a long way. . . . It seems as though the essence of success was to have got further than one's father, and as though to excel one's father was still something forbidden."

25. Freud (1900), p. 205. Strachey notes that the allusion is to Shakespeare's Henry IV: "Thou owest God a death."

26. Pfrimmer (1982).

27. Byck (1974), p. 270; Freud (1980), p. 15.

28. Freud/Fliess (1985), p. 265; (1986), p. 284.

29. Heller (1956), p. 419.

30. Freud/Fliess (1985), p. 409; (1986), p. 449.

31. Freud's letter to Emil Fluss, March 17, 1873, in E. Freud (1969), p. 423.

32. See the entire letter, dated Sunday, July 23, 1882, in Freud (1960), no. 7, pp. 17–21; (1980), pp. 27–32.

33. Though never mentioned, at least in the extant published documents of Freud's life, it is almost inconceivable that he should not have prepared for and experienced the Bar Mitzvah ceremony at age thirteen. His father's orientation (see below), the norms of the time and of his parents' Jewish milieu, his studies with Samuel Hammerschlag are sufficient warrant for such an assumption. Simon ([1980], pp. 200f.) has found an additional, if circumstantial, clue to support it. In his "Note on the Prehistory of the Technique of Analysis" (Freud [1920], pp. 264f.) Freud writes, in the third person, of the strong influence upon him of Ludwig Börne. He refers specifically to the 1863 edition of Börne's collected works, which appeared in three volumes, and recalls that "in his fourteenth year [im vierzehnten Jahr; not, as Strachey has it, 'when he was fourteen'] he had been given Börne's works as a present, that he still possessed the book now, fifty years later, the only one he had retained from his childhood." Simon points out that indeed the thirteenth birthday falls in the "fourteenth year" and claims that he was able to convince Anna Freud that this passage contains a screen memory of Freud's Bar Mitzvah, for "nur zur Bar-Mitzwa bekam man Klassiker geschenkt."

34. See also his message on the occasion of the opening of the Hebrew University (Freud [1925b]): "Historians have told us that our small nation withstood the destruction of its independence as a State only because it began to transfer in its estimation of values the highest rank to its spiritual possessions, to its religion and its literature."

35. Byck (1974), p. 270.

36. Jones (1953–57), vol. 1, pp. 5f.; Krüll (1986), pp. 58–60, 119–22.

37. Letter of February 20, 1930, German text in Roback (1957), p. 227; English tr. in Freud (1960), no. 248, p. 395. Similar remarks on his ignorance of Hebrew in his preface to the Hebrew translation of *Totem and Taboo* (Freud [1934]). See also his letter of April 30, 1936, to the executive board of YIVO in Vilna, printed "instead of an introduction" at the beginning of the first fascicule of Max Weinreich's Yiddish translation of the *Introductory Lectures* (Freud [1936a]): "I have been very pleased at your news that the first part of my *Vorlesungen* in the Yiddish translation will appear very shortly, and with great respect I have taken into my hand the first signature which you have forwarded to me. It is a pity, but more than this I could not do with it. In that time when I was a student no attention was paid to cultivating the national tradition; so that I learned to read neither Hebrew nor Yiddish, something I very much regret. Nevertheless I still became a good Jew although, as you probably know, not a believing one" (my translation from the Yiddish; I do not know if the German original has survived).

38. On Freud's studies and relations with Hammerschlag see Rainey (1975), ch. 2, pp. 35–60. See also Freud's glowing tribute to Hammerschlag in his obituary (Freud [1904]). Rainey's conjecture that, before entering the Gymnasium at age nine, Freud was enrolled in a private Jewish *Volksschule* is plausible.

39. See Freud (1960), pp. 110, 164f., 216; Freud/Fliess (1985), pp. 254, 285f., 315, 335, 367, 369, 384, 406. Despite its title, Max Kohn's *Freud et le Yiddish* (1982) has, by the author's own avowal (p. 12: "Ce travail n'a pas le Yiddish pour objet"), nothing to do with the subject as understood here. I take it to be a neo-Lacanian meditation on "Yiddish" as an unconscious interlingual space and its purported relation to Freud's pre-psychoanalytic articles. The latter, along with a general repertory of Jewish jokes (not those in Freud's *Der Witz*), are surveyed in some detail, but the connection eludes me. Perhaps because of an inner resistance of my own to such modes of discourse, I find the book to be impenetrable.

40. Freeman (1971), p. 80.

41. Freud (1900), p. 442.

42. J. and W. Grimm (1897), vol. 4, column 4023: "GESEIER, n. laute klagende oder scheltende rede, geschrei, durcheinander von stimmen: *mach kein geseier*, das ist ein geseier wie in einer judenschule . . . ; aus dem hebr. *gesera, geseira*, plur. *geseraus* [sic] . . . östr. *gseres machen* . . . lärm, viel aufheben machen." The appearance of "Gezeires" in *Mein Kampf* has been noted by Gilman (1986), p. 242.

43. Freud/Zweig (1970), pp. 130f.

44. Freud/Zweig (1968), pp. 140f.

45. Facsimile and English translation in Aron (1956–57), p. 289; Roback (1957), pp. 92f.; with German translation in E. Freud et al. (1976), p. 134; for my own reading of the text see below, appendix II. After this lecture was written, and before I delivered it at Yale, Dr. Mortimer Ostow sent me the galleys of his article

entitled "Sigmund and Jakob Freud and the Philippsohn Bible" (Ostow [1989]), which contains a transcription, translation, and analysis of the birthday inscription. Each of us, as both can testify, did his work independently of the other, and I have changed nothing as a result. The reader is invited to compare our analyses, which, in my opinion, complement and sustain one another. Dr. Emanuel Rice of New York informed me some time ago that he was writing a book on Freud's Jewish identity in which he has closely studied the inscription. I have not seen his work, which, I have been told, is to be published shortly.

46. In this regard it is important to recall that Jakob's "Gedenkblatt" (see above, n. 19) had recorded his father's death and Sigmund's birth and circumcision in both Hebrew *and* German.

47. Wilder first met Freud in 1935. According to his journal, Freud told him that when he had read his *Heaven's My Destination* he had thrown it across the room, and explained, "I come from an unbroken line of infidel Jews. My father was a Voltairian. My mother was pious, but one day my father took me out for a walk in the Prater, I can remember it perfectly, and explained to me that there was no way we could know that there is a God; that it didn't do any good to trouble one's head about such; but to live and do one's duty among one's fellow men" (quoted by Harrison [1983], p. 139). This can, of course, be interpreted in a number of ways. I will merely point out that, considering the Hasidic background of his father's family (see Freud's letter to Roback in Roback [1957], p. 227), Freud's absurd reference to an "unbroken line of infidel Jews" only shows his public persona at work in a way that casts his entire statement in doubt.

48. Babylonian Talmud, *Menaḥot*, 99b. Cf. *Berakhot*, 8b; *Baba Bathra*, 14b.

49. Freud (1914), pp. 230, 233.

50. Ibid., p. 213.

51. In this connection it may be appropriate to take note of Freud's "sacrificial act" in shattering a small marble statue of Venus in his collection of antiquities during the grave illness, in 1905, of his eldest daughter, Mathilde. On another occasion he deliberately broke a newly acquired Egyptian figurine in order to preserve a friendship that seemed threatened. (See Freud [1901], pp. 169f.; these passages were added in 1907). Though both incidents are usually classed among Freud's numerous "superstitions," the possibility of a vestigial link, whether conscious or not, to the biblical prohibition and traditional Jewish abhorrence of "idols" should not be ruled out.

52. Freud (1925), p. 8; my italics.

53. Freud (1912–13), pp. 143, 145. Cf. Freud (1909a), p. 35; (1911), p. 55; (1923), p. 88.

54. Freud/Salomé (1972), pp. 206f.; (1980), p. 225.

55. Robert ([1974], pp. 276f.; [1976], pp. 166f.), basing herself here on Freud's remark in *M.M.* (in the section entitled "The Return of the Repressed") that "even the great Goethe, who in the period of his genius certainly looked down upon his unbending and pedantic father, in his old age developed traits which formed a part of his father's character" (Freud [1939], p. 125). Since Freud identified with Goethe, he must be speaking of himself and his own father. The syllogism, though slippery, is in itself not implausible. Indeed, one could attempt to decode the entire passage on a personal level. The lines that follow, on the young man who first rebelled against his worthless father and became a "capable, trustworthy and honor-

able person," but whose character was later reversed on the model of the same father, has been interpreted as a veiled allusion to Otto Rank and his father, Simon Rosenfeld (Lieberman [1985], pp. 321f.). By the same token the lines that precede the statement about Goethe, on the girl who becomes totally unlike her mother, but later, after marrying and having children, reestablishes her identification with her, may have their root in Freud's image of his own wife, Martha. But within the manifest context of the section in which these passages appear, Freud is merely describing such returns of the repressed as an inevitability of the human condition. Even if we provisionally accept Robert's syllogism, it does not follow that the paternal traits that Freud now discovered in himself were anything more than those of character and temperament, precisely as in Goethe's own case.

Chapter 5. Monologue with Freud

1. Freud (1930), p. 212.

2. Baron (1939), p. 477.

3. Freud (1912–13), p. 100.

4. Freud (1939), p. 107.

5. Ibid., p. 131.

6. Freud/Abraham (1965), p. 36; (1980), pp. 48f.

7. I formulated this question spontaneously, long before I had read any of the secondary literature on *M.M.* Subsequently I found a very similar approach in Yehezkel Kaufmann's little-known but very important Hebrew review, though I do not share some of his other strictures. See Kaufmann (1940).

8. *Wayyikra Rabbah*, 10:3; cf. *Tanhuma*, Ki-tisa, 13.

9. *Midrash Aggadah* on Numbers 30:11.

10. *Bamidbar Rabbah*, 16:13; *Tanhuma*, Shelah, 22.

11. *Midrash 'Asseret ha-Dibrot*, in Jellinek (1967), vol. 1, pt. 1, p. 63.

12. Freud (1939), p. 128.

13. Ibid., p. 127.

14. Yerushalmi (1988), p. 12.

15. Mann (1948), pp. 215–23; (1958), pp. 965–69.

16. Freud (1939), pp. 99f.

17. Eusebius (1965), vol. 1, pp. 11, 31, 39, 43.

18. Chrysostom (1979), pp. 5f.

19. Augustine (1966), vol. 4, p. 427.

20. Augustine (1975), pp. 29f.

21. Freud's acceptance, dated Vienna, December 29, 1929, and the letter of thanks from the executive board, initialed "MW" and "SR" and dated Vilna ("Wilno"), January 7, 1930, are in the archives of the YIVO Institute in New York and are reproduced below, appendix III. The appointment and composition of the honorary Praesidium were announced in the Vilna *Yedies fun YIVO* (News from YIVO), no. 28, January 24, 1930. A worldwide appeal for support of the YIVO, signed by the members of the Praesidium (including Freud), was published ibid., no. 31, May 30, 1930.

22. The letters of Stendig and Freud, on which the account that follows is

based, are in the YIVO archives in New York. For the texts see below, appendix III.

23. My observations derive in part from my participation in the Research Group on the Psychoanalytic Study of Anti-Semitism but do not necessarily reflect the opinions of its other members. Over the years I have been struck more than once by the fact that in their search for clinical material relevant to our theme, various analysts in the group, both Jews and gentiles, would return to cases in their files with a new and heightened awareness of anti-Semitic elements in some analysands that had elicited no special attention while the analyses were taking place.

As for the attitudes of Jewish analysts to their own identity or of non-Jewish analysts toward Jews, I know of no literature on the subject. An admittedly extreme instance of the pent-up rage suddenly discharged by a distinguished non-Jewish analyst against his Jewish colleagues and Jews in general has recently surfaced in M. Masud R. Khan's shocking account of his treatment of a Jewish homosexual (see Khan [1989], preface and ch. 4, esp. pp. 90f., 92f.). I certainly do not suggest that the case of Mr. Khan, tragic in itself, is anything but idiosyncratic. My point is simply that if there are other non-Jewish analysts who harbor much milder resentments (or, for that matter, far greater affections) regarding Jews, such feelings seem beyond the pale of discourse, whether polite or psychoanalytic.

24. Quoted from an unpublished letter of Anna Freud by Steiner (1988), p. 276.

25. A. Freud (1978), p. 148. Although the Jerusalem Congress is mentioned by Elisabeth Young-Bruehl in her comprehensive biography of Anna Freud, no mention is made of Anna's speech, whose full text was published in the *International Journal of Psycho-Analysis*. Nor, in writing of Anna's attendance at the Paris Congress of 1938 (Young-Bruehl [1988], p. 236), does she state that Anna's specific task on that occasion was to read publicly her father's "Der Fortschritt in der Geistigkeit" from *M.M.* (see above, ch. 3, n. 46). From the tenor of the biography in dealing with Jewish matters (there is a fine summary of *M.M* on pp. 204–07) I have no doubt that these omissions were inadvertent. Interesting for our present context is Young-Bruehl's observation (pp. 375f.) that the appointment of Clifford Yorke in 1966 to administer the Hampstead Clinic "represented the Clinic to the outside world as what it largely was not—he was male, non-Jewish, native British. . . . In the 1960s, Anna Freud had taken care with her hiring to assure that the Clinic was not isolated . . . by remaining a largely female, Jewish emigré enclave, with thickly accented 'Hampstead English' as the predominant language."

26. The Jerusalem Congress was vividly described in an eyewitness account by Paul Schwaber (1978), emphasizing the depth of Freud's personal Jewish identity, the enthusiasm and symbolic significance of this meeting of "the children of Herzl and the children of Freud," and especially the conclusion of Anna Freud's speech, of which he wrote, "People hesitated, turned, wondered: a Jewish science! It came from nowhere in the speech. Yet under the circumstances of the Hebrew University a title of honor. Maintaining her reserve, but emphatic at the climax, Anna Freud faced down the old issue, unexpectedly transvaluing values. The very quality of unencumbered statement suggests that the tension has not been resolved but dealt with differently. Nonetheless, with proximate distance still, she bespoke a changed attitude. An historical moment."

On November 7, 1989, following the delivery of these lectures at Yale, I met for a luncheon discussion with members of the Gardiner Program in Psychoanalysis and the Humanities. The discussion turned to my remarks about Anna Freud's Jerusalem speech. At that point Professor Schwaber intervened to state that he had sent his aforementioned article to Anna Freud when it was published and that she had responded in a letter from London on June 8, 1978, which he now produced. At my request he kindly sent me a copy of the letter, which I reproduce here:

Dear Dr. Schwaber,

Thank you very much for your essay on the Congress. I read it with the greatest pleasure and I admired your quite wonderful way of describing not only events, but bringing out their meaning. Thank you also for what you said about my contribution. You understood what I meant, but I know that not everybody did.

Yours sincerely,

Anna Freud

27. Freud (1960), no. 219, p. 365; (1980), p. 380.

Bibliography

Note: *S.E.* refers to the *Standard Edition of the Complete Psychological Works of Sigmund Freud*, tr. under the general editorship of James Strachey in collaboration with Anna Freud, assisted by Alix Strachey and Alan Tyson, 24 vols. (1953–74). London: The Hogarth Press and the Institute of Psycho-Analysis.

Manuscript sources:

Freud, Sigmund. *Der Mann Moses: Ein historischer Roman*. Manuscript draft dated September 8, 1934. Freud Archives, Library of Congress, Washington, D.C.

———. Letter to Theodor Herzl, September 28, 1902. Central Zionist Archives (Herzl Archive H VIII 247), Jerusalem.

———. Letter to the Yiddish Scientific Institute, Vilna. Archives of the YIVO Institute for Jewish Research, New York.

———. Exchange of letters with Dr. Samuel Stendig, January 6 and January 21, 1939. Archives of the YIVO Institute for Jewish Research, New York.

Published works:

Abraham, Karl (1912). Amenhotep IV (Ichnaton). Psychoanalytische Beiträge zum Verständnis seiner Persönlichkeit und des monotheistischen Atonkultes. *Imago,* 1:334–60.

——— (1935). Amenhotep IV (Ikhnaton). A Psychoanalytic Contribution to the Understanding of His Personality and the Monotheistic Cult of Aton. *Psychoanalytic Quarterly,* 4:537–69. Reprinted in Abraham (1955), 262–90.

——— (1955). *Clinical Papers and Essays on Psycho-analysis.* New York: Brunner/Mazel.

Albright, William Foxwell (1940). *From the Stone Age to Christianity.* Baltimore: Johns Hopkins University Press.

Alt, Albrecht (1929). *Der Gott der Väter.* [Beiträge zur Wissenschaft vom Alten und Neuen Testament, III, 12].

Altmann, Alexander (1973). *Moses Mendelssohn: A Biographical Study.* Philadelphia: Jewish Publication Society of America.

Aron, Willy (1956–57). Notes on Sigmund Freud's Ancestry and Jewish Contacts. *YIVO Annual of Jewish Social Science,* 11:286–95.

Auerbach, Elias (1932). *Wüste und Gelobtes Land.* Vol. 1: *Geschichte Israels von den Anfängen bis zum Tode Salomos.* Berlin: Kurt Wolf.

Augustine [Aurelius Augustinus] of Hippo (1966). *The City of God against the Pagans,* tr. George E. McCracken [Loeb Classical Library], 7 vols. Cambridge: Harvard University Press.

—— (1975). *Against Faustus the Manichaean.* In *Disputation and Dialogue: Readings in the Jewish-Christian Encounter,* ed. Frank E. Talmage. New York: Ktav Publishing House and Anti-Defamation League of B'nai B'rith.

Bach, Hans I. (1974). *Jacob Bernays: Ein Beitrag zur Emanzipationsgeschichte der Juden und zur Geschichte des deutschen Geistes im neunzehnten Jahrhundert.* Tübingen: J. C. B. Mohr (Paul Siebeck).

Bakan, David (1958). *Sigmund Freud and the Jewish Mystical Tradition.* Princeton: D. Van Nostrand.

Balmary, Marie (1979). *L'homme aux statues: Freud et la faute cachée du père.* Paris: Grasset.

—— (1982). *Psychoanalyzing Psychoanalysis: Freud and the Hidden Fault of the Father,* tr. Ned Lukacher. Baltimore: Johns Hopkins University Press.

Baron, Salo Wittmayer (1939). Review of Freud's "Moses and Monotheism." *American Journal of Sociology,* 45:471–77.

Beer, Georg (1912). *Mose und sein Werk.* Tübingen: J. C. B. Mohr.

Benjamin, Walter, and Gershom Scholem (1980). *Briefwechsel 1933–1940.* Frankfurt am Main: Suhrkamp.

—— (1989). *The Correspondence of Walter Benjamin and Gershom Scholem,* tr. Gary Smith and Andre Lefevere. New York: Schocken.

Bergmann, Martin (1976). Moses and the Evolution of Freud's Jewish Identity. *Israel Annals of Psychiatry and Related Disciplines,* 14:3–26. Reprinted in Ostow (1982), 115–42.

Bericht über den XV. Internationalen Psychoanalytischen Kongress. *Internationale Zeitschrift für Psychoanalyse und Imago,* 24 (1939): 360–70.

Bettelheim, Bruno (1983). *Freud and Man's Soul.* New York: Alfred A. Knopf.

Bieber, Hans, and Moses Hadas (1956). *Heinrich Heine: A Biographical Anthology.* Philadelphia: Jewish Publication Society of America.

Bin Gorion, Micha Josef (1926). *Sinai und Garizim: Über den Ursprung der Israelitischen Religion. Forschungen zum Hexateuch auf Grund rabbinischer Quellen,* ed. Rahel Bin Gorion and Emanuel Bin Gorion. Berlin: Morgenland-Verlag.

Blüher, Hans (1922). *Secessio Judaica. Philosophische Grundlegung der historischen Situation des Judentums und der antisemitischen Bewegung.* Berlin: Der Weisse Ritter.

Blum, Ernst (1956). Über Sigmund Freuds: Der Mann Moses und die monotheistische Religion. *Psyche,* 10:367–90.

Bori, Pier Cesare (1979). Una pagina inedita di Freud: la premessa al romanzo storico su Mosè. *Rivista di storia contemporanea,* 7:1–16.

—— (1989). *L'estasi del profeta ed altri saggi tra ebraismo e cristianesimo dalle origini sino al "Mosè" di Freud.* Bologna: Il Mulino.

Bornemann, Fritz (1954). Verzeichnis der Schriften von P. W. Schmidt S.V.D. (1868–1954). *Anthropos,* 49:385–432.

Bourguignon, André, Pierre Cotet, Jean Laplanche, and François Robert (1989). *Traduire Freud.* Paris: Presses Universitaires de France.

Brandt, Lewis W. (1959). Freud and Schiller. *Psychoanalysis and the Psychoanalytic Review,* 46:97–101.

Breasted, James Henry (1933). *The Dawn of Conscience.* New York: Charles Scribner's Sons.

Brecht, Karen (1988). La psychanalyse sous l'Allemagne nazie. *Revue internationale d'histoire de la psychanalyse,* 1:95–108.

Brecht, Karen, et al. (1985). *"Hier geht das Leben auf eine sehr merkwürdige Weise weiter . . ." Zur Geschichte der Psychoanalyse in Deutschland,* ed. K. Brecht, V. Friedrich, L. M. Hermanns, L. Kaminer, D. H. Juelich. Hamburg: Verlag Michael Kellner.

Brome, Vincent (1981). *Jung: Man and Myth.* New York: Atheneum.

——— (1983). *Ernest Jones: Freud's Alter-Ego.* New York: W. W. Norton.

Byck, Robert, ed. (1974). *Cocaine Papers by Sigmund Freud.* New York: Stonehill Publishing Co.

Carotenuto, Aldo (1982). *A Secret Symmetry: Sabina Spielrein between Jung and Freud,* tr. Arno Pomerans, John Sheply, Krishna Winston. New York: Pantheon Books.

Chamberlain, Houston Stuart (1977). *Foundations of the Nineteenth Century,* tr. John Lees, introd. by George L. Mosse. New York: Howard Fertig.

Chandler, Tertius (1962). Ikhnaton and Moses. *American Imago,* 19:127–39.

Chasseguet-Smirgel, Janine (1988). Quelques réflexions sur l'attitude de Freud durant la période nazie, "Jo, comme Juif." *Revue internationale d'histoire de la psychanalyse,* 1:13–31.

——— (1988a). Some Thoughts on Freud's Attitude during the Nazi Period. *Psychoanalysis and Contemporary Thought,* 11:249–65.

Chemouni, Jacquy (1988). *Freud et le Sionisme: Terre psychanalytique, terre promise.* Malakoff: Solin.

Chrysostom, John (1979). *Discourses against Judaizing Pagans,* tr. Paul W. Harkins. Washington, D.C.: The Catholic University of America Press.

Clark, Ronald (1980). *Freud: The Man and the Cause.* New York: Random House.

Cocks, Geoffrey (1985). *Psychotherapy in the Third Reich: The Göring Institute.* New York: Oxford University Press.

——— (1988). Continuités et développement de la psychanalyse en Allemagne depuis 1939. *Revue internationale d'histoire de la psychanalyse,* 1:51–70.

Dalma, Juan (1963). La catarsis en Aristóteles, Bernays y Freud. *Revista de psiquiatría y psicología médica,* 6:253–69.

David, Michel (1970). *La psicoanalisi nella cultura italiana,* 2d ed. Turin: Editore Boringhieri.

Delitzsch, Friedrich (1902). *Babel und Bibel.* Leipzig: J. C. Hinrichs.

Dolles, Wilhelm (1921). *Das Jüdische und das Christliche als Geistesrichtung* [Beiträge zur Kinderforschung und Heilerziehung, Heft 179]. Langensalza: Hermann Beyer & Söhne.

Doryon, Israel (1940). *Mamlekhet Linkeus* [The kingdom of Linkeus], prefaces by Sigmund Freud and Albert Einstein. Jerusalem: Reuben Maas.

Edelheit, Henry (1978). On the Biology of Language. Darwinian/Lamarckian Homology in Human Inheritance (With some Thoughts about the Lamarckism of

Freud). In *Psychoanalysis and Language* [Psychiatry and the Humanities, vol. 3, 45–74]. New Haven: Yale University Press.

Eliade, Mircea (1969). *The Quest: History and Meaning in Religion.* Chicago: University of Chicago Press.

Engelman, Edmund (1976). *Berggasse 19: Sigmund Freud's Home and Offices, Vienna 1938.* Introd. by Peter Gay. New York: Basic Books.

Eusebius of Caesarea (1965). *The Ecclesiastical History,* vol. 1, tr. Kirsopp Lake [Loeb Classical Library]. Cambridge: Harvard University Press.

Ferenczi, Sándor (1988). *The Clinical Diary of Sándor Ferenczi,* ed. Judith Dupont, tr. Michael Balint and Nicola Zarday Jackson. Cambridge: Harvard University Press.

Ferenczi, Sándor, and Georg Groddek (1982). *Correspondance (1921–1933),* tr. into French and ed. by Judith Dupont, Susanne Hammel, Françoise Samson, Pierre Sabourin, Bernard This. Paris: Payot.

Fraenkel, Michael, ed. (1932). *Jacob Bernays: Ein Lebensbild in Briefen.* Breslau: M. & H. Marcus.

Freeman, Erika (1971). *Insights: Conversations with Theodor Reik.* Englewood Cliffs: Prentice-Hall.

Freud, Anna (1978). Inaugural Lecture for the Sigmund Freud Chair at the Hebrew University, Jerusalem. *International Journal of Psycho-Analysis,* 59:145–48.

Freud, Ernst L., ed. (1969). Some Early Unpublished Letters of Freud. *International Journal of Psycho-Analysis,* 50:419–27.

Freud, Ernst L., et al. (1976). *Sigmund Freud: Sein Leben in Bilder und Texten,* ed. Ernst Freud, Lucie Freud, and Ilse Grubrich-Simitis. Frankfurt am Main: Suhrkamp.

Freud, Martin (1983). *Sigmund Freud: Man and Father.* New York and London: Jason Aronson.

Freud, Sigmund (1900). *The Interpretation of Dreams. S.E.,* 4–5.

———— (1901). *The Psychopathology of Everyday Life. S.E.,* 6.

———— (1904). Obituary of Prof. S. Hammerschlag. *S.E.,* 9.

———— (1907). Obsessive Actions and Religious Practices. *S.E.,* 9.

———— (1909). Family Romances. *S.E.,* 9.

———— (1909a). Analysis of a Phobia in a Five-Year-Old Boy. *S.E.,* 10.

———— (1911). Psycho-Analytic Notes on an Autobiographical Account of Paranoia (Dementia Paranoides). *S.E.,* 12.

———— (1912–13). *Totem and Taboo. S.E.,* 13.

———— (1914). The Moses of Michelangelo. *S.E.,* 13.

———— (1914a). *On the History of the Psychoanalytic Movement. S.E.,* 14.

———— (1916–17). *Introductory Lectures on Psycho-Analysis. S.E.,* 15–16.

———— (1917). A Difficulty in the Path of Psycho-Analysis. *S.E.,* 17.

———— (1920). A Note on the Prehistory of the Technique of Analysis. *S.E.,* 18.

———— (1923). Josef Popper-Linkeus and the Theory of Dreams. *S.E.,* 19.

———— (1923a). A Seventeenth-Century Demonological Neurosis. *S.E.,* 19.

———— (1925). *An Autobiographical Study. S.E.,* 20.

────── (1925a). Letter to the Editor of the *Jüdische Presszentrale*, Zurich. *S.E.*, 19.

────── (1925b). On the Occasion of the Opening of the Hebrew University. *S.E.*, 19.

────── (1930). Address delivered in the Goethe House at Frankfurt. *S.E.*, 21.

────── (1931). *Schriften zur Neurosenlehre und zur psychoanalytischen Technik.* Vienna: Internationaler Psychoanalytischer Verlag.

────── (1932), My Contact with Josef Popper-Linkeus. *S.E.*, 22.

────── (1934). Preface to the Hebrew Translation of *Totem and Taboo*. *S.E.*, 13.

────── (1935). Postscript to *An Autobiographical Study*. *S.E.*, 20.

────── (1936). A Disturbance of Memory on the Acropolis. *S.E.*, 22.

────── (1936a). *Araynfir in Psykhoanalyz* [Yiddish translation by Max Weinreich of Freud (1916–17)], Heft I [all published]. Vilna: YIVO.

────── (1938). Anti-Semitism in England. *S.E.*, 23.

────── (1938a). A Comment on Anti-Semitism. *S.E.*, 23.

────── (1940 [1938]). *An Outline of Psycho-Analysis*. *S.E.*, 23.

────── (1939). *Moses and Monotheism*, tr. James Strachey. *S.E.*, 23.

────── (1939a). *Moses and Monotheism*, tr. Katherine Jones. London: The Hogarth Press and the Institute of Psycho-Analysis. New York: Knopf.

────── (1939b). *Der Mann Moses und die monotheistische Religion. Drei Abhandlungen.* Amsterdam: Verlag Allert de Lange.

────── (1939c). *Der Mann Moses und die monotheistische Religion. Drei Abhandlungen.* New York/Toronto: Longman's Green and Co. Alliance Book Corporation.

────── (1939d). Der Fortschritt in der Geistigkeit. *Internationale Zeitschrift für Psychoanalyse und Imago*, 24:6–9. [Delivered by Anna Freud, 15th International Psychoanalytic Congress, Paris, August 2, 1938. See ibid., pp. 363f].

────── (1941 [1926]). Address to the Members of the *B'nai Brith*. *S.E.*, 20.

────── (1960). *Letters of Sigmund Freud*, ed. Ernst Freud, tr. Tania Stern and James Stern. New York: Basic Books.

────── (1978). *Mosheh ha-ish ve-'emunat ha-yiḥud.* [Hebrew tr. of Freud (1939b) with "Afterword" by Mosheh Atar]. Tel-Aviv: Dvir.

────── (1980). *Briefe 1873–1939*, ed. Ernst Freud and Lucie Freud. Frankfurt am Main: S. Fischer.

────── (1986). *L'homme Moïse et la religion monothéiste. Trois essais*, tr. C. Heim, préface de Marie Moscovici. Paris: Gallimard.

────── (1987). *A Phylogenetic Fantasy: Overview of the Transference Neuroses*, ed. Ilse Grubrich-Simitis, tr. Axel Hoffer and Peter T. Hoffer. Cambridge: Harvard University Press.

Freud, Sigmund, and Karl Abraham (1965). *A Psycho-Analytic Dialogue: The Letters of Sigmund Freud and Karl Abraham (1907–1926)*, ed. Hilda C. Abraham and Ernst L. Freud, tr. Bernard Marsh and Hilda Abraham. London: The Hogarth Press and the Institute of Psycho-Analysis.

────── (1980). *Briefe*, ed. Hilda C. Abraham and Ernst L. Freud. Frankfurt am Main: S. Fischer.

Freud, Sigmund, and Wilhelm Fliess (1985). *The Complete Letters of Sigmund Freud to Wilhelm Fliess 1887–1904,* tr. and ed. Jeffrey Moussaieff Masson. Cambridge: Harvard University Press.

―――― (1986). *Sigmund Freud Briefe an Wilhelm Fliess 1887–1904,* ed. Jeffrey Moussaieff Masson, German editor Michael Schröter, transcription by Gerhard Fichtner. Frankfurt am Main: S. Fischer.

Freud, Sigmund, and Carl Gustav Jung (1974). *The Freud/Jung Letters,* ed. William McGuire, tr. Ralph Manheim and R. F. C. Hull. London: The Hogarth Press and Routledge & Kegan Paul.

―――― (1974a). *Sigmund Freud/C. G. Jung Briefwechsel,* ed. William McGuire and Wolfgang Sauerländer. Frankfurt am Main: S. Fischer.

Freud, Sigmund, and Oskar Pfister (1963). *Briefe 1909–1939.* Frankfurt am Main: S. Fischer.

―――― (1963a). *Psychoanalysis and Faith: The Letters of Sigmund Freud and Oskar Pfister,* ed. Heinrich Meng and Ernst L. Freud, tr. Eric Mosbacher. London: The Hogarth Press and the Institute of Psycho-Analysis.

Freud, Sigmund, and Lou Andreas-Salomé (1972). *Letters,* ed. Ernst Pfeiffer, tr. William Robson-Scott and Elaine Robson-Scott. New York: Harcourt Brace Jovanovich.

―――― (1980). *Briefwechsel,* ed. Ernst Pfeiffer, 2d rev. ed. Frankfurt am Main: S. Fischer.

Freud, Sigmund, and Arnold Zweig (1968). *Briefwechsel,* ed. Ernst L. Freud. Frankfurt am Main: S. Fischer.

―――― (1970). *The Letters of Sigmund Freud and Arnold Zweig,* ed. Ernst L. Freud, tr. Elaine Robson-Scott and William Robson-Scott. New York: Harcourt Brace & World.

Freudiana (1973). *Freudiana: From the Collections of the Jewish National and University Library.* Jerusalem: Jewish National and University Library.

Gager, John G. (1972). *Moses in Greco-Roman Paganism.* Nashville and New York: Abington.

Gamwell, Lynn, and Richard Wells (1989). *Sigmund Freud and Art: His Personal Collection of Antiquities.* Introd. by Peter Gay. New York: Harry N. Abrams.

Gay, Peter (1978). *Freud, Jews and Other Germans: Masters and Victims in Modernist Culture.* New York: Oxford University Press.

―――― (1982). Six Names in Search of an Interpretation: A Contribution to the Debate over Sigmund Freud's Jewishness. *Hebrew Union College Annual,* 53:295–307.

―――― (1987). *A Godless Jew: Freud, Atheism, and the Making of Psychoanalysis.* New Haven: Yale University Press.

―――― (1988). *Freud: A Life for Our Time.* New York: W. W. Norton.

Gilman, Sander L. (1986). *Jewish Self-Hatred: Anti-Semitism and the Hidden Language of the Jews.* Baltimore: Johns Hopkins University Press.

Goethe, Johann Wolfgang von (1888). Israel in der Wüste. In *Werke,* 7:156–82. Weimar: Hermann Böhlau.

Goldhammer, Leo (1937). Theodor Herzl und Sigmund Freud. *Theodor Herzl-Jahrbuch,* ed. Tulo Nussenblatt. Vienna: Dr. Heinrich Glanz Verlag.

———— (1958). Herzl and Freud. *Herzl Year Book,* 1:194–96.

Graetz, Heinrich (1975). *The Structure of Jewish History and Other Essays,* tr. and ed. with introd. by Ismar Schorsch. New York: Jewish Theological Seminary of America.

Graf, Max (1942). Reminiscences of Professor Sigmund Freud. *Psychoanalytic Quarterly,* 11:465–76.

Gressmann, Hugo (1913). *Mose und seine Zeit: Ein Kommentar zu den Mose-Sagen.* Göttingen: Vandenhoeck & Ruprecht.

Griffiths, J. C. (1953). The Egyptian Derivation of the Name Moses. *Journal of Near Eastern Studies,* 12:225–31.

Grimm, Jakob, and Wilhelm Grimm (1897). *Deutsches Wörterbuch,* vol. 4. Leipzig: S. Hirzel.

Grubel, Fred (1979). Zeitgenosse Sigmund Freud. *Jahrbuch der Psychoanalyse,* 11:73–80.

Grunwald, Max (1952). Memories and Letters: Chapters from an Autobiography. 1. Encounters with Freud [in Yiddish]. *YIVO Bletter,* 36:241–43.

Harrison, Gilbert A. (1983). *The Enthusiast. A Life of Thornton Wilder.* New Haven and New York: Ticknor & Fields.

Heine, Heinrich (1982). *The Complete Poems of Heinrich Heine: A Modern English Version,* tr. Hal Draper. Boston: Suhrkamp/Insel.

Heller, Judith Bernays (1956). Freud's Mother and Father. *Commentary,* 21:418–21.

Herder, Johann Gottfried (1903). *Vom Geist der ebräischen Poesie,* Erster Teil. In *Werke,* ed. Theodor Matthias, vol. 3. Leipzig and Vienna: Bibliographisches Institut.

Hermanns, Ludger M. (1988). Conditions et limites de la productivité scientifiques des psychanalystes en Allemagne de 1933 à 1945. *Revue internationale d'histoire de la psychanalyse,* 1:71–93.

Hirsch, Shelomoh (1873). *Korot Yisrael ve-'emunato* [History of Israel and its faith], pt. 1. Vienna: Leopold Hahn.

Huber, Wolfgang (1977). *Psychoanalyse in Österreich seit 1933.* Vienna and Salzburg: Geyer Edition.

———— (1978). Katholiken und Psychoanalyse in Österreich bis zum Ständestaat. In *Beiträge zur Geschichte der Psychoanalyse in Österreich,* ed. W. Huber, 61–105. Vienna and Salzburg: Geyer Edition.

Ibn Verga, Solomon (1947). *Sefer Shevet Yehudah,* ed. A. Shohat, introd. by Y. Baer. Jerusalem: Mosad Bialik.

Jaffé, Aniela (1989). C. G. Jung and National Socialism. In *From the Life and Work of C. G. Jung,* tr. R. F. C. Hull and Murray Stein. Einsiedeln: Daimon Verlag.

Jellinek, Adolph (1967). *Bet ha-Midrasch: Sammlung kleiner Midraschim und vermischten Abhandlungen aus der ältern jüdischen Literatur.* 6 pts. in 2 vols. Jerusalem: Wahrmann Books.

Jones, Ernest (1951). The Psychology of the Jewish Question. In *Essays in Applied Psycho-Analysis,* vol. 1, 284–300. London: The Hogarth Press and the Institute of Psycho-Analysis.

——— (1953–57). *The Life and Work of Sigmund Freud.* 3 vols. New York: Basic Books.

——— (1959). *Free Associations: Memories of a Psycho-analyst.* New York: Basic Books.

Josephus Flavius (1978). *Jewish Antiquities,* books I–IV, tr. H. St. John Thackeray [Loeb Classical Library]. Cambridge: Harvard University Press.

Jung, Carl Gustav (1961). *Memories, Dreams, Reflections,* ed. Aniela Jaffé, tr. Richard Winston and Clara Winston. New York: Pantheon.

——— (1970). *Civilization in Transition* [*Collected Works,* vol 10]. 2d ed. Princeton: Princeton University Press.

——— (1973–76). *Letters,* ed. Gerhard Adler and Aniela Jaffé, tr. R. F. C. Hull. 2 vols. London: Routledge & Kegan Paul.

——— (1973–80). *Briefe,* ed. Aniela Jaffé and Gerhard Adler. 3 vols., 2d ed. Olten and Freiburg im Breisgau: Walter-Verlag.

——— (1974). *Zivilisation im Übergang* [*Gesammelte Werke,* Bd. 10]. Olten and Freiburg im Breisgau: Walter-Verlag.

——— (1977). *C. G. Jung Speaking: Interviews and Encounters,* ed. William McGuire and R. F. C. Hull. Princeton: Princeton University Press.

Kaufmann, Yehezkel (1940). Sifro shel Freud 'al Mosheh ve-'al 'emunat hayiḥud [Freud's book on Moses and on the monotheistic religion]. *Moznayim,* 10:199–211.

——— (1954). *Toldot ha-'emunah ha-yisraelit* [History of Israelite religion], 3 vols. Tel-Aviv: Mosad Bialik-Dvir.

——— (1960). *The Religion of Israel,* tr. and abridged by Moshe Greenberg. Chicago: University of Chicago Press.

Kerr, John (1988). Beyond the Pleasure Principle and Back Again: Freud, Jung, and Sabina Spielrein. In *Freud, Appraisals and Reappraisals,* ed. Paul E. Stepansky, 3:3–79. Hillsdale, N.J.: The Analytic Press.

Khan, M. Masud R. (1989). *The Long Wait and Other Psychoanalytic Narratives.* New York: Summit Books.

Kiell, Norman, ed. (1988). *Freud without Hindsight: Reviews of His Work 1893–1939.* Madison, Conn.: International Universities Press.

Klein, Dennis B. (1985). *Jewish Origins of the Psychoanalytic Movement.* Chicago: University of Chicago Press.

Knoepfmacher, Hugo (1979). Sigmund Freud and the B'nai Brith. *Journal of the American Psychoanalytic Association,* 27:441–49.

Kobler, Franz, ed. (1935). *Juden und Judentum in deutschen Briefen aus drei Jahrhunderten.* Vienna: Saturn-Verlag.

Kohn, Max (1982). *Freud et le Yiddish: Le préanalytique.* Paris: Christian Bourgois.

Kroeber, A. L. (1920). Totem and Taboo: An Ethnological Psychoanalysis. *American Anthropologist,* 22:48–55.

——— (1939). Totem and Taboo in Retrospect. *American Journal of Sociology,* 45:446–51.

Krüll, Marianne (1979). *Freud und sein Vater: Die Entstehung der Psychoanalyse und Freuds ungelöste Vaterbindung.* Munich: C. H. Beck.

—— (1986). *Freud and His Father,* tr. Arnold J. Pomerans. New York: W. W. Norton.

Kürschner (1931). *Kürschners deutscher Gelehrten-Kalender,* ed. Gerhard Lüdtke. Berlin and Leipzig: Walter de Gruyter.

Lévi-Strauss, Claude (1962). *Le totémisme aujourd'hui.* Paris: Presses Universitaires de France.

—— (1963). *Totemism.* Boston: Beacon Press.

Lévy-Valensi, Eliane Amado (1984). *Le Moïse de Freud ou la référence occulté.* Monaco: Éditions du Rocher.

Lieberman, E. James (1985). *Acts of Will: The Life and Work of Otto Rank.* New York: The Free Press.

Loewenberg, Peter (1970). A Hidden Zionist Theme in Freud's 'My Son the Myops . . .' Dream. *Journal of the History of Ideas,* 31:129–32.

Lohmann, Hans-Martin, ed. (1984). *Psychoanalyse und Nationalsozialismus. Beiträge zur Bearbeitung eines unbewältigten Traumas.* Frankfurt am Main: S. Fischer.

Mahler, Raphael (1985). *Hasidism and the Jewish Enlightenment: Their Confrontation in Galicia and Poland in the First Half of the Nineteenth Century,* tr. E. Orenstein, A. Klein, and J. Machlowitz Klein. Philadelphia: Jewish Publication Society of America.

Mann, Thomas (1948). *Joseph, der Ernährer.* Stockholm: Berman-Fischer.

—— (1958). *Joseph the Provider.* In *Joseph and his Brothers,* tr. H. T. Lowe-Porter. New York: Alfred A. Knopf.

Maylan, Charles E. (1929). *Freuds tragischer Komplex: Eine Analyse der Psychoanalyse.* Munich: Ernst Reinhardt.

—— (1931). Die Psychoanalyse am Scheidewege. *Suddeutsche Monatshefte,* 28:772–76.

McGrath, William J. (1986). *Freud's Discovery of Psychoanalysis: The Politics of Hysteria.* Ithaca: Cornell University Press.

Meitlis, Jacob (1951). The Last Days of Sigmund Freud. *Jewish Frontier,* 18:20–22.

Meyer, Eduard (1906). *Die Israeliten und ihre Nachbarstämme: alttestamentliche Untersuchungen von . . . mit Beiträgen von Bernhard Luther.* Halle: M. Niemeyer.

Meyer, Michael (1988). *Response to Modernity: A History of the Reform Movement in Judaism.* New York: Oxford University Press.

Midrash Aggadah 'al Hamishah Humeshey Torah, ed. S. Buber, Vienna, 1894.

Midrash Tanhuma, ed. S. Buber, 2 vols. Vilna, 1885.

Miller, Justin (1981). Interpretations of Freud's Jewishness, 1924–1974. *Journal of the History of the Behavioral Sciences,* 17:357–74.

Nunberg, Herman, and Ernst Federn, eds. (1962–75). *Minutes of the Vienna Psychoanalytic Society.* 4 vols. New York: International Universities Press.

—— (1976–81). *Protokolle der Wiener Psychoanalytischen Vereinigung.* 4 vols. Frankfurt am Main: S. Fischer.

Oehlschlegel, Lydia (1943). Regarding Freud's Book on 'Moses': A Religio-Psychoanalytic Study. *Psychoanalytic Review,* 30:67–76.

Oring, Elliot (1984). *The Jokes of Sigmund Freud: A Study in Humor and Jewish Identity*. Philadelphia: University of Pennsylvania Press.

Ostow, Mortimer, ed. (1982). *Judaism and Psychoanalysis*. New York: Ktav.

—— (1989). Sigmund and Jakob Freud and the Philippsohn Bible (With an Analysis of the Birthday Inscription). *International Review of Psycho-Analysis*, 16:483–92.

Oxaal, Ivar (1988). The Jewish Origins of Psychoanalysis Reconsidered. In Timms and Segal (1988), 37–53.

Pawel, Ernst (1989). *The Labyrinth of Exile: A Life of Theodor Herzl*. New York: Farrar, Straus & Giroux.

Petazzoni, Raffaele (1958). Das Ende des Urmonotheismus. *Numen*, 5:161–63.

Petrie, W. M. Flinders (1906). *Researches in Ancient Sinai*. New York: E. P. Dutton.

—— (1924). *Religious Life in Ancient Egypt*. Boston: Houghton Mifflin.

Pfrimmer, Théo (1982). *Freud, lecteur de la Bible*. Paris: Presses Universitaires de France.

Popper-Linkeus, Josef (1899). *Phantasieen eines Realisten*. Dresden and Leipzig: Carl Reissner.

Puner, Helen Walker (1947). *Freud: His Life and His Mind*. New York: Howell, Soskin.

Rainey, Reuben B. (1975). *Freud as a Student of Religion: Perspectives on the Background and Development of His Thought*. Missoula: American Academy of Religion and Scholars Press.

Rank, Otto (1909). *Der Mythus von der Geburt des Helden. Versuch einer psychologischen Mythendeutung*. Leipzig and Vienna: Deuticke.

—— (1959). *The Myth of the Birth of the Hero and Other Writings*. New York: Vintage Books.

Reik, Theodor (1954). Freud and Jewish Wit. *Psychoanalysis*, 2:12–20.

Richmond, Marion B. (1980). The Lost Source in Freud's "Comment on Anti-Semitism": Mark Twain. *Journal of the American Psychoanalytic Association*, 28:563–74.

Ricoeur, Paul (1965). *De l'interprétation: essai sur Freud*. Paris: Éditions du Seuil.

—— (1970). *Freud and Philosophy: An Essay on Interpretation*, tr. D. Savage. New Haven: Yale University Press.

Rieff, Philip (1959). *Freud, the Mind of the Moralist*. New York: Viking Press.

Roback, Abraham A. (1957). *Freudiana. Including Unpublished Letters from Freud, Havelock Ellis, Pavlov, Romain Rolland, et alii*. Cambridge, Mass.: Sci-Art Publishers.

Robert, Marthe (1974). *D'Oedipe à Moïse: Freud et la conscience juive*. Paris: Calmann-Levy.

—— (1976). *From Oedipus to Moses: Freud's Jewish Identity*, tr. Ralph Manheim. Garden City: Anchor Books.

Rossi, Paolo (1984). *The Dark Abyss of Time: The History of the Earth and the History of Nations from Hooke to Vico*, tr. Lydia G. Cochrane. Chicago: University of Chicago Press.

Sachs, Hanns (1944). *Freud, Master and Friend*. Cambridge: Harvard University Press.

Schiller, Friedrich (1962). Die Sendung Moses. In *Sämtliche Werke*, 4:783–804. Munich: Carl Hanser.

Schmidt, Wilhelm (1912). *Der Ursprung der Gottesidee. Eine historisch-kritische und positive Studie.* [Bd.] I. Munster i. W.: Aschendorffsche Verlagsbuchhandlung.

———— (1928–29). Eine wissenschaftliche Abrechnung mit der Psychoanalyse. *Das Neue Reich* [Vienna-Insbruck-Munich], 11:266–77.

———— (1928–29a). Prof. Dr. Freuds psychologische (psycho-analytische) Theorie zum Ursprung der Familie und der Religion. *Schönere Zukunft* [Vienna and Regensburg], 4:263–65, 287–89, 308–10.

———— (1929). Der Ödipus-Komplex der Freudschen Psychoanalyse und die Ehegestaltung des Bolschewismus. Eine kritische Prüfung ihre ethnologischen Grundlagen. *Nationalwirtschaft* [Berlin], 2:401–36.

———— (1930). *Handbuch der vergleichenden Religionsgeschichte zum Gebrauch für Vorlesungen an Universitäten, Seminarien usw. und zum Selbststudium. Ursprung und Werden der Religion. Theorien und Tatsachen.* Munster i. W.: Aschendorffsche Verlagsbuchhandlung.

———— (1931). *The Origin and Growth of Religion: Facts and Theories*, tr. H. J. Rose. London: Methuen.

———— (1931–32). Das Rassenprinzip des Nationalsozialismus. *Schönere Zukunft*, 7:999–1000.

———— (1933–34). Zur Judenfrage. *Schönere Zukunft*, 9:408–09.

———— (1936). Blut-Rasse-Volk. In *Kirche im Kampf*, ed. Clemens Holzmeister, 43–81. Vienna: Seelsorger Verlag.

Schorske, Carl E. (1973). Politics and Patricide in Freud's *Interpretation of Dreams*. *American Historical Review*, 78:328–47. Reprinted in *Fin de Siècle Vienna*, ch. 4, pp. 181–207. New York: Vintage Books, 1981.

Schur, Max (1972). *Freud: Living and Dying*. New York: International Universities Press.

Schwaber, Paul (1978). Title of Honor: The Psychoanalytic Congress in Jerusalem. *Midstream*, 24:26–35.

Schweitzer, Albert (1954). *The Quest of the Historical Jesus*. 3d ed. London: Adam and Charles Black.

Sellin, Ernst (1922). *Mose und seine Bedeutung für die israelitisch-jüdische Religionsgeschichte.* Leipzig and Erlangen: A. Deichertsche Verlagsbuchhandlung.

———— (1928). Hosea und das Martyrium des Mose. *Zeitschrift für die Alttestamentliche Wissenschaft*, 46:26–33.

———— (1929). *Das Zwölfprophetenbuch*, 3d ed. Leipzig: A. Deichertsche Verlagsbuchhandlung D. Werner Scholl.

Shengold, Leonard (1972). A Parapraxis of Freud in Relation to Karl Abraham. *American Imago*, 29:123–59.

Simon, Ernst (1957). Sigmund Freud, the Jew. *Leo Baeck Institute Yearbook*, 2:270–305.

———— (1962). Priester, Opfer und Arzt. Zu den Briefen Wolfskehls, Kafkas und

Freuds. In *In zwei Welten: Siegfried Moses zum fünfundsiebzigsten Geburtstag*, 414–69. Tel-Aviv: Verlag Bitaon.

——— (1980). Freud und Moses. In *Entscheidung zum Judentum. Essays und Vorträge*. Frankfurt am Main: Suhrkamp.

Smend, Rudolf (1959). *Das Mosebild von Heinrich Ewald bis Martin Noth*. Tübingen: J. C. B. Mohr.

Sombart, Werner (1911). *Die Juden und das Wirtschaftsleben*. Munich and Leipzig: Duncker & Humblot.

Steiner, Riccardo (1988). 'C'est une nouvelle forme de diaspora . . .' La politique de l'émigration des psychanalystes. *Revue internationale d'histoire de la psychanalyse*, 1:263–321.

Stern, Menahem, ed. (1976–80). *Greek and Latin Authors on Jews and Judaism*. 2 vols. Jerusalem: Israel Academy of Sciences and Humanities.

Strachey, James (1939). Preliminary Notes upon the Problem of Akhenaten. *International Journal of Psycho-Analysis*, 20:33–42.

Strachey, James, and Alix Strachey (1985). *Bloomsbury/Freud: The Letters of James and Alix Strachey*. New York: Basic Books.

Thompson, R. J. (1970). *Moses and the Law in a Century of Criticism since Graf*. Leiden: E. J. Brill.

Timms, Edward (1986). *Karl Kraus: Apocalyptic Satirist*. New Haven: Yale University Press.

Timms, Edward, and Naomi Segal, eds. (1988). *Freud in Exile: Psychoanalysis and Its Vicissitudes*. New Haven: Yale University Press.

Velikovsky, Immanuel (1941). The Dreams that Freud Dreamed. *Psychoanalytic Review*, 28:487–511.

Viereck, George S. (1930). *Glimpses of the Great*. London: Duckworth.

Vitz, Paul C. (1988). *Sigmund Freud's Christian Unconscious*. New York and London: Guilford Press.

Wallace, Edwin R. (1977). The Psychodynamic Determinants of *Moses and Monotheism*. *Psychiatry*, 40:79–87.

——— (1983). *Freud and Anthropology: A History and Reappraisal*. New York: International Universities Press.

Wayyikra Rabbah, ed. Mordecai Margulies. 3 vols. Jerusalem, 1953–56.

Weber, Max (1952). *Ancient Judaism*, tr. Hans H. Gerth and Don Martindale. New York: The Free Press.

Weiss-Rosmarin, Trude (1939). *The Hebrew Moses: An Answer to Sigmund Freud*. New York: The Jewish Book Club.

Wilson, John A. (1951). *The Culture of Ancient Egypt*. Chicago: Phoenix Books.

Wittels, Fritz (1924). *Sigmund Freud: Der Mann, die Lehre, die Schule*. Leipzig: Tal.

Yahuda, Abraham S. (1946). Sigmund Freud 'al Mosheh ve-torato [Sigmund Freud on Moses and his teaching]. In *'Eber ve-'Arab*. New York: Histadrut Ibrit be-Amerikah.

Yerushalmi, Yosef Hayim (1982). *Zakhor: Jewish History and Jewish Memory*. Seattle: University of Washington Press.

——— (1982a). Assimilation and Racial Anti-Semitism: The Iberian and the German Models [*Leo Baeck Memorial Lecture* no. 26]. New York: Leo Baeck Institute.

——— (1988). Réflexions sur l'oubli, tr. Éric Vigne. In *Usages de l'oubli (Colloque de Royaumont, 1987)*, 7–21. Paris: Editions du Seuil. [English version in Yerushalmi, *Zakhor*, 2d ed. (1989), 105–17. New York: Schocken.]

——— (1989). Freud on the 'Historical Novel': From the Manuscript Draft (1934) of *Moses and Monotheism. International Journal of Psycho-Analysis*, 70:375–95.

Young-Bruehl, Elisabeth (1988). *Anna Freud: A Biography.* New York: Summit Books.

Zweig, Arnold (1927). *Caliban, oder Politik und Leidenschaft. Versuch über die menschlichen Gruppenleidenschaften dargetan am Antisemitismus.* Potsdam: Gustav Kiepenheuer.

——— (1934). *Bilanz der deutschen Judenheit 1933: Ein Versuch.* Amsterdam: Querido.

Zweig, Stefan (1987). *Briefwechsel mit Hermann Bahr, Sigmund Freud, Rainer Maria Rilke, und Arthur Schnitzler,* ed. Jeffrey B. Berlin, Hans-Ulrich Lindken, and Donald A. Prater. Frankfurt am Main: S. Fischer.

Index